C. J. Peers

in appreciation & with Ruidert thoughts

Helena Deneke

Jan 1961

GRACE HADOW

GRACE HADOW, 1920

GRACE HADOW

By

HELENA DENEKE

London

OXFORD UNIVERSITY PRESS

Geoffrey Cumberlege

OXFORD UNIVERSITY PRESS
AMEN HOUSE, E.C. 4
London Edinburgh Glasgow New York
Toronto Melbourne Cape Town Bombay
Calcutta Madras
GEOFFREY CUMBERLEGE
PUBLISHER TO THE UNIVERSITY

FIRST PUBLISHED MARCH 1946
REPRINTED   JULY 1946

PRINTED IN GREAT BRITAIN

PREFACE

THIS book is the result of the friendship of a lifetime and is a labour of love. But it would not have been possible without the help of friends of Grace Hadow who met my requests in that same spirit. I have named most of them in the text, but there are others to whom I am indebted, and I should like here to put on record my warm thanks to them all. The personal records left by Grace Hadow were of the scantiest: a short childish journal, her observations on the War (1914–18), the letters she wrote when on holiday, which some friends fortunately preserved, necessarily determine the proportions of this biography.

I owe a special debt of gratitude to members of Grace Hadow's family who placed letters and journals at my disposal in a most generous way and were ever ready to answer questions or discuss points: foremost among these the late Canon Edgecumbe Hadow, Miss Enid Hadow (Grace Hadow's executors), and Mrs. John Cornish (her eldest sister). Lady Balfour too helped me by memory and criticism. Lady Tweedsmuir and Miss M. Sidgwick encouraged me to undertake the memoir, and to Miss M. G. Skipworth and Mrs. Kreyer I am indebted for most of the material recording holidays. Miss Helen Darbishire and Dr. W. G. S. Adams read the whole manuscript and contributed valuable suggestions, and Miss Kate Lea went through it to its advantage when completed. Miss Darbishire has added to her kindness by reading the proof-sheets and Dr. Ernest Walker has allowed me to consult him on particular points. Professor Edgar L. Collis provided the focus for the chapter on the Ministry of Munitions. The Hon. Eleanor Plumer and Miss M. D. R. Leys read the chapter concerning St. Anne's Society and Mr. Lionel Curtis the chapter on the British Commonwealth Conference. I owe special thanks to the Hon. Elsie Corbett, whose interest in this publication has made it possible; and to Dr. John Johnson, kindest and most understanding of printers, who has advised on the final form.

H. C. DENEKE

GUNFIELD,
  NORHAM GARDENS, OXFORD,
   25 *November* 1945.

'Wisdom which is the worker
Of all things taught me, for in
her is an understanding spirit.
Holy, Subtil, Clear in utterance,
loving the thing that is good.
Quick, steadfast, ready to do good.'

WISDOM, vii.

CONTENTS

LIST OF ILLUSTRATIONS

CHAPTER I

FOREBEARS, SURROUNDINGS, AND CHILDHOOD
1875–1891

GRACE ELEANOR HADOW was born on 9 December 1875 in Gloucestershire, the youngest child of the Rev. William Elliott Hadow and his wife, Mary Lang Hadow, at the vicarage of South Cerney near Cirencester. On his father's side Mr. Hadow's people had mostly been clergy, and he himself was born in 1826 at Elstree Vicarage, Herts., the son of the Rev. W. Hadow and his wife, Eleanora Anna Drinkwater. On his mother's side his forebears were soldiers and sailors. Her two brothers stand out: Colonel Drinkwater was in command of a regiment at Gibraltar and wrote an account of the siege that is extant in a manuscript copy, while his brother took the name of Bethune on inheriting a small estate, Balfour, in Scotland, became an Admiral, and was the father of Sir Edward Bethune of the 'Bethune Horse'. Mrs. Hadow was born in 1833 at Tavistock, where her father Henry Cornish was a lawyer. Her mother, Grace Rundle, was sister to John Rundle, M.P. for Tavistock for many years and a local landowner. His daughter, Elizabeth Rundle, afterwards Mrs. Rundle Charles, was author of the *Chronicles of the Schönberg Cotta Family*, a best seller in its day, and of many other books that had a religious flavour or a religious subject.

The married life of the Rev. W. E. and Mrs. Hadow had begun in 1859 at Ebrington, a tiny hill village in the Cotswolds, where the three eldest children were born and a baby daughter, the fourth child, was buried. After an interval in an unwholesome city vicarage at Bristol, where a second son was born in 1871, the Rev. W. E. Hadow brought his wife and children in that same year to the open country of South Cerney. It is a district of water-meadows drained by a canal and dikes. A curving road winding its way to Wiltshire forms the backbone of the village, and at a central spot where the waters gush forth from the sluice of a mill there rises a hump-backed bridge across the Churn. All-round greyness characterizes the rows of low, rather unlovely cottages along the road, although a few Cotswold gables convey some distinction to them. Portions of the village were known

B

as the Upper-Up and the Upper Upper-Up. Green banks and broad edges of grass set off the houses and the dikes. There has been building since those earlier days and the status of the village has risen; what were farm-houses have become residences, and those who live in the village are no longer necessarily altogether of it. The finest Cotswold house is now a stately place on a somewhat small scale. Behind it, away from the road, there is still to be found, hiding almost shamefacedly, the most interesting feature of the village, its church. Long ago its fine spire was destroyed by lightning, and the remaining base provides a somewhat squat tower. The church porch is approached through a group of old trees, some of the few now in Cerney, and inside the porch there is a lovely doorway with beaked Norman carving in good preservation. On the north side of the church, from an open spacious churchyard there is seen, across meadows, the front of a grey building that extends in not inelegant length: the so-called 'college'.

This peculiar institution gave a special flavour to Cerney in old days. It was originally endowed for the widows and unmarried daughters of clergy from the dioceses of Gloucester, Worcester, and Hereford. Since ladies were not then expected to work for their living and could hardly attempt it without disgrace, the institution was a boon to its gentle-born inhabitants who contributed some accomplishments and some intellectual interest to a village consisting exclusively of farmers, craftsmen, and labourers. There were twelve residences in the college. One set of elderly ladies struck awe into the vicarage children by getting up at 5 a.m. each day to study Greek. Others had families with them. Many claimed help and sympathy in growing infirmity. Naturally the college ladies were in close touch with the vicarage. This lay opposite the college on the other side of the long village road, away from the church. The house has the air of a gentleman's residence of the plain post-Georgian type. It abuts at right angles on the road, its more pretentious front seeming to peer outwards in a wrynecked way: at the back the house shrinks down comfortably under a sloping stone roof to two irregular floors with all the appearance of a farm-house. There it has a good porch, an orchard close by, and fields beyond. The road curves back by the front of the house so that this stands at a slightly acute angle and the upper windows command the road right up to the hump-backed bridge. What passes through Cerney can be seen from them. The disproportion of the house is suggestive of an effort that has been imposed on it to keep up appearances, and must have made it difficult to manage. However, before the days of much traffic its closeness to the road was no disadvantage. Even in those days farm-carts passed by rather than carriages, and what the windows saw was mostly village history.

Tradition in South Cerney was strong, alive, and unselfconscious. People observed old customs and kept to their fathers' ways. They were shy and reserved with new-comers, but if you were born in the place, you belonged.

'A dear little daughter born' is the entry in Mrs. Hadow's journal on 9 December 1875 and, soon after, 'the new little daughter is bright and well', followed on 6 January 1876 by 'our gentle treasure christened and my own dear boy godfather. May God so guide and help him that he may indeed aid us in teaching this new little soldier in Christ's army.' With this welcome the child came into a united family where the children were dearly loved and things of the mind and spirit were held in high esteem. The mother's remarkable personality dominated the home. The eldest child, Grace's godfather, was then sixteen and a scholar at Malvern College, from where he was soon to proceed as a scholar to Worcester College, Oxford. His mother's hopes, fears, and ambition centred on him; every slightest step in his subsequent distinguished career was watched with proud tenderness and recorded with thanksgiving. All her children were dedicated to the service of God, but in the early efforts and the later success of this eldest son she found most compensation for hardships borne. Two other sisters, closer to him in age, completed the group of older children. Grace Hadow and two brothers, her elders by four and three years, were looked on as the 'little ones'.

The children of a vicarage share, in a miniature way, something of the privileges and the obligations of royalty. They are in a sense public property; for the parishioners feel they have a right to them. Yet it would be difficult for an intelligent child so placed to grow up with an overweening sense of self-importance; many others have claims upon their parents' time and sympathy, and quite naturally the lives of people from various

ranks of life enter into theirs. There can hardly be a better way of
being educated in the sense of responsibility for one's fellows than
is found in such a parsonage home. Mrs. Hadow shouldered
parish work with a will, and the children inherited its obligations.

Within her own walls she had troubles to face. 'Poverty, illness,
sorrow' are noted in her journal, and soon after Grace's birth
hardships became acute. Loss of money through unfortunate
or imprudent investment saw the family in a poor living and
virtually cut off from possible resources of work in a wider world,
and this just at the time when a family is expensive, the eldest
of the six children being only sixteen. Mrs. Hadow had not been
brought up to managing on restricted means. How to secure ways
and means to give to the children an adequate education was a
hard problem which persisted for some years. 'But for the great
blessing of our children I do not know what we could do or how
support the sorrows of our present life', she writes in the years of
Grace's babyhood, and later when Grace is eleven: 'God's blessings
very great. He has given us very dear children from whom we
have no anxiety beyond their health. In other things the difficulties are very great, much more than we have ever known, but
doubtless the discipline is necessary and inside it there is a blessing.
My great prayer is "O God in thy loving mercy show us what to
do". ' To her mind the children covered everything.

One of the expedients not infrequently practised by country
parsons who were not well off was the taking of resident pupils,
and during Grace's childhood there were older boys at the vicarage
who came to be coached for examinations by her father and were
also taught and cared for by her mother. Many of them gratefully
remember her influence and help. The direction of the family's
welfare was mainly in Mrs. Hadow's hands and she did the con-
triving and planning. Her husband seems to have been more
passive in these ways; he was a preacher rather than a parish
priest, and it was as a preacher that he made his mark in the
district. His reading aloud had won him a gold medal at Cambridge. To hear him was an experience, and Grace always
associated passages in the Bible with his voice and heard it in the
novels of Scott. He was a mine of exact information on many
subjects, a scholar above all things, and something of an authority
on heraldry and brasses. His wife tells how on one occasion his
study was put in order 'for the first time since the memory of

THE VICARAGE AT SOUTH CERNEY (THE FRONT)

From a drawing by HECTOR WHISTLER

THE VICARAGE AT SOUTH CERNEY (THE BACK)

From a drawing by HECTOR WHISTLER

men', recording his 'never again' and her own 'I hope not'. Always accessible to his family, to whom he was a real person, he had little interest in practical things.

'I used to put food and education first', Mrs. Hadow would say in talking of the difficulties of those days; 'other things such as clothes matter only for the time being.' Tiny Grace is remembered at one stage as wearing her mother's clothes cut down for her, in accordance with a practice of the day; but she wore them long 'like a little Dutch girl' and is remembered as a quaint little figure running about in the garden in long skirts—partly to satisfy her mother's Puritan instincts, partly to keep the child from cold. If circumstances were narrow and there were many things which could not be afforded (though happily the children were not oppressively aware of it), there was no shortage of necessaries. Mrs. Hadow was resourceful in providing little treats that appeal to a child's imagination: she made a happy home for the family, and the vicarage managed always to dispense the simple charity to poorer neighbours which is one of the functions of a country parson's household. If the absence of luxuries was not felt by little Grace, she none the less learnt early to feel the serious side of life, and there grew within her a strong instinctive sympathy with the underdog and with those who were up against things. But troubles were not allowed to cloud happiness. Hers was a happy childhood in the natural delights and freedom of the country. 'I was born under a briar bush' was her description, and she would recall riding through the fields on the shoulder of Granville Coole, a village boy, remarkable for his devotion to the family. The boy's father was a character, and it was his work to drive the village fly to Cirencester and back, a queer vehicle, a so-called Coburg, known at the vicarage as the 'Shandarydan'. All who could not walk the four miles from South Cerney used it, and Mrs. Hadow used it also for paying calls.

The Cooles were a noteworthy family, and Granville was greatly trusted. Starting off with the vicarage children, the little one on his shoulder and the two boys by his side, he would show them how to fish for minnows or explore fields and hedges. The boys, especially Gerald, became ardent naturalists, storing collections in various parts of the premises, and they developed a passion for experiments, infesting the house with smells on inconvenient occasions, inventing and making ingenious machines, and sometimes injuring themselves. Their little sister took a wondering and sympathetic interest in these things and shared as much of them as she was allowed. They gave her a distaste for games that were considered right for little girls. And her mother had no prejudices about these ways; on the contrary she entered into the children's ideas and had great powers of sympathy with each of them. She also believed in real games as a means of teaching children, encouraged them to take a hand at serious whist when the college ladies came in, and invented ways of turning their lessons into games that were enjoyed.

The monotony of days sits lightly on country children interested in their surroundings. Yet romance is needed. Here it lurked within, and Grace, at her mother's hand, learnt how to make an adventure of each first time of doing or seeing something that went beyond the ordinary routine. The first visit to London at the age of eight brought a first ride in an omnibus, a first sight of Hyde Park and of the Gas Works, the first ice eaten, and the Zoo visited and a Circus seen. Nearer home there was the first visit to the annual theatricals at the Agricultural College in Cirencester, and there was the excitement of the local fairs; the Mop[1] in Cirencester, with its fire-eater and other marvels and its strange custom of hiring servants; and the little Mop too on a less ambitious scale which was called the runaway Mop. In Cerney itself there was the Whitsun procession on Monday and Tuesday when the Odd Fellows met at the Royal Oak Inn at the Upper-Up and marched down to the vicarage to fetch the vicar, who joined the procession, taking his place immediately behind the big drum and processing with them to church where a service was held. After the service they returned to the inn for a dinner at which the vicar presided. In the afternoon there was a fair. The children loved this exciting medley of impressions when their church and

---

[1] Footnote by Margaret E. Cornish: 'The "Mop" was the big fair held annually in the market place at Cirencester, and in our young days servants both men and women were hired at it. You could tell what job the men wanted by noticing what they wore on their hats: a piece of whipcord for a coachman, a sponge for a groom, a straw for a carter, and so on. The women met in Corn Hall where they were interviewed by their would-be employers. The Mop was held on the Monday nearest the 11th October, the day on which the Church was dedicated to St. John the Baptist. A second Mop was held a week later, the runaway Mop. It was so called because on that day the hired servants could all leave the places they had taken if they found they did not suit them. If the 11th October fell on a Monday there were three Mops, but that did not often happen.'

village practised worship and revelry side by side yet in due order. The church, of course, they felt to belong to them. It was part of the ordinary equipment and routine of life which was taken for granted and which involved a little bit of responsibility now and then. On these days of village festivity their father appeared as the highest public dignitary, and then they themselves could glow with reflected glory and next could plunge into the delight of stalls and booths and roundabouts. This Whitsun event was greatly looked forward to year by year. A pale reflection of it also made a great day for the children when the women's clubs held their festival, going in procession to church for service and returning to the school for tea and dancing.

At Christmas there was another annual delight: the visit of the Mummers who came to the vicarage regularly for many years and acted 'St. George and the Dragon' in the kitchen, or on occasion a special mumming play, 'Robin Hood and the Tanner'.[1] On Christmas Eve the ringers came with handbells and played carols at midnight, standing on the lawn beneath the vicarage windows—a thrilling performance. A quaint, possibly unique custom at South Cerney in the children's days was the so-called candle auction at the George Inn. This, too, was visited by the small Hadows. It was conducted for one Cutts of long ago who had owned land, mainly allotments, at Upper-Up, which was let annually by being put up for auction. As each allotment or piece of land was put up a small piece of candle was lighted, and the man who made the last bid before the candle went out got it.[2] There were traditional local recipes too. There is a story of a cottager who knew how to make mead in the traditional way and gave some to little Grace which she, as a child, accepted, not knowing its potency till she found herself struggling home hardly able to walk.

Unconsciously Grace Hadow's imagination was fed in childhood

[1] First printed in the *Oxford Treasury of English Literature*, vol. ii, edited by G. E. and W. H. Hadow, 1907.
[2] 'The ancient custom of auction "by the candle" survived in this village until 1913. As Chairman of the Trustees of Cutts Charity, one of the oldest in England (I have deeds dating back to 1426), it devolved on me to conduct the letting of land held by this charity, an inch of candle being used. The chief difficulty was to spot the last bid before the candle finally burnt out, leaving the room in darkness till the next lot w as put up. It is interesting that the names of the fields are the same as described in the earliest deeds 500 years ago.' Captain E. T. Cripps, South Cerney Manor, Cirencester (*The Times*, 25 April 1933).

with native lore and legend, and she had a quick sense for the romance of these as providing a link between one generation and the next, a token handed down that sometimes kept its meaning and sometimes lost it on the way, and yet remained as a trace of what our forefathers thought and did and felt.

Such a home setting left indelible impressions on her mind, and meanwhile the intellectual atmosphere of the vicarage was stimulating, and her mother's teaching and companionship gave her mind its bent. She inherited her mother's quickness and sense of fun and her habit of making the most of every ray of sunshine and yet exercising a keen and delicate sense of criticism of what is not perfect. From her mother, too, she imbibed terse and impressive English almost in babyhood, for Mrs. Hadow had a sense of language and enjoyed her youngest daughter's vivid words; she notes the four-year-old's first pun—by no means a bad one— when on being told 'Miss Knight is coming to-day' she remarked 'funny Miss Night coming by day', and she records the child's ingenuity and aptness for repartee. When told not to ask for things at the tea-table she was heard to mutter at the appropriate moment, 'I am staring at that cake', and at five she had a flash of pregnant critical intelligence in disapproval of her Reader: 'I do not like this book, it is very silly'; then starting to read aloud: 'I am to go in. Am I to go in? Let me go in' she then decides: 'There is no story in it—it must be a hymn.'

Her natural companions were the two brothers, her seniors, nearest to her in age, and her taste in occupations and games was theirs as far as possible. Gerald's interest in beetles and snakes and scientific experiments had a spice of adventure and he roused her especial devotion. The brothers dared her to feats in which she was determined not to be outdone. In holding her own she showed she could be ingenious as well as resourceful.

Mrs. Hadow believed in rules, and we may take it for granted that implicit obedience was expected of her children, though at the same time the response was in love. Demands were not unreasonable and opposition does not seem to have occurred to them. There was religious education based on Scripture in accordance with the ideas of the time and the tradition of a vicarage household; part of the day's events were church services, and Sunday was strictly kept. Long before its meaning went home Grace Hadow became familiar with the sound of scriptural language which roused puzzled thoughtfulness: 'May I say, O Lord God of Israel, and may I forgive a little boy when I have promised to be revenged on him? he quite roused me up.' And this tradition of a religious education continued throughout her schooldays. An interesting, and it would seem, rather unusual idea of her mother's was to conduct an argument with a child on a given topic, potentially an excellent way of training an intelligent young mind to accept a reasoned conclusion that goes against the grain and is nevertheless convincing. The little girl may well have experienced something of this at a very early age. At less than five, having begged her mother for an argument and being asked which side she would like to take, she decided 'the right side'. Another time there was her retort which became a family saying: 'I am not arguing, I am telling you.' An instance of this method of convincing her when she was nearly twelve is an 'argument' on the child's own most immediate concerns: 'I came away from Miss Ramsay's to-day to have a tooth out it was 6*d*. and did not cry a bit. Mother and I are to have an argument as to whether or no it is right to have gas Mother no me yes. I have two more to come out and which ever side wins has it.' In this case the issue must have been a drawn battle for the decision turned out to be 'if two at once gas else none'.

The quotation is taken from a diary of Grace Hadow's written in a childish hand, with very imperfect spelling and few stops. It begins at Cerney when she is eleven and continues with some gaps till 1892, and was her mother's gift. Evidently it is modelled on Mrs. Hadow's journal with brief daily entries in the style of a log-book, and dealing with happenings at the moment. The whole fills no more than a portion of an ordinary exercise book with a shiny black cover, but it is altogether characteristic. Clear, crisp, objective, this little record even at its earliest stage shows her mind in its lucidity and her character in its directness; and there are moments in which it shows more. The little historian keeps a careful check upon her statements and aims at exact truthfulness; the form in which the entries are made also lends itself admirably to a training in thought and expression. But whether or not it was supplied as an educative aid, the diary is wholly the child's own. Her relation to her mother and her brothers is reflected; when the diary starts abruptly on 23 September 1887 the two brothers nearest to her in age, Gerald and Edgie, are at

boarding-schools, Granville Coole has left the village—he became
a policeman—the older sisters Maggie (or Pearl) and Cottie are
mostly at home. Her godfather brother, Harry, is rarely there and
comes at fleeting moments to play with his little god-daughter
on the vicarage lawn and plait her fuzzy hair into many tiny
plaits, or he returns from Italy and brings her a *pomgranet*, or he
introduces a strange foreign artiste to the village who has fallen
on unfortunate days and is no doubt glad of a performance, or, as
she gets old enough to observe these things, he casts reflected
glory on the family by staying at as grand an address as the Palace,
Gloucester, or comes to visit her at her first boarding-school and
relieves all her troubles by a gift of 10*s*.

Meanwhile some permanent features of character are seen in
this little record; for instance, there is her intense joy in having
Edgie's old watch for her very own, her disappointment at
missing a magic lantern through jaundice, her impressions of a
winter walk alone, and her interest in people and in everything
slightly unusual that happens in the village. And on one occasion
there is the child's candour on receiving a gift—she is 'deeply
obliged' but she has 'no room'.

We find ourselves in touch with an eager, vivid, and sensitive
child; we are aware of her ardour and her loving nature; we
realize her power of repressing her feelings. And the child
develops perceptibly in this little record. Between 1888 and 1889
some pages of the diary have been removed which may or may not
have recorded more personal matters; however that may be, the
entries expand, the child takes herself in hand and is severe with
herself, there is more expression of opinion. Throughout there is
the striking sense of detachment with which events are set down.
The log-book style may have accustomed her to it. After minding
very much that she would not see the magic lantern the entry is:
'there was a full meeting, the lantern was splendid, I believe',
and the next day her mother's providing a 'chicken to carve
myself and everything' is entered; it is obviously the treat which
was intended to make up for the disappointment, and though
the impression remains that it did not do so, there is no further
comment.

As the only child left at the vicarage when her brothers went
to school, it must have been felt that she needed companions of
her own age. The pupils, Charlie and Marshall, with whom she

went for walks, or blackberrying or skating, were of an age to be coached for examination and too old for her. Gerald followed in his eldest brother's footsteps by gaining a scholarship at Malvern College, after which he obtained one at Caius College, Cambridge; the youngest son Edgecumbe also went to Malvern College and later to Oxford. Grace Hadow remained at home. Girls' education was not usually much thought of; partly for this reason, partly because it was difficult enough to scrape together means for the education of the boys, hers was somewhat haphazard. However, she acquired the most important things at home: a love of reading and a faculty for using her observation and intelligence. On expeditions in the 'Shandarydan' to Cirencester with her mother she would be allowed to sit on the counter of the shop while her mother was busy, and to look at the books for sale; it was there she learnt to peep into the uncut pages and acquired her faculty for 'reading a book without cutting it'. Evidently her mother realized the child's gifts and was determined to do for her what she could. At twelve she was sent to Cirencester once a week for French, German, Music, and Drawing to a school kept by a Miss Ramsay. Arithmetic she learnt from the schoolmaster at South Cerney; there were also intermittent German governesses at the vicarage.

In what circumstances a scholarship became possible for Grace Hadow is not clear; for scholarships were unusual at girls' schools at the time. Nevertheless she obtained one at Brownshill Court near Stroud, a school of some thirty girls, and went there as a boarder at the age of thirteen and nine months. For a small private school of that time Brownshill may have been ambitious in its teaching since this included Latin, Euclid, and Algebra, which were not necessarily 'girls' subjects' in those days. Grace Hadow as a scholar, perhaps a prize pupil, whose record was to be of value, was told off to pass examinations. She was ordered to write something original for the *Budget*, presumably the school magazine, by a given date and was urged to join the school essay club in place of the outside one to which she had belonged. Towards the end of her time at school it is reported: 'I was third in the history exam. Miss A. says I ought to be in the first class but I am too young—thank goodness (conceit).'

The ways of girls' schools have changed greatly since the nineties: particularly perhaps in matters of discipline and in 'marking'. Whether Grace Hadow quite lived up to the expectations of the authorities it would be hard to say. Very possibly they were prepared for the small misdemeanours that would seem calculated to occur under the accepted system of assessing conduct. Losing her 'term character' was by no means unusual for this little girl, or 'having a squeak' for it by throwing water against form-room windows from a window above: 'music lesson. Now for a row' is noted; or being reported for 'talking in Devo' time. Result a row' is a characteristic entry; or 'I am getting low in Sunday exams. Only 19 last time.' It is to be inferred that the religious teaching in the school was low church. 'Mr. T. . . . preached for the first time. He horrified Miss Z. so, that we are going to leave Pitchcombe. He mentioned praying for the souls of the dead, and said something about the Athanasian Creed. It was fine. He belongs to the class of barrel-organ-with-the-works-gone-wrong clergyman. They are a variety to people who work on strings and whose arms and legs fly about in all directions like Mr. A's.' By the side of amusement in watching gestures there is the voice of the fourteen-year-old enjoying something that defies what is considered the proper thing.

It is clear that the school did not get hold of young Grace Hadow; probably it was not constructed to make an appeal to the public spirit which was so strong in her in later years; perhaps she was too young or too independently critical of authority. She was given to laughter rather than condemnation, but critical she became and critical she remained, and impatient about things that savoured of routine rather than conviction. And yet she believed in rules where they helped self-discipline. At Brownshill she greatly enjoyed the fun, the expeditions, the charades, the games; what seems to have interested her most was the other girls, and when she admired them there was an over-anxious desire to stand well in their esteem: one Margaret whom she 'adores' and who is 'so nice', with whom she reads Milton on one occasion and discusses heaven, and Marjorie whom she steadily loves and admires and whose affection she is anxious to hold. She longs to have her to stay at Cerney; she is protective towards her and very steady in her attachment; finally she became a lifelong friend.[1]

Meanwhile Grace's short-sightedness had become confirmed. She learned to live with it and always wore glasses, and she deve-

[1] Mrs. Campbell, *née* Hope.

loped so good a faculty of seeing in spite of it that it was hardly felt as a disability. But nature gave her remarkable deep blue eyes which eagerness could set on fire, and it was a pity that this feature of her countenance should have been robbed of its full effect.

Most interesting is the growth in character which is seen over an episode of a ghost that intruded upon the peace of Browns-hill with noises and rumblings. Partly she was fascinated by the mystery of this affair, partly very ready to consider and to advance reasonable explanations. Marjorie was very frightened, and in the effect that it must have had upon the girls the interlude of the ghost may well have done the school harm at the time. Whether Brownshill was really haunted or whether the supposed ghost was someone's trick or a misunderstanding is not clear; what is noteworthy is the discovery made by this excitable and imagina-tive child of fourteen about keeping courage. She never loses her head; when afraid herself she finds she can keep up her courage by helping Marjorie to keep up hers : 'I am inclined to feel queer at times but then I am sure to have to look under the beds or some-thing to comfort her and the very act makes me alright again.'

Grace stayed at Brownshill till just after she was fifteen, when her mother became dissatisfied with the school and removed her. It is doubtful whether school could have given her an intellectual stimulus to supplement home, let alone rival it. Her interest in 'Parnell and Pigott' and still more in the case of the Bishop of Lincoln does not appear to have been shared, but if she was left longing for a good talk on such matters, there were compensa-tions; she had learned something about living under a routine devised for numbers, she had tried herself in various ways, she had found a friend of her own age and had learnt in a new way to stand on her own feet. In school subjects she had done well. As to finding her level among girls of her own age, it would be hard to say what happened; probably she was head and shoulders above them in most respects and quite unaware of it.

CHAPTER II

TRANSITIONAL YEARS

1891–1900

THE years from adolescence to full womanhood were not marked by incidents for Grace Hadow, but they were vivid in inward experience. Her affections were centred in her family, where her mother was the dominating influence and the background. The feeling for Mrs. Hadow on the part of her children was unusual in its undeviating character, composed of deep-rooted affection and of the attraction of a very remarkable personality. Bound up with it there was the consciousness of how much she had toiled and suffered for her children's education and future, and the natural wish to make life easier for one to whom they owed everything. Grace was a hero-worshipper eager to devote herself, and in her sight one hero never eclipsed another. As the youngest of a large family she had found scope for admiration of others at home, of her brothers, especially her godfather; during her later teens this faculty radiated outwards. When the outside world begins to assert its claims and to make inroads upon childhood's instinctive acceptance of things at home there must be conflicts. Grace was direct and ardent and shy, and in some ways very young for her age; like others of her generation, she experienced the familiar conflict between home duties and promptings to follow up her own development and remoter desires. How far was it right to choose a life of her own, staying away from home where a devoted mother longed for her daughter's presence and where there was much to do to ease a heavy routine? Would her affections let her compromise over such an issue?

At the age of fifteen Grace left Brownshill Court and spent the next nine months at home, first suffering an illness, described as 'suppressed jaundice', then going back to the old groove of Cerney. A German governess undertook part of her instruction, who was something of an infliction: 'a great, fat, ugly German with a bad temper', but this did not hinder Grace from progressing in French, German, and music under her direction. Inklings of her powers began to assert themselves, though as yet they were neither analysed nor understood: 'I *do* so want to be an actress. I wonder if they will ever let me. Mater would never be content, I am afraid, unless I did Shakespeare and was always a heroine. I think one could do God's work. It does not sound a noble life but I can't think God would give one such an intense desire else. I used to want to be a nurse or Home Missionary, but not as I want to be an actress. It can't be wrong. I admire the other lives so, but one could try to do others good in a quiet way anywhere. Of course if Cottie marries or anything I must stay at home and teach so as to help Mother. God helping me, I will always do what she wishes, she bears so much for us.'

When she was approaching sixteen there was a change which opened up a new world to her; it was decided to send her to Truro High School. Her mother's brother, Archdeacon Cornish, afterwards Bishop of St. Germans, was then vicar of Kenwyn, a small place one mile from Truro. His wife was an intimate friend of the headmistress of the High School, Miss Arnold. Grace was to live with her uncle and aunt and attend the school which lay at the other end of Truro, about two miles off. The atmosphere of the vicarage was quiet, entirely of its time, full of good works. Mrs. Cornish, a leader in everything that went on and possessed of great powers of sympathy, spent her time in parish work and things connected with the diocese; the Archdeacon, fond of children, full of fun, kindness itself, was busy all day, seeing little of the family except at meals and in the evening. Both were real Victorians of the best type. Their daughter Margaret, then a child of nine, also attended the High School. The Vth and VIth forms of the school, however, together numbered only sixteen, and Grace's arrival among these older girls stands out in the memory of a contemporary, partly perhaps because it was rare to have a new girl in the upper part of the school: 'She had regular features, a faultless complexion, and fair wavy hair— but this she drew back from her high forehead so tightly as to make it as nearly as possible invisible: I remember her in a long woollen dress with its stiff bodice buttoned to the neck and its high collar neatly fastened by a large round brooch. Nobody could call it a becoming outfit for a girl of fifteen, but in spite of it Grace managed to look quietly impressive. . . . It was not till the day of the school play when we saw her taking a man's part, in peruke and ruffles, that we realized how very distinguished she could look and that perhaps she was not so desperately serious as we had supposed.'

Another schoolfellow, who has only met her twice since, retains a clear impression of her in early days, remembering her as 'intellectually gifted and full of cheerful vitality' but outstanding in the complete self-discipline, lovableness, and tender sympathy of her character. She describes her as 'a strong soul'.

Grace did not at once like school: 'I hate it, I hate it, I hate it!! now I am better' is a note in her diary on returning to Kenwyn after her first holidays at home. Soon she was to find her imagination captured by Miss Arnold, whose influence upon her at a formative and impressionable age was deep, and must have done much to form her later ideas. Miss Arnold was a remarkable personality who made the strong impression which she undoubtedly did make by sheer force of character. The school was immersed in the influence that radiated from her; all her VIth form worshipped her—and this in a perfectly healthy way, for she would have stood no nonsense. Formed largely by Miss Beale, in the tradition of Ruskin, she was an intellectual and cultured woman of deep and strong affections and sincerely religious: 'if she had a fault, it was perhaps that she lived on too intense a plane with very little relaxation, she seemed to us, in spite of all her love and kindness, a being of another world.'[1] Born in 1859, she belonged to the earlier generation of mid-Victorians, and when Grace came to Truro she was thirty-two years old and had been headmistress for three years, having taken over a school of forty-five girls which had since then grown in numbers. The school was badly housed, but deficiencies in buildings and equipment were not allowed to interfere with the quality of the work done. 'Expect perfection: you will not get it, but you will get far better work than if you make moderate demands' was Miss Arnold's advice to a teacher, and she herself was an inspiring one. A lover and reader of Browning, she lived and imparted the philosophy of the 'Grammarian's Funeral' which she taught her pupils to love. And she read them poetry of the day, the Brownings, Rossetti, Tennyson, Matthew Arnold, besides Milton and Wordsworth.

The school had been started by Archbishop Benson when he was Bishop of Truro and the cathedral services were part of its life. Miss Arnold's was one of those minds for which it is essential to

[1] Mrs. Tweedy (*née* Margaret Cornish).

find truth for themselves. Like others of her generation she went through religious doubts and difficulties. At sixteen she had been baptized in the sea near St. Leonard's by a representative of the Plymouth Brethren; as she 'watched the sun sparkling on the tiny waves and heard them breaking gently on the beach' the beauty of the scene possessed her and she felt herself baptized 'in the name of the Father and Maker of Heaven and of Earth but not of the Brethren'.[1] Mental struggles that ensued were eased with her release from the doctrine of eternal punishment and she found peace of mind in the gospel of love. At the age of twenty-five, in 1884, she was confirmed in St. Paul's Cathedral, 'not as a formal entry into the Church of England' but belonging 'to the Holy Church throughout the world' and wishing her confirmation to be at St. Paul's since 'there is nothing parochial about the Cathedral, the confession of ages is still vibrating in the air: it lies at the heart of *working* London, and working men and women pass in and out all day, and find rest and comfort in its music and quiet'. The Bishop of St. Germans recalled Miss Arnold's 'deeply religious spirit that made the life (at the school) a unity in itself, and all ideals and pure aims seem natural and almost commonplace'. Her religious teaching is remembered by her pupils as inspiring and inspired; it 'cast out fear' and helped them understand the words 'thy service is perfect freedom', and they testify that her influence remained a living force in after life. Grace left no record; but it is certain that she was devoted to Miss Arnold heart and soul, and she must have owed to her a great deal of what remained central in her outlook.

'The importance of education consists in its effect on character', said Miss Arnold. 'To train in unselfishness, in devotion to truth, in self-control, is more difficult than to train the reason and memory; it is also more important; and it is not for success in the next examination that we are teaching, it is not even in success in their future career that we train these children; and we are looking to eternity for the judgement on our work.'

To many of her friends in later life it might seem strange to hear Grace Hadow described as religious. She did not keep to observances that were part of her life at home and at school and did not discuss religion except on rarest occasions and for special reasons, yet there remained a steady anchorage.

[1] Quoted from *Notes and Letters* by *Clare Robinson* (printed for private circulation).

Grace stayed at Truro from 1891 to 1894, was very happy there, and loved the life at school. She threw herself into school activities, became robust and a player of cricket, often coaching other girls in the game. As head girl she was long remembered for her distinction, and she continued her interest in the school in later years.

In May 1893 Grace's pluck and resolution caught the attention of observers when she saved one of the little girls from an accident. Miss Arnold, reporting it, writes that the foreman of a shop had told her he thought she ought to know 'how nobly one girl acted' when a little one fell down as a carriage and horses came down the road, and must have been seriously hurt had not a 'big one, with extraordinary presence of mind, clutched her and dragged her between her knees though the effort upset her, and the carriage went over her own foot'.[1] The damage, if painful, was not serious. 'We may feel rather proud of belonging to the same family', remarks her godfather-brother in expressing concern to his mother, whose mind had been put at rest before it could be anxious.

The conclusion that Grace's career at the High School became a signal success is not difficult to draw, even if she had not obtained prizes and done well in some outside examinations and been offered a further opening at the school. Miss Arnold was seriously and disinterestedly concerned in her pupil's future and, in May 1893, she made a formal offer that Grace should continue for a further year or more at the school as a student-teacher, a post hitherto not contemplated for anyone there; instead of leaving in that summer she was to return to the school in September, for lessons only, till Christmas, and after Christmas she was to teach some music and have some music lessons given, while all her mornings were to be free to work at languages and literature. The new music mistress had picked Grace out as the one girl to whom specialization would be worth while and was disposed to give her full attention; Miss Arnold evidently cared also about her other gifts.

Grace herself was thrown into conflict by the proposal. Her return home had been taken for granted, and she was torn between gratitude to Miss Arnold and the wish to do what was best for her mother. A letter written to her eldest sister when this subject

[1] Recorded by Mrs. Hadow. The 'little one' was her cousin Margaret Cornish.

was first raised eight months earlier is so characteristic in its feeling and outlook that it seems worth while to reproduce it in full. The mature Grace Hadow remained as sensitive to the claims of those she loved, and in the first place those of her mother, though she no longer expressed herself in the way of the girl of nearly seventeen; what is, however, most striking is the effort to rid herself of an emotional crisis in her personal concerns by seeing them as impersonally as possible; her innocent diplomacy, also characteristic, plays round the one point on which she was clear; her personal liking was not to weight the scales, if she could feel satisfied in this regard the rest could be left to fate. In intensity of feeling, and in this particular approach to a problem, Grace Hadow did not change in later years when she had long arrived at keeping her conflicts to herself.

> Kenwyn Vicarage,
> Truro.
> Sept. 26th, 1892.

My dear Margaret,

I am going to send you a very uninteresting letter all about myself, but I am rather miserable and I want you to help me. Miss Arnold spoke to me to-day about my leaving. I hardly know what I told her, but I said Mother wanted me, and though I knew she would let me stay if I very much wished it, I explained that I could not ask her. Miss Arnold was so kind, she quite understood, but she asked if I would mind her writing to Mother about it (wasn't it sweet of her to ask) and she spoke so kindly and promised me such a triumphant future at School that I am afraid she carried me away. Anyhow she is going to write to Mother, but she is not going to tell her how much I want to stay. I am sorry now I said she might write at all. But I thought it probably would not affect Mother very much. But I want you to shew Mother the other side; to do what Miss Arnold wants I should have to stay at school at least two years more and it would not do. I suppose I ought to have told her I wanted to leave but I couldn't, and between that and the fear of letting her think Mother was dragging me away against my will, which she most certainly is not, I don't know what impression I left on Miss Arnold's mind. It was so tempting to listen to her, I never had the least idea I was likely to do as well as she says before. Indeed I can't believe it now, but if there was twice as good a future waiting for me I think I ought to come home. Speaking purely selfishly I should be *miserable* if I thought of Mother working so hard, and longing for me, and I able to come and not coming. Miss Arnold spoke of my being more use to her bye and bye if I stayed, but I don't think so. I know it was frightfully selfish of me to let Miss Arnold write, I am very sorry now. It ought not to be hard to give up anything for Mother. It is not, but God knows it felt *so* hard to decide which was most useful. One only wants to relieve and help her. I don't know whether this letter is in the least intelligible but I felt I must talk to someone and I think you understand. Impress on Mother that I am *glad* to come home at Christmas. I have thought and prayed and wrestled over it and I think it must be best. It is no real sacrifice, it could not be one to do anything for her. I should never forgive myself if I neglected any chance of making her life easier. I must leave. I *want* it. Please forgive such an egotistical letter, but I am afraid of Miss Arnold's letter upsetting Mother and I want you to counteract it.

Good night

My darling, darling sister

from

Grace.

Clearly Grace was wanted at home at the time; with her eldest daughter removed by marriage and the second claimed by Mrs. Rundle Charles at Hampstead, Mrs. Hadow was left single-handed to deal with the duties of the parish, the household, and the resident pupils who needed her time and attention for their leisure hours and for lessons other than those provided by the vicar. The higher education of women did not altogether appeal to Mrs. Hadow, whose strong intellect was satisfied by wide and various reading, by mother-wit, by practical duties, and by religion as comprising everything else. However, Grace's godfather was alive to the importance of taking this opportunity for his young sister, and in June 1893 he urged upon his mother to re-arrange matters at home, to give up the pupils and take no others, and to allow him to make up for any loss of income: 'Do remember that if you would feel remorse at missing an opportunity for us (which you never have and never could) we should feel just as bad if trouble came to you from any decision of ours. If you had one over-worked day in consequence of Grace's absence, we should be very unhappy indeed. So please reflect that we can't discuss this question at all except you are going to be good and not do too much. Do drop those pupils.' If Mrs. Hadow could manage without her youngest daughter, Grace had better accept Miss Arnold's offer; it was an honour to her, she was very happy and popular at the school, was getting 'plenty of play and plenty of incident' and was leading a good, useful, and healthy life, and one of which she was really fond. 'Her hero-worship for Miss Arnold is another point in favour of acceptance.'

And so it was decided. Mrs. Hadow let the pupils go except one boy who depended upon her for passing an examination, and Grace, for the time being, was started on music as a step towards a profession in which her brother, having visions of her as a cultured artist, hoped to help her, but which was not truly her vocation. In July 1894 both she and her pupils passed their examinations. She returned to home duties varied by visits to her brother in Oxford or elsewhere. Days, in her absence, had been 'quiet, not to say a little dull'. Two years later, in August 1896, Miss Arnold was married to Canon C. M. Robinson and went to live first in Ripon, where her daughter was born, and then in Limpsfield in Surrey. She died in 1906 at the age of forty-seven.

In 1939 Grace Hadow, then Principal of a Women's College in Oxford, visited her old school at Truro at the opening ceremony of the newest building. When the service had been held and the children had performed their dramatic entertainment, she gave them a description of the school in her day and spoke of her affection for it: 'Truro High School fifty years ago: what is the picture that that brings? A tall house in Strangways Terrace, with tall elms opposite. People used to condole with Chancellor Worledge who lived next door, for having "a rookery on one side and a girlery on the other". Dinner was in the basement, and was wheeled in a go-cart all the way from Kenwyn.[1] I can see the then charwoman with an old Liberty hat of Miss Arnold's slightly over one eye, trundling it down Pydar Street. The "Gym" was an old stable, and our playing field a small meadow across the way, so that fielding not infrequently involved plunging through the hedge into the road.

'But Truro fifty years ago stood for many other things besides a certain old-fashionedness. My mind goes back to those brief

[1] The boarding-house, 'Trevosa', was at Kenwyn (close to the vicarage). Grace went on to live there presumably when she became a pupil teacher at the school.

ten minutes before school when Miss Arnold read poetry to us, and laid the foundation of a love of Wordsworth which has been one of the lasting joys of life. Now-a-days Cornwall is a summer haunt of trippers. In those days at the summer half-term a little group of mistresses and older girls used to sally forth, descend upon some fishing village in a heavenly cove and just stay there: though I own I still remember the farm which turned Miss Caldwell and me away on the ground that "we only take gentlefolk".

'What are the changes that a very old Girl sees when she comes back? They are such as must delight her. I shall always have a very real if wholly sentimental affection for the actual building which has so many associations for me, but no one could pretend it was suited for a school, and the difficulties with which headmistress and staff must have had to contend were enough to have broken any less intrepid spirits. The first feeling I always have when I come to the present school is of light and space. I suppose the sun must have shone into Strangways Terrace, but my recollection of it is always of something faintly resembling an aquarium. Now we are set on a hill, and sun and wind are what I think of when I picture us. The gay colours of the new wing are just right, they "belong to be there". We were anything but gloomy or repressed, but atmosphere does tell and the abounding vitality of the new school, although no doubt largely a reflection of Miss Coate's,[1] must also be in part due to airy, sunny buildings, and a general sense of being on top of the world. What one is tempted to call the sun deck on the roof of the newest building is typical of the spirit of the place—something still sunnier, still airier, still higher than before, with a yet wider outlook and fresher air to breathe.

'One thing struck me at the opening ceremony. Truro High School has always stood for religion as an integral part of normal daily life. The religious ceremony of the dedication blended absolutely naturally with scenes from *Alice in Wonderland*. At one moment the Bishop in full canonicals was giving us his blessing, at the next he was watching the Pied Piper charming rats. That simplicity and sincerity of outlook have always been characteristic of the Truro I know and love, and as long as they remain we Old Girls can only rejoice in the changes that mean life and growth

[1] Miss Dora Coate, the present headmistress (1945), who kindly allowed me to quote from the school magazine of 1940.

GRACE HADOW AS A CHILD

Reproduced from a 'Ferrotype' of the time

THE 'LITTLE WINDFLOWER'

and the power to meet new conditions. We have always been proud to belong to Truro: we find that pride increases.'

Grace's connexion with Cornwall did not come to an end when she left Truro in 1894. In the same year when she first went to Kenwyn her eldest sister Margaret had been married to her cousin John Cornish, a lawyer in Penzance, and their house became a holiday home for her at times when the journey to Cerney was too far, and it remained so in subsequent years.

John Cornish, a lawyer by circumstance, was a sailor by vocation and a passionate yachtsman, and Grace became devoted to him. He introduced her to the Cornish coast and Cornish sea, and to the peculiar history and customs of Cornwall and its smugglers' tales, which were as intimately known to him as were the fisherfolk and the country people of his home.[1] From him she learnt in later years to sail the 16-ton *Little Windflower* sufficiently well to be commended by him for the way in which she handled her. No coast could ever satisfy her compared to the Cornish coast, no other district appealed to her imagination more passionately than this country with its wonderful scenery, its sea, its dangerous rocks, its sheer black cliffs, its marvellous fish. To go to Cornwall with Grace in later years was to watch her romantic side taking grip of her. Scrambling on the cliffs and bathing when the waves were very high were an exultation, and learning, rather laboriously, to swim an achievement; and then there were walks inland across the moors and fields, with their kindly rubbing-stones for cattle, and luscious farm-house teas with cream and jam and saffron cakes. And there were endless tales of Cornish people; to her it was a region haunted by beauty and romance, and she had roots of her own in it.

Six months after her return from Truro in 1894 there was to be another venture for the sake of education in languages and music; she was sent to Germany for a year to board with a family at Trier and take lessons. Her old friend 'Marjorie', of Brownshill days, shared her stay and remembers as an outstanding event how they saw *Lohengrin* performed and were both transported by the wonderful acting of a Munich star. For the rest their stay was 'desperately boring'. Grace worked very hard at music and singing lessons; during those months she joined a choral

---

[1] He discovered and edited the manuscript of the autobiography of Harry Carter, a Cornish smuggler of Prussia Cove (1749–1809).

society, and was greatly surprised when the performers 'did not stand up for the Hallelujah Chorus'; besides German conversation in the house, she also had French lessons outside. Their Hausfrau hostess was a provincial who was easily offended in trivial ways, whereupon it usually fell to Grace to placate her by some special mark of attention, so that she came to be regarded as a 'schöne, stattliche Dame'. A visit from Grace's sisters when they went to see Strasbourg, another from her brother Harry who took her on a walking tour in Luxembourg and other parts, broke the time, and Grace herself was incapable of being bored; she acquired a good working knowledge of the German language and retained an understanding and liking for Germans of the best sort. However, the time in Germany does not appear to have brought lasting personal contacts. An ancient picture map of Trier hung in her bedroom for many years, but the impression left by life in Germany was not one of enthusiastic admiration of the country and its ways. On 25 February 1896 she returned to South Cerney 'thin and tired, but very dear and bright and well'.

Meanwhile circumstances at home had improved and the wheels of life were eased. The end of resident pupils is noted by Mrs. Hadow, as it were with a sigh of relief, in 1895. 'That chapter has been fully written, every word finished.' Mrs. Rundle Charles, the authoress, 'Cousin Bessie', with whom she lived on sisterly terms, had died appointing her executrix with a bequest of £4,000; her own eldest son had been appointed tutor at Worcester College and was now able and eager to help, and the struggle for her children's education was over. Among events most treasured and much looked forward to were the visits of this eldest son in vacations; to these the routine of the vicarage gave way. For Mrs. Hadow they became festive days of scintillating talk when her son and his friends had discussions in which she and other members of the family took part and of which the topics ranged over things read, heard, seen, reflected upon: the world of books, new and old, and of music in the young Oxford of those days, travel in Italy and elsewhere, scientific discoveries, card games, odd ideas; and always the visitors were arrested by the vivacity of their hostess, and her eager look, while she herself was aware chiefly of her son, anxious to draw him out, or to let him have his silences when there was no occasion for talk. Less intellectual visitors found all this formidable. But there was no posing or standing on tiptoe. If the standard of conversation in that little vicarage drawing-room approximated to a small salon of wits, all round there were fields and the stolid agricultural and sporting world. And this world had entered into the consciousness of the Hadows who had grown up in it, and while it gave occasion for humorous observations and good stories, it also held fresh air. At the edge of the field was the 'Snakarium', an institution due to Gerald Hadow's scientific interest in snakes. There, if the spirit so moved them, the younger Hadows might pick up a snake to take with them to the railway station on meeting a train and to startle the porters. In years not long gone by, her godfather-brother and his friend Graham Balfour[1] had found it sport to play with little Grace on the vicarage lawn. Now, just returned from Trier, she sat both vivid and demure, a grown-up young lady to be introduced to Graham Balfour's young wife, who was amazed at these unusual vicarage folk, listening to their startling discussions till bit by bit shyness wore off. In the minds of the home party of the vicarage Oxford stood for a culture that they longed to share, and to Grace Hadow her brother, her nearest hero, became a prototype.

Records of Grace between 1892 and 1900 are very scanty. There must have been a period when some religious beliefs for which her school or home circle stood were questioned and assailed. Whether this happened as a process of natural growth in intercourse with her brother Gerald, the scientist, and her eldest brother, Harry, the philosopher, or whether it came as a shock and inward dramatic crisis it is impossible to say, though this last seems unlikely, considering her known relation to Miss Arnold. It is certain that she had arrived at firmly based convictions and developed clear thought by 1900, when her friends in Oxford felt her to be a 'co-ordinated and mature being'. Her transitional years may be said to have ended in 1899, a year that decidedly tested her and brought out qualities. She accepted a junior post at Cheltenham Ladies College which in the event proved hard. It seems to have been entered upon with a view to further qualification as a teacher; anyhow, it was there she attended some lectures of Ernest de Selincourt, who came to the college

[1] Graham Balfour: Assistant Secretary to the Delegacy for Oxford Local Examinations, 1897–1902; Director of Education, Staffordshire, 1902–1926; author of *History of Education*, Clarendon Press, Oxford, 1898, and of the Life of his cousin, Robert Louis Stevenson, 1901. Born 1859, died 1929, married 1896, Rhoda, daughter of Leonard D. Brooke of Oxton, Birkenhead.

each week from Oxford, where he was exerting himself to build up the status of the English School and to give a high standard to the study of English literature. He soon found Grace Hadow 'head and shoulders above the rest' in his class, and his interest in her roused her eldest brother to decide that his own belief in her powers was not only 'brotherly partiality'. She was encouraged to read with a view to the English School in Oxford and to prepare herself for the so-called 'Women's First',[1] an obsolete examination especially designed for women, which excused them from Responsions, admitting them to read an Honour School and to present themselves for the Final Examination. There was an understanding with Cheltenham that she was to be allowed some time for her own work, the time reserved for this proving to be 6.30 a.m.

Her duties included supervision at meals, which led to a standing request on the part of the children for a story. While they listened spellbound and eager, but still able to eat, Grace herself could do little more than look at her meals or bolt them at top speed. However, she passed the 'Women's First' easily in December 1899, and next July passed the Cambridge Higher Local, which last may well have been her original objective in taking the Cheltenham post. In July 1900 she gave up the work at Cheltenham and returned to South Cerney.

Meanwhile the autumn of the previous year had brought a crushing sorrow at home which drew her united family together closely and imprinted its mark of reserve on Grace herself. Her brother Gerald, full of promise and brilliantly gifted in ways quite other than the rest of the family, succumbed to consumption when he had just begun medical practice and died at the age of twenty-eight, in August 1899, at Penzance. She shared the experience of his illness and was present at his death, but her grief went too deep for her to be able to speak of those days. Gerald's memory was unforgettable. Mrs. Hadow records stages in his illness and recalls his gentleness and the measure of his suffering. Years later she recurs to the thought of him as of yesterday. A tablet in South Cerney Church commemorates him. Grace buried her grief.

---

[1] After the M.A. degree had become accessible to women she availed herself of the privilege of qualifying for it retrospectively. This meant preparing for Responsions, for Divinity Moderations, and for Groups B2 and B5 which she passed in succession. She was meanwhile engaged in all the activities implied in her Secretaryship of Barnett House. She took her degree in 1922.

CHAPTER III
OXFORD
1900–1903

IN October 1900 Grace Hadow came to Somerville College, Oxford, to read the Honour School of English Language and Literature and to expand like a plant in congenial soil. Work and society in Oxford seemed suited to every faculty of hers, and she was soon to feel the satisfaction of a life lived under such circumstances. Oxford with its deep and varied historical stamp and its unique intermixture of young and old in people and institutions could not fail to attract her. Through her brother she had long felt its glamour; now she was to see it with her own eyes from within and from quite a new point of view. To go to a women's college in those days was to become a member of a comparatively small and privileged society most of the members of which were serious-minded hard-working people who knew they had a common cause. Their colleges were still small. In comparison to the present day there was not the difficulty of competition for entrance to college, since there were not appreciably more candidates for admission than it was possible to accommodate. Students were drawn almost exclusively from professional and business classes with a tradition of culture. The secondary schools throughout the country were themselves in process of being built up and were not yet making their full contribution. It was then twenty-one years since the first 'Ladies' colleges' were opened in Oxford. Women's education had outgrown the experimental stage. Only four years before, in 1896, however, a proposal to confer degrees upon women had been rejected by Congregation. With the assistance of members of the University, who supported their education, women were nevertheless penetrating peacefully all the while, but they remained on sufferance. While distinguished members of the University made time to take them as pupils, serve on the councils of their colleges, and advise on policy in the cause of gaining their establishment in the University by right, the women for their part were put on their mettle; they felt responsibility for living up to the privilege of study and becoming truly fit in themselves to take their place in Oxford and belong. They were allowed the full privileges of study and were admitted to university examinations, but not to the degree.

Grace Hadow came to Somerville after hardship. She had seen a dearly beloved brother on the eve of a brilliant future stricken down by disease and die; she had gone through drudgery in a pupil-teacher's post. She knew the hunger and thirst for opportunities to meet people who cared for things of the mind and spirit and belonged to a wider world than her own. The high lights of her life had come for the most part through her eldest brother whether in reading or talk, or in interesting people or in travel abroad; for remarkable as her own home circle was, life in Cerney offered little outside interest, and so the freedom of college and the wealth of opportunities now open to her were delightful. Here her time was her own to overtax; close at hand there was a greater choice of interesting people than she had ever known, with ways and ideas many of them unlike any which she had hitherto encountered; further, there was the exhilaration of discovering that she had it in her to do things successfully which she had never yet attempted, and as a background to her college life there was still her eldest brother taking an interest in her progress, giving her his companionship when time allowed and the entry to the homes of his oldest friends. In 1899 he had become a member of Somerville College Council.

Founded in 1879 on an undenominational basis when this implied a certain militancy and strong individual conviction, Somerville College stood for liberalism as well as for scholarship and culture. A liberating spirit of confident achievement permeated its atmosphere, and the college had the reputation of cultivating in women professionalism in the best sense, and of fitting them for a life in which women must fight women's battles. Recently it had produced a remarkable generation, which became well known later in parliamentary circles—women such as Eleanor Rathbone and Mrs. H. A. L. Fisher (Lettice Ilbert), leading reformers such as Margery Fry, or those who acquired professional status for high scholarship such as Mildred K. Pope, for many years tutor of the college and afterwards professor at Manchester University. All of these were Grace's seniors, ardent Somervillians who had left their mark on the college, so that when she came into residence there was already an eager spirit abroad. The atmosphere of Somerville proved excellent for her.

She entered into the feeling that Somervillians had for Somerville and became a leader, perhaps in the view of some a partisan, for she could not be other than eager or enthusiastic about people and causes. Soon she was 'simply pouring herself into college life, fizzling and bubbling with high spirits'.

The 'students'—as they were then called—numbered some eighty and were grouped into two houses, 'West' and 'Hall'—which were presided over by the Principal, Miss Maitland, and the Vice-Principal, Miss Bruce,[1] respectively. Grace was assigned to 'Hall' and quickly made friends with Alice Bruce, supporting her in college matters. Through her brother-in-law, Augustus George Vernon Harcourt,[2] Alice Bruce had known W. H. Hadow for a good many years; she had stayed at South Cerney and knew the Hadows' home circle. When Grace arrived in Oxford as a rather silent person and distinctly shy, she found in Alice Bruce the directness and simplicity that always appealed to her and that set her at her ease, and she found a friend who could help her overcome her shyness. Grace arrived 'tall, slim, fair, speaking with a Gloucestershire burr with a roll on the *r*'s which gave it a special flavour' with little idea of dressing to advantage and little small talk. Soon she began to discover the use of her many-sided gift. 'Everything was there, it only needed bringing out,' said Alice Bruce, who saw this happen with interest and used opportunities to assist the process, taking Grace to Scotland in vacation to join her brother, General Bruce, on a month's holiday, and there to discover her passion for mountain-climbing and her fearlessness. 'Oxford seems to suit Grace wonderfully well,' writes her brother on 10 February 1901; 'she is at present a standing advertisement for the place, full of multifarious occupations, doing them all successfully and looking the picture of health.' A month later he writes to their mother suggesting she should be allowed the full three years at college instead of two years as first planned:

'March 10, 1901.

'Since writing this morning I have had a walk with Grace. Her Somerville authorities have suggested that she should stay up for three years, instead of two, and have hinted that if she does,

---

[1] The Hon. Alice M. Bruce, daughter of Lord Aberdare and sister of General Bruce of Everest fame.

[2] F. R. S. Lee's Reader in Chemistry at Christ Church, Oxford.

and gains the general experience of the place which that entails, there may be more chance of their offering her work after schools. If this came off it would be about the best thing that could happen to her, and it seems worth while her staying on. . . .

'The part that Grace is taking in college life will be most useful to her hereafter in any case: but it crowds her time a little as present conditions stand. Another year for literature would relieve the pressure. She is looking very well and is in the highest of spirits, but it would do no harm if she could take things a little more at leisure.

'She is very happy and doing extremely good work all round. At the next meeting of the "joint" Debating Society (to which all the women's colleges belong) she is being put up for two out of three offices: her dons all seem to be fond of her. It really looks as though she had found her proper billet.'

The third year was agreed upon for Grace. Alice Bruce drew her into college problems, as was natural in those earlier days when seniors and juniors often lived together more closely than more complete organization now allows, and as was doubly natural perhaps at a time when her brother was on the Council of the College.

It was an interesting moment in college history. Somerville College was then taking the lead in developments that permanently affected the position of women in Oxford. Miss Maitland had been Principal for eleven years and if, as has been said, she 'frankly wanted Somerville to inherit the earth', she wanted it in a way that proved to be statesmanlike. She planned provision for research which she was to see established as the first for women in Oxford,[1] and planned the extension of the college buildings. She saw the Library erected, a building connecting 'Hall' and 'West', completed in 1904 as the first in a women's college. Most important of all, perhaps, she fostered a policy of internal tutorships. What had been a Hall of residence was developing into a real college with an organization analogous to the Oxford pattern. When Miss Maitland retired in 1906 Somerville's leadership in the general movement towards obtaining recognition for women in the University was continued by her successor Miss Penrose, a great Principal and a fine scholar, who carried with her not

[1] The Somerville (afterwards called Mary Somerville) Research Fellowship founded by old students in 1902.

only her own college but the growing body of women tutors in Oxford.

In 1901 W. H. Hadow was serving on the Committee of the Somerville Council to arrange preliminaries for building the Library. He speaks of being exercised with the matter of a compromise between the 'idealists (who want the best possible building) and the financiers (who want to keep down the cost)', and this a little anxiously at first and then in satisfaction at the acceptance of his proposals. The venture claimed the practical sympathy of old Somervillians who financed it by a loan and gifts. When the Library stood complete there was an opening ceremony for which Robert Bridges wrote his masque *Demeter*. W. H. Hadow set it to music and members of the college performed it in 1904. Grace was well sponsored in Somerville, and the knowledge of persons and the measure of insight into college dealings that she gained there stood her in good stead in later days.

Among her contemporaries, as a student she was distinguished mainly as a speaker, with a reputation for brilliance that was somehow challenging and which, whether it moved others to shyness or to opposition or to enjoyment, remained exhilarating. However, she was not aware of being notable. Her gift as a speaker came as a discovery to herself, and she had a touching simplicity in assuming this to be merely a matter of conquering shyness and so attainable by all. Certainly she stimulated others to try. Soon after she came to college she was shining at the Oxford Women Students Debating Society, which then met weekly in the Hall of the Girls' High School, and in her second term she was elected its Treasurer, the first time that such an office was conferred on anyone in her first year. In due course she became President. By November 1901 her brother reports: 'Grace presides next Tuesday over a debate in which the chief speakers are Miss Fry and Miss Rogers,[1] one of them a Somerville don and the other the ultimate authority of Women's Education in Oxford. She is looking forward to it with pleasure.'

In Somerville itself she took a leading share in a Parliament which was inaugurated in her day, largely under the inspiration of Margery Fry, and which became a feature. Conducted as a debating society but in accordance with strict parliamentary procedure, it was carried through with zest. Members of the Senior

[1] A. M. A. H. Rogers. Cf. Chapter IX.

and Junior Common Room stook part, and the whole thing became an enjoyable game which was taken seriously. In October 1901 Grace was acting as Colonial Secretary (vice Mr. Chamberlain). Now and then 'Parliament' took a dramatic turn, as when the impeachment of Wyndham was acted, in which Grace is especially remembered by her fellows. It was in debate in particular that she was outstanding at this time—in later years her speaking developed further powers—quick in mind, witty, resourceful, clear in argument, she was a formidable opponent and yet was enjoyed by her opposers. As regards other college activities she took part in the ordinary ones with ardour and with few exclusions: she boated, played games, went for country walks; she took part in college societies, she helped with a girls' club in East Oxford. She was full of vitality and had many friends. These last she did not pick for remarkable distinction, but acquired through doing things together with them or because of some personal quality or appeal that made her seek them out, or just because they came. The shyness which had first beset her soon seemed incredible to her fellows and yet it was a deep-rooted characteristic, and to the end her reluctance to speak of personal matters about which she really cared amounted almost to an inhibition. And so it was not altogether easy to become intimate with her: 'I used sometimes to wish she would not talk so fast and so well, for I sensed an extraordinary depth in her silences,' writes one who knew her well; 'it sometimes seemed as if she talked in defence to keep people from getting too near—and she certainly talked faster and with more brilliant edge when she was tired.' Some of her more outstanding contemporaries who knew her well in later life knew little of her then beyond her striking talk.

Helen Darbishire, later Principal of Somerville, was her exact contemporary, reading the same subject. Mrs. H. A. L. Fisher knew her both in Somerville and outside: 'We had both known W. H. Hadow for some years', she writes, 'and it was therefore natural that he should ask us to make friends with her. "I think you will like her", he said with his half shy and altogether attractive smile. Of course we did, and we all four were upon the friendliest terms. I think the first thing that struck us was the very strong resemblance between the two, in looks, in speech, in manner, and the next the very close relationship between them and their deep and satisfying affection for one another. They were delightful together, their quick minds and neat tongues acting and reacting, each bringing out the best of the other and each obviously so much enjoying the other's company. Grace's enthusiasm and vitality, her quick identification of herself with Somerville and also Oxford, her gaiety and powers of enjoyment are what I remember in those early days. It was great fun to go to tea with her in college, to hear all the college news and all the college jokes, even more fun when we were all four together and the two Hadows sparkled away, ready to talk about music or poetry or letters or indeed anything that occurred to anyone of us and to talk remarkably well. And underneath all the sparkle one was always conscious of solid rock.'

Her closest friend in her first year was Frances Hiley,[1] a weekly correspondent of hers for the rest of her life. Later she was associated with a group of friends, humorously self-dubbed the Clique, who enjoyed themselves together. These remember 'utterly carefree days' with her at a time when Oxford in its loveliness was a small and quiet city and the country was reached by a walk across fields: her birthday picnic on the river in the winter, when her health was drunk in champagne sent from home; or a May morning before sunrise near Magdalen Bridge with the sudden hush when the hour has struck and quiet voices float down from the tower in song, and then the abrupt change to the clatter of boats and punts getting ready to move to the bank for breakfast. To this same group of friends among others Grace would sing unaccompanied in a spirited way 'Monday night, my washing night', 'Long nights call', and other good old songs.

Coming to Oxford at twenty-four, rather older than most students and after knowing responsibility, she immensely enjoyed sheer fooling. She could keep somewhat solemn women in fits of laughter by squatting on the floor to act the 'great O.M.', an imaginary idol who bowed and nodded, uttering ominous words. She liked making mock of herself. A memorable going-down party for her year in 1903 became the first of a long series of such entertainments of a topical sort in which college characters were mimicked or parodied. It was conceived as a menagerie shown off

---

[1] Afterwards headmistress of Newcastle Central High School. Frances Hiley has supplemented recollections of my own; for the rest I am mainly indebted in this chapter to Helen Darbishire, Lucie Savill, and Alice Bruce.

by a showman, each animal having an appropriate description [1] with which each of those going down was presented as an animal or bird she was supposed to be like. Grace appeared as a Gosling—her nickname—in a tight-fitting yellow dress with a suggestion of wings, while her hair, which never grew long, was let down and looked very fluffy, sticking out almost at a right angle to her head. Certainly Grace never stood on her dignity, though she had it in her to look impressive, merely by qualities that shone through. At times there were pranks of her own enjoyed as they came; she was known to try roof climbing out of her attic window in 'Hall', and her demonstrations, be it of resolution or of iconoclasm, became a legend at least on one occasion when she smashed the glass handle of E. M. Atkinson's umbrella. Her friend and cousin at Somerville had lamented being afflicted with the valuable and hideous thing, the gift of a respected relative (such possessions never met with an accident); whereupon Grace seized a hammer and with a deliberate attack upon the handle did the deed.

The friends who so greatly enjoyed Grace's fun grudged the time she would spend over students whom they thought dull, but recognized that even in those days she wanted to serve people who she saw needed her help. While at college she touched life at many points. Her brother drew her into his interests: 'Grace and I perform at a reading society on Wednesday. It ought to be rather fun' (17 Nov. 1901), after which we hear she 'read excellently and was a great success'. In the spring of 1902 she sang for his lecture at the Teachers' Guild and had 'a first rate reception'. She might go up to London with him for a very special concert, or to dinner parties with him in Oxford. There were regular weekly lunches with the H. A. L. Fishers given alternately at their house or by W. H. Hadow at Worcester College; there was the household of the Graham Balfours with literary and other interests and two small boys and their quaint sayings. With Rhoda Balfour Grace could share and conceal the disappointment that her first Oxford evening-dress given to her by her mother and chosen by her with such loving care was in white silk! With these oldest of friends there was the closest intercourse till Graham Balfour's appointment as Director of Education in 1902 removed them to Staffordshire. Apart from society in Oxford there were regular

[1] Many of these were written by Helen Darbishire.

"The S·C·R"!

A FANCIFUL SKETCH OF A PICNIC BY THE CHERWELL IN WHICH THE 'GOSLING' APPEARS

concerts, there was the theatre for her continued pleasure, and in
vacations there were journeys or visits, a stay at the Rieder Alp in
Switzerland in 1901, a visit to the Vernon Harcourts in the Isle
of Wight in April 1902 when 'wonderful moonlight flooded the
trees below them and the level sea beyond', as from the tower of
St. Clare they saw 'the whole fleet outlined in light; hulls, funnels,
rigging hung with tiny electric lamps, a wonderful sight'. It was
a prelude to the great naval review for the Coronation of King
Edward VII. Both Grace and her brother loved 'to live history'.
Early in her second term at college she had heard the deep
sound of 'Tom', the great bell at Christ Church, tolling to
announce the death of the old Queen and had felt a pang at the
passing of the Victorian age, and she must have watched the
streams of two processions meet by the porch of St. Mary's
Church: fur-gowned aldermen and dignitaries of the University
in scarlet or black, to hear the double proclamation and 'God
save the King'. Grace enjoyed her student days with delightful,
infectious enjoyment, drinking in every moment. In spite of
her many engagements and activities she managed to maintain
concentration, burning her candle at both flaming ends in order
to work at her books.

Intellectually she depended upon the stimulus of other minds,
whether by contradiction or agreement. Consciously or unconsciously her thinking was shot through by the self-determination
that marked her personality. There was quick insight into the
core of books and the core of persons and a strong instinct to
approve or not. She was fond of throwing out challenging statements which she might another time challenge herself. She was
impatient of hesitation and disliked indecision. But with all this
she had fine and sensitive understanding and a faculty for observ-
ing and fixing upon particulars and relating them to central
characteristics by the right word. Her flashing power of rapid
description or definition was not, as it might have been, a sign of
superficiality; it was often the fruit of thoroughness and exactness
of reading and showed a fine sense for first-hand sources. Always
there was imagination, though it was possible for sensitiveness to
be smothered by advocacy of some issue or by impatience of
offence against common sense. Yet common sense must have been
in some measure an acquired quality in Grace. There remained in
her a shining streak of something the very reverse of the common-

sensible in the ordinary interpretation of the term. Common sense alone does not lead to the values that were truly hers.

When at her books she occupied herself with philology just as much as was essential for the Honour School and no more, while she thoroughly enjoyed literature. The Elizabethans were then her first love both in drama—so close to life and so rich in imagination—and in lyric song with music in support. She was also attracted by medieval times. On the whole she steadily preferred a naïve outlook to complexity, and thinking that goes hand in hand with doing. Milton's grand Puritanism appealed, George Herbert was a lifelong friend, Traherne's *Centuries of Meditation*, when later discovered, became a favourite, as did Wordsworth, whose poetry grew upon her so that she confessed to feeling deeply ashamed of ever having yielded to the temptation to make fun of him. She was a lover of Dickens, with penetrating perception for his fine touches, and she disliked Thackeray without ever revising this opinion. Sensitive as she was to sound and imagery in poetry and retentive of expressions, on the whole it would be true to say that content and thought meant more to her than form. She could extract gold from books that were not, properly speaking, literature at all.

Among university tutorials the hours when Dr. (afterwards Canon) A. J. Carlyle taught her on the eighteenth century left a lasting impression on her mind, and he, for his part, recalled her fine literary sense. She also studied with Ernest de Selincourt, afterwards D.Litt. of Oxford and Professor in Birmingham, who had discovered her at Cheltenham and who may well have deepened her love of Wordsworth. In 1903 he was one of her examiners in the Honour School of English Language and Literature when she was placed in the First Class. Revising for schools had been a strain and a weariness, and the many other engagements in previous terms took their toll. Much depended upon her actually getting the right class and many eyes were fixed upon her which made her anxious. Her brother received the news by cable in Toronto. He had obtained leave of absence for the summer term in 1903 and was spending from April to October travelling in America. In sending loving congratulations to his mother he writes: 'I know how glad and proud you feel about it, as glad and proud as I feel myself.' He was even then planning to shepherd her into the next venture. Her pastors and masters at Somerville judged that it would be well for her to take the opportunity of a temporary teaching post at Bryn Mawr, U.S.A., for the sake of experience and still with a view to ultimate work in Oxford. Since her brother intended to be in America at the time, Mrs. Hadow was reconciled to such a plan, and in urging that it was a good one in view of his sister's future, he undertook to meet her boat in New York and settle her in at Bryn Mawr.

After a journey to the West through Canada and U.S.A. and very happy days in New England, mainly at Concord, he went over to Philadelphia in September to see 'that imposing place Bryn Mawr' and to report that 'Grace's apartment consists of two rooms, an adequate bedroom and a sitting room, very like that which she occupied at Somerville, upstairs, and a pleasant "wooded" view from the windows', Philadelphia, not far off, being 'a red brick city set in oaks and chestnuts'. The Principal, Miss Thomas, was absent, but he saw a competent Secretary and Bursar resembling 'Cousin Bessie'. His friends, Mr. and Mrs. Surette, living alternately in New York and Philadelphia, had agreed cordially to allow Grace to consult them if she wanted anything. Mrs. Hadow's anxiety was so far allayed, but her son had yet to confess that he reached New York an hour too late, and when he got to the dock—having learnt that the boat had arrived a day before its time—a New York friend of his, head of Novello's, 'had seen the announcement and by pure inspiration had gone down to the dock, sent up his card to Grace and by the time I arrived (panting) from the train he had cleared her through the customs house and taken her up to the hotel. So there was no tragedy after all. But I didn't meet that boat!' He found Grace 'looking very well, her usual normal self much interested in every-thing and alternately amused and delighted'. They spent three days together at Bay Head, a watering-place on the sand-dunes of New Jersey, and, after settling her in at Bryn Mawr, he took her on to Philadelphia for a week-end visit. Soon after he sailed for home.

CHAPTER IV

AN INTERLUDE AND OXFORD AGAIN
1903–1910

LIFE at Bryn Mawr did not prove altogether easy in the event. However, it resulted in pleasant contacts and in at least one friendship which lasted for the rest of the friend's life. Grace liked teaching. Her first class of about twenty freshmen is described as 'an extremely nice set: very young but very keen and intelligent, and they seem to enjoy being laughed at. You would smile if you saw me holding forth and the dear babes sitting round me, with great wide-open eyes. I made them open their eyes still wider several times, but now I find that I can make them laugh, when I want to, I am not afraid of them.'

Grace was critical of Miss Thomas and at war with her methods. The contrast between the highly sophisticated life in the college and primitive savagery within reach beyond the woods stuck in her mind and troubled her. She was frankly intolerant of the imitation of Magdalen's May morning ceremony which was carried out by girl students every year on the tower of Bryn Mawr. Perhaps in itself this had an independent value of grace and beauty, but uprooted and divorced from its own setting it could not be other than artificial to one who measured it by the real thing.

Nevertheless America caught her imagination as it had caught her brother's. She loved and responded to American warm-heartedness, and her delight in the quick intelligence of Americans and her respect for their enterprise began with this first visit to the U.S.A.

Meanwhile her friends in Oxford had not abandoned their plans for her, and she came home in 1904 to take the place of the English tutor at Somerville, Miss Sheavyn, during her sabbatical year. It was a natural and easy transition to become a member of the Senior Common Room and soon she was established in rooms on the ground floor of 'West', as a don in her own old college, picking up the threads of her life there. Her life in Oxford with her brother and his circle went on much as before.

A good deal was expected of her teaching. Josephine Coning, of Somerville, recalls the impression it made on her and how her personality was felt by her pupils: 'as far as I can remember, it was in my second year as a student that I first met Grace—I think she had then been for a year at Bryn Mawr in U.S.A.—and she must have been acting as English Tutor in Miss Sheavyn's absence. I saw her first, with an armful of books, walking swiftly from the West Wing through the garden—very straight and tall and fair, and with purpose and life in every movement. In the strong sunlight she looked, as she often did, transparent or translucent without in the least suggesting fragility. Hers was a robust fineness. I remember too that in the Common Room after dinner she would sing to us. She sang with great enjoyment in a voice like a choir boy's, mostly old traditional songs, "My Johnnie was a shoe-maker", "Come I will sing to you" (with Miss Kempson) and other such lovely old things.

'I had two terms of coaching with her. In the first of these she conducted a Chaucer Seminar, and I can recall to this day the delicious atmosphere of spring and gaiety, of humour and tolerance in which those readings were invested. Grace loved Chaucer, and it was not I think a bad shot on our part when we decided that in Chaucer's "Guide Fair Whyte" we found more than a passing resemblance to our tutor. For of her too "Dullness was ydrad", she too was debonair and gay, and yet

> "She nas to sobre ne to glad;
> In alle thinges more mesure
> Had never, I trowe, creature."

'Later, she coached me on pre-Shakespearean drama—I think our discussions may have been psychological rather than literary, for I remember her passionate defence of Webster's Vittoria in whom she was interested as a person. I also have occasion to remember that during a coaching on Marlowe's *Edward II*, Grace seized the poker and flourished it with such conviction that I had finally to move my place, to her great mirth. Everything she touched became at once alive and real. There must always, I imagine, have been the danger, if danger it can be called, that the human interest might outweigh every other, and I remember her telling me, not long ago, that she felt somewhat taken aback by the point of view offered on one occasion by a class of women (Women's Institutes, I think). She had been reading *King Lear* with them, "and I wanted them to say *why* it was that Shakespeare always chose Kings, Princes, or people of importance as his tragic heroes. For instance, if anything happened to *me*, it would make no great difference"—when a woman interrupted with "We'd much rather it happened to King Lear, Miss, than to you".

'When I saw Grace last, at the Gaudy (and she was never surely in greater form than in her after-dinner speech of Reminiscences that night) she took me home with her, and we had, after many years of not meeting, a couple of hours' talk, from which I came away, as one did always, soundly exhilarated. She talked mostly of present-day youth, which she loved and understood, and I realized afresh, not her youth, for that would have implied immaturity, but her agileness. We strolled across to L.M.H. and found ourselves in the midst of an Oxford Group meeting—in temporary occupation—and before I knew where I was, I was incredibly being introduced to Frank Buchman, whom apparently, though not his movement, Grace took in her swift stride.

'We very seldom wrote in those later years, though we punctually greeted each other at Christmas—her card this Christmas (1939) I kept. It bore St. Augustine's words: "To my God a heart of flame; to my religion a heart of love; to myself a heart of steel." Flame and Steel and Love were all three in her, as light, as steadfastness and as beauty—they can never die.'

When the year as a tutor at Somerville drew to its close, Grace Hadow was appointed resident English tutor at Lady Margaret Hall, then a college of some sixty students and considered to be the contrasting counterpart to Somerville. The contrast went back to the foundation of both. Lady Margaret Hall had been founded in 1878 by Bishop Talbot as a Hall of residence on a Church of England basis with provision for the liberty of other religious bodies; 'high training and intellectual culture under the elevating influence of religious principles' was envisaged at the foundation, and the working out of this ideal was entrusted by the distinguished churchmen and women who formed the first Council to Elizabeth Wordsworth, the first Principal, possessed of personality that was truly remarkable. There can be no doubt that Miss Wordsworth's personality was responsible for the early character of the Hall. She was the centre and the inspiration, and her broad humanity set its seal upon the college. Her family heritage of scholarship and wisdom and churchmanship was further leavened by a streak of genius with which she was gifted. It was difficult to foresee in what small ways she might feel convention to be important or where no thought of it would occur to her; those who lived with her were stirred by suggestions profoundly wise or maybe rather odd but mostly unexpected. Talks with her took those engaged in them into a world of ideas which was hers and no one else's, and which nevertheless reflected the generation of mid-Victorians to whom she belonged. It would have been alien to her to concentrate upon a policy of improving the status of women in Oxford, and in this respect her leadership stood in strong contrast to Miss Maitland's. However, she believed that the true life is one of development and that progress should come by applying old principles to new conditions, and in this she agreed with the founder of the Hall.

L.M.H. was situated on the verge of the town as it then was. With the University Parks adjacent and the Cherwell bounding the college grounds and open fields beyond, it seemed to be in the country, and its fresh air and freedom were in keeping with this setting. The Hall had an atmosphere of its own; to join it meant becoming a member of a society conscious of its traditions and outlook.

Where Somerville had a reputation for professional efficiency, the Hall risked the epithet 'ladylike' with the underlying values and enjoyed the joke; its character was founded on a sense of obligation, upon 'tradition to maintain and examples to admire, and, if possible to imitate, an esprit de corps to live up to, a Sparta to adorn', as Miss Wordsworth has said. 'A good society to be in and full of delightful people' was a Somervillian's description in 1912. It would have been difficult to have escaped being happy there, and Grace soon felt at home.

'A vivid impression of a delightful casualness at the Hall' remained with her of the days when she first came there. She resided during the last three years of Miss Wordsworth's principalship when, intellectually alert, she was present with her wit and her wisdom but no longer took active part in college affairs. The burden of these rested on the Vice-Principal, Eleanor Lodge. She and Grace became intimate friends. Eleanor Lodge was an unusual personality; she was a fine scholar, able to live up to the demands of scholarship and of a very full practical life. She was possessed of the simplicity and directness of character that always appealed to Grace. With it there was a certain unquenchable youthfulness and buoyancy urging her to live up to her ideal of 'unimpeded activity' which had much in common with Grace's temperament. The Hall and its people were everything to her; she had grown up with it, remaining there since her student days, and was altogether identified with its concerns. She fostered the 'spirit of comradeship, the close bond between teacher and taught' which Grace attributed to her at L.M.H. and which had always existed there, and she was able to include in it many generations. Grace became her right hand, made much of her leadership, and did much to strengthen it, and it may be inferred that Nellie Lodge's vision of the college and its place in Oxford was broadened and that her purposes were strengthened by her friend's stimulating companionship and by her wider experience. Her help and influence meant much to Nellie Lodge. When she wanted a home in vacation, she would go regularly to Cirencester or to Penzance to Grace's people; at other times she and Grace undertook cycling tours together through various parts of England or along the Cornish coast. After 1909, when Grace had given up residence and could no longer do as much at the Hall, Nellie Lodge rose many a time 'with the lark' or earlier to bicycle the thirty-six odd miles between Oxford and Cirencester to get there for breakfast and spend a long day before riding back in the evening.

To Miss Wordsworth Grace had a personal relation of her own, for they shared qualities. To know Miss Wordsworth was a liberal education in itself, and in later days this became true also of Grace Hadow. Miss Wordsworth had been a great figure in Oxford society; at Oxford dinner parties, those occasions for brilliant talk, she would still be received with a little stir of expectation when she entered the room. Her delight in good talk became a bond between her and Grace; inevitably they attracted one another; both had brilliance and both took the same fundamental ideas for granted. Grace could satisfy Miss Wordsworth's pleasure in a person who is natural and thinks for herself, and they enjoyed one another in talks on books, on life, on ideas, on happenings in the great world. Grace, however, was at home in college affairs which did not then mean much to Miss Wordsworth. On occasions when it became necessary to win Miss Wordsworth's sympathy for college problems that arose from modern notions Grace was a good person to send.

The collegiate life of L.M.H. was passing through the evolutionary stage when personal co-operation was giving way to the delegation of offices and to settled organization. With her quick insight, her ready sympathy, her experience, and her independent contacts in Oxford Grace worked as a conservative liberator. Her very appointment had become an occasion for raising the standard of living for dons. A don with a brother who visited her frequently could reasonably demand two rooms in place of the usual bed-sitter; that was obvious and must be arranged for her. As a result the housing accommodation was raised to a higher level for all tutors, the bursar alone remaining the exception, for whom this amenity was gained in the time of Miss Wordsworth's successor, Miss Jex-Blake, when the new building of 1909 made it possible. Her Somervillian experience was most useful to Grace's L.M.H. colleagues. She could be depended upon to lose no opportunity, however casual or informal, of helping to establish the position of Vice-Principal and members of the Senior Common Room. As regards women's work and status the tradition of the Council was old-fashioned; privileges were never grudgingly withheld, but the need for them was often not realized. In these days of self-government it is strange to remember that Senior Common Rooms in the women's colleges were represented on the Council by one or more members, and that mediation was often called for. At L.M.H. the Vice-Principal represented the rest of the S.C.R., whose position remained analogous to that of a school staff in this respect. Nellie Lodge was altogether conservative by temperament, but the development of the Hall into a real college was a cause she had at heart. When L.M.H. decided to build a Dining-Hall and Library, which were completed in 1909, the experience of Somerville in raising a loan from their own members was a useful precedent, and it fell to her to see the details of this plan through.

A picture of Grace Hadow as seen by a colleague in the setting of the Hall in the years 1906 to 1909 remains in the memory of Evelyn M. Jamison, then Bursar and Librarian (later Vice-Principal and history tutor) at L.M.H.:

'G. E. H. came to the Hall as its first resident English Tutor in October, 1906. She has been described by A. E. Levett, then in her third year, as "our first non-indigenous Don, bringing with her a puzzling vocabulary, and an infectious gaiety, and readiness of friendship". The vocabulary did indeed raise doubts at first when "the other building" was referred to as "the other end", and, low be it spoken, we heard of such foreign mysteries as "scouts" and "nondescript". But that phase was soon over, and the Hall took G. E. H. to its heart, and she took it, with all the warmth and generosity of her nature. It was the fashion then to refer to dons by their surnames prefixed by "S". And so Miss Lodge became to many generations S'lodge; and Miss Hadow was honoured by the appellation of S'hadow. Indeed Gray S'hadow (Grace Hadow) was not unknown, inappropriate no doubt, but full of affection. She came like a fresh breeze with her keen intellect, her witty speech and humorous anecdotes, her boundless activity, but it was warmed like a sunny day by the kindliness of her criticism, her instinctive readiness to think the best of people, and her gift of inspiring with her own hopefulness and high purpose all with whom she found herself, whether they were thoroughbreds or only lame dogs. She always lavished her care on lame dogs. She captured the confidence and affectionate respect of her pupils in the English School; she was fortunate in them and in her co-adjutors, M. C. Campbell and Octavia Myers, from 1909 to 1911 when she ceased to be resident, but it was to her leadership and teaching that in great measure was due the seven first classes in English of the years 1908 to 1911. During these years she prepared two books: *The Oxford Treasury of English Literature* (jointly with her brother W. H. Hadow),[1] and *Chaucer and his Times* (1914).[2] The work of preparation undoubtedly reacted well, as it always does, on the work of teaching and tutoring.

'The period of G. E. H.'s residence was a time of activity and enterprise among an able set of students. Just before, Hall Meeting and the Constitution of Resident Members of the Hall had been reorganized and Essay Club was a new and vigorous effort at bringing members of different Schools together—otherwise, as Miss Wordsworth said, they were "parallel straight lines that never met". Now "Sharp Practice" was to blossom into "Political" and hold a joint debate with the Somerville Parliament; O.S.D.S. was at its most vigorous, thanks to such speakers as G. E. H. herself, S. M. Fry, R. Sidgwick, and A. E. Levett. The Women Students' Suffrage Society was founded in 1907, and

---

[1] Published by the Oxford University Press.

[2] Published in the Home University Library series (Oxford University Press).

members bore its magnificent banner in the great procession of 1908 to the Albert Hall. In all these activities there was fruitful and steady co-operation between Dons and Students, to use the language of the period, and in all G. E. H. played a noted part. She stimulated the musical talent of the Hall, whether in Chapel where she trained the choir or in "Sociable" where her singing was a constant delight. Sometimes she would go on singing for an hour or two to a special audience later in the evening, including in her repertory the "Lyke Wake Dirge", and many another. She played hockey and tennis and I can see her now contesting a hard set with Miss Lodge on the old gravel courts under the Words-worth Building windows. I have a vision too of her speeding off for the weekly lunch party given by her brother and herself at Worcester and I remember her well in a dark grey-blue cloth dress with bands of velvet, and a hat to match, which became her admirably. She was well-known in Oxford society and much in request for parties with or without her brother, W. H. Hadow. The bond between them was very strong and they spent as much time together as they could snatch from their multifarious duties. It was a common sight to see them walking and talking round the Parks at amazing speed. We used to say that they walked so fast that they went in front of themselves, and talked before their mouths had time to open.

'An enterprise which she inspired and helped to carry to success was the notable performance of Lyly's *Campaspe* in 1908 by the members of the Hall, the first performance since the XVIth Century. Miss Wordsworth prophesied that it would be, as it certainly was, "of very great literary interest", adding that "the music and dances, fortunately, are not Greek but Elizabethan; if this can be held to include a very dainty song composed for the occasion by Mr. Hadow". The performance was part of a great effort to raise funds for the extension of the Hall by the building of Dining Hall, Library and kitchens (the present Talbot Building), and it was therefore a notable departure from Hall practice in that it was the first public dramatic effort of the Hall and was given in the Masonic Building. Hitherto shows had been limited to an invited audience, chiefly female, in the dining room or garden, and G. E. H. had succeeded in winning Miss Wordsworth's consent and her approbation for the new venture. The years 1906–9 were the last of Miss Wordsworth's long reign as Principal; her mind was ever open to new developments and she decided every question on its merits, but the Hall was growing rapidly in size, conditions were changing, and I cannot but think that G. E. H. did not a little to win the peaceful passage to fresh ways in some respects. She had Miss Wordsworth's confidence and affection because they had much in common in their characters and upbringing—the family life of the country vicarage and the strenuous academic tradition of the University. They had the same mental vigour and witty speech, and the same independence and originality of outlook. Above all, G. E. H. never bored her!

'Things were undoubtedly moving in the Women's Societies and in L.M.H. The Delegacy for Women Students, after much preparation, came actually into being in 1910; Somerville and L.M.H. were building. Incidentally, the anticipated moving of the Library to its new habitat required a fresh classification of the books, and this was carried out in the Long Vacation of 1908. G. E. H. found time, as she always did, not only to provide the scheme for English Literature, but to help for some weeks in the actual labour of labelling, listing and numbering. The S.C.R. was very small in those days—there were four of us—and very young as S.C.R.'s go—all of us under forty. But it was beginning to cohere and to take shape as a distinct entity. The original notion that the Hall should consist of separate buildings each under a Vice-Principal on the Newnham model, had recently given way to the ideal of a single college with one Vice-Principal only, as the Principal's deputy, and this conception naturally led to a homogeneous body of Dons, whose sense of corporate responsibility for the working of the Hall was increased by the fact that Miss Wordsworth to a certain degree withdrew to Gunfield from the everyday life of the college. It was G. E. H. who fostered the incipient Common Room by introducing the custom of coffee after lunch in the "little drawing-room" at the door of Wordsworth Building, and creating together with the Vice-Principal, Miss Lodge, the first very informal "Dons' Meeting" one evening a week. . . . G. E. H. too introduced the daily Hall messenger, an immense boon in days when there were no telephones, no motor buses (much less private cars) and a post of proverbial slowness. It was a relief to be able to *send* notes, business or social, and essays and papers, instead of dashing off in person on a bicycle just before dinner to the other end of Oxford. The first messengers were small boys confided to the care of G. E. H. by a club-leader in St. Ebbe's; some were excellent, but there was also the urchin who, when the addressees lived up the Iffley Road, hid the notes behind the soup-tureen in Mrs. Bunce's kitchen, or scattered the torn-up fragments of an essay over the Parks.

'In 1909 G. E. H. was called home by her mother's illness and ceased to be resident, but for another eight years she took part in different capacities in the work of the English School. Her interest and her affection for the Hall never ended and she continued to pour out of her treasure things new and old. Her spirit seemed still to live in her room at the S.E. corner of Wordsworth Building, with its keen fresh air tempered by the warm sunlight; the roses round the windows and the ting of tennis balls outside always brought her to the mind of memory.'

The performance of *Campaspe* was charming. Dances, dresses, and colour were carefully planned and correct; shoes and accessories were well made and of the right period, while the setting was simple as in the sixteenth century. Some study of these matters was therefore demanded of the producers. However, no one could have been more alive to the incidental humour of the whole undertaking than was Grace herself: 'Miss Jamison and I', she writes, 'read the instructions for Elizabethan dances in the Upper Reading Room of the Bodleian, our top halves immovable and discreet, our feet practising steps under the table. Have you ever tried practising steps when you can't see your feet and the upper half of you had to look like that of a person immersed in study?

'The performance was in the Masonic Hall. On the first night, as the audience was assembling and the company in various stages of undress were painting their faces and sunburning their arms and legs, a message came to me; "Mr. —— wants to see you *at once*." I went into the vestibule where I found an indignant Mason hung with aprons and sashes and medals and ribbons dancing with fury. It appeared that an initiation ceremony was about to take place in the Masonic Temple. There was a door leading from our dressing-room into the Temple and the Masons said it was quite impossible for them to proceed with us there. Obviously we could glue our eyes (in turn) to the key-hole and see all their mysteries. We must leave instantly.

'I pointed out that it was really not feasible for twenty imper-
fectly clad and browned Greek soldiers to wander out into the
street, and after some discussion the Masons very kindly met us.
We might continue dressing if we would allow a Brother with a
drawn sword to guard the door on our side. We had no objection
whatever, and a shy, elderly Mason, bald and tubby, stood
blushing hotly as he clasped a drawn sword in an obviously unaccustomed hand, while we continued our dressing. The next
night I asked the caretaker if we were again to expect an angel to
guard the Masonic Paradise. "No," he said, "Brother —— says
he wouldn't go among these young ladies again, not for £100."

'Two other pictures of that performance come to my mind.
Elsie Drew, in a long white satin frock with the train that people
wore for evening dress in those days, standing on her head in the
middle of the stage between the acts, with the most perfect pro-
priety, her skirt caught neatly between her ankles, so that she
looked like Lot's wife upside down; and one of the largest Greek
soldiers hemstitching a very small pocket-handkerchief as she
waited to go on.'

Actually Grace went through a heart-breaking emotional
strain while Lyly's *Campaspe* was being produced. Her mother
had been taken dangerously ill at home and the illness dragged on
for a good many months. When immediate anxiety was removed
there came a time of severe heart-searching when Grace found it
hard to see her way. For life in Oxford and at L.M.H. had compelling claims on her, even apart from the fact that it was the life
she loved and in which she had found herself; yet she felt drawn
with all the ardour of her nature to go home and devote herself to
her mother. To give up residence in Oxford would be to take
her hand from the plough when there was work that needed her
particularly; it further meant loss of her brother's companionship
at a moment when their minds had grown together closely and
when, tutors both, he at Worcester College and she at L.M.H.,
they were living, as it were, upon the same pattern; his position
in the University had opened up to her a fuller and wider Oxford
than she would have known without him and she for her part
was bringing freshness into her brother's life.

To her friends Grace seemed marked out for a brilliant career.
She had made her reputation as a teacher and a sparkling lecturer;
work with her brother for the *Oxford Treasury of English Literature*

BANNER, DESIGNED BY EDMUND NEW

Everyman

Strength, Knowledge, Everyman, Good Deeds, and Discretion

CHARACTERS FROM 'EVERYMAN'

had launched her as an editor and an interpreter with keen human insight and speech that had an edge to it; her mind was working on the intellectual background of literature, and she had thoughts of further books. Her personality had made itself felt not only in Somerville and L.M.H. Members of those two Senior Common Rooms were being drawn together and closer co-operation was replacing that instinctive rivalry which results from ignorance of one another's ways. E. M. Jamison of L.M.H. had been the first holder of the Mary Somerville Research Fellowship in 1903–6, and research was to associate E. C. Lodge and M. K. Pope; Oxford women were moving towards intercollegiate understanding all round. This was widening the horizon, the development of women's education being more clearly felt as a common cause, and, with personal contacts, there came more intellectual co-operation in research and teaching. It was an interesting movement of growth which called for direction : and which offered the very opportunity for qualities of mind and character that were Grace Hadow's special gifts. Her friendships in the Common Rooms of Somerville and L.M.H. were helping in this movement, her galvanizing strength giving her a leading part. Against all these claims came her mother's. It was a hard choice between competing instincts. Her decision was one of those that determine a life. She gave up residence in L.M.H. in 1909, and continued as tutor for two years with a junior resident colleague; then she resigned the tutorship and became a visiting lecturer spending two days at L.M.H. each week.

The same renunciation of things greatly cherished was to be required of her in later years more than once. It never made her care less for those things in themselves, but her natural instinct for casting her bread upon the waters was strengthened into a principle that became altogether characteristic. For those who knew her well a striking performance of *Everyman* at Somerville College became symbolical. It was set in the charming little garden of Radcliffe House and staged on its terrace; dons from L.M.H. and from Somerville took the parts. Grace was Everyman, dressed first in gay clothes, then in grey monastic habit with a thick penitential rope round her waist and with bare feet, and her fluffy gold hair flowing; the finely cut features and broad forehead more expressive than ever, and her eyes with an inward gazing look. As Everyman, confronted by the warning of death, appeals to one friend after another for help and finds Riches, Good Fellowship, Kindred, Knowledge, Strength, Beauty, and others leave him, while his Good Deeds lie on a mattress too feeble to rise he does penance for his past error and his prayers grow in intensity with his distress. Some friends realized the 'Everyman side' in Grace as they put it, Grace who ever set light store by official or social distinctions. 'None who saw this performance could fail to be moved by it, perfectly simple—unpretentious as it was', writes L. C. Kempson. 'But all who took part in it seemed to be living again in spirit the "heart-breaking realities of Everyman". When, the play being over, actors and audience mingled in the Somerville garden in the prosaic business of tea and talk, those who had taken part in the play experienced the curious sensation of leaving a world of reality to enter a world that was artificial. In the brief span representing the pilgrimage of Everyman "into the heavenly sphere" the eternal truths had manifested themselves in the simple symbolism of the old play, and something of Grace Hadow's own spiritual quality had entered into that symbolism and clothed it with life.'

EVERYMAN

In Radcliffe House Garden, Oxford, June 4th, 1910

CAST

Everyman	G. E. Hadow	L.M.H. & S.C.	*Strength*	O. M. Myers	L.M.H. & S.C.
God-Adonai	A. M. Bruce	S.C.	*Discretion*	E. M. Jamison	S.C. & L.M.H.
Death	H. Walton	S.C.	*Five-Wit*	Erica Lindsay (Mrs.)	S.C.
Messenger	L. C. Kempson	S.C.	*Beauty*	O. Rhys	O.H.S.
Fellowship	E. N. Overend (Mrs. Lorimer)	S.C.	*Knowledge*	H. Escreet	S.C.
Cousin	L. C. Kempson	S.C.	*Confession*	A. M. Bruce	S.C.
Kindred	E. C. Lodge	L.M.H.	*Angel*	M. Keeling	S.HILD.H. & S.HUGHS
Goods	O. M. Myers (Mrs. Adler)	L.M.H. & S.C.	*Doctor*	L. C. Kempson	S.C.
Good Deeds	H. Darbishire	S.C.			

Music—Misses Price

'This ae night'

CHAPTER V

BETWEEN OXFORD AND CIRENCESTER

1909–1914

AT the death of the Rev. W. E. Hadow in 1906 his widow and home daughter had moved to the neighbouring town of Cirencester. It was a place little touched by the twentieth century and little visited by sightseers. Its fine old church and spacious grey-stone market-place gave the little town a peculiar dignity; more-over, except on market-days when animated bustling life transformed the scene, the old-fashioned houses spread abroad a delusive air of quiet decorum, revealing nothing of the shamefaced little slums that here and there hid behind them. Close by was a further glory of the place, the Great Park belonging to Lord Bathurst with its long symmetrical avenues of receding trees and their surprise vistas of distant churches. In the circumstances it was an excellent place of retirement. South Cerney Vicarage had been the hub of a tiny universe in days when Mrs. Hadow, besides being the parson's wife, was often consulted as doctor or lawyer by the village. Now at seventy-three the burden of village concerns had become too heavy for her and parish work had passed on to her second daughter, Constance, who had long been her father's right hand in these ways. No doubt it was a wrench to break up a home of thirty-five years' standing, but at Cirencester the Hadows remained in their own neighbourhood, where they were well known and of the soil. Constance Hadow was soon absorbed in local activities and did not find it too hard to make the new start in life, while Cirencester bid fair to offer a vacation home within convenient reach of the Oxford son and daughter.

The family settled in Foss Lodge, a squarish and uncompromising house of grey stone that stood in a row with others abutting on the foot-path of Sheep Street on the edge of the town, and facing the railway. Trains were few and far between and Cirencester the last station on the line, so its situation was quiet enough. At the appointed hour the chimes of the old church of St. John the Baptist could be heard playing the old 113th.[1] The house itself had good wood-work and Georgian windows and was not without character. At the back there was a surprisingly pleasant

[1] 'From highest Heav'n the Eternal Son' (*Hymns Ancient and Modern*, 171).

garden surrounded by walls; in the dark dining-room, which was situated to the right of the narrow entrance-passage, the shadowy portraits of forebears looked down on you; the table, unless a long row of tea-cups and a white cloth adorned it, was covered with red baize patterned in black; stuck in the mirror over the mantel-piece were cards indicating manifold activities; two vases on the mantelpiece held spills folded to save matches. The drawing-room at the back of the house had the look of preciseness that a well-worn suite of Victorian furniture can give, but it allowed of a piano and had good windows that looked out on the garden, and it was the setting for animated talk. Below the windows there was a stone terrace where one could put up a camp bed on starlit nights. In and out of Foss Lodge there was a good deal of local traffic. The hospitable habits of the Hadows held sway, and it was their way to be involved in jobs that appealed to local patriotism.

However, apart from the weekly visits to Oxford and her work as lecturer, Grace's life now, in 1909, centred on her mother. Though never robust, Mrs. Hadow had marvellous recuperative powers, and at seventy-six she recovered to the semi-invalidism of an old lady whose mind was altogether alert, suffering a danger-ous illness once more in 1914, which she again withstood. The hardships of earlier days were over. From her children there had come to her contacts and interests for which she had long starved, and their high tradition of deference, service, and devotion to-wards her never swerved. She herself kept an open mind for new friendships. Her critical and appreciative sense of people and things had not faded, her eyes lighting up at moments with most attractive innocence and fun. Grace and her mother understood one another; their hours together were happiness. Grace washing caps and shawls; Grace brusquely refusing help as she pushed the wicker chair (Harry's gift)—Mrs. Hadow was only partially resigned to being wheeled—Grace on the floor in the drawing-room at Foss Lodge talking to her mother eagerly, while the old lady was eagerly responsive: these scenes are vivid in the mind of memory. For joy and stimulation her mother lived on Grace like a lover. She could do for her what no one else could do.

L. Leslie Brooke's three-quarter length drawing of her in 1910 gives an excellent idea of Mrs. Hadow at this time. She is seated, as she pauses from knitting, with hands resting on her knees.

There is a suggestion of resolve in the dignified poise of head and shoulders; the white cap and streamers, the *ruche*, the white shawl lightly worn over the shoulders set off a face instinct with recollection and inward refinement. The features are clear cut; in the expression there is tranquillity after effort. The artist consulted Grace in deciding on the pose for that portrait, and she threw herself into contributing to its success. The weariness of sitting was not felt while Grace read *The Times* aloud, and, if the old lady flagged, Leslie Brooke found he need only mention 'Lloyd George' to produce the desired effect instantly. Formerly she had described Gladstone as 'England's scourge' and a radical government never seemed anything short of 'wicked'. Uncompromising both in her loyalties and the reverse, she was ever an ardent patriot and politician. She was keenly interested in ideas, in people, and in new inventions, and was deeply religious. Latent talents of her own had remained uncultivated because of the demands of practical life and because she had lived in her children. It was given to her youngest daughter in greatest measure to make her latter days happy, and Grace did it ardently, resourcefully, and with steadiness of purpose.

Each summer she would take her mother from Cirencester to Penzance for a long stay. Her eldest son provided a G.W.R. saloon-carriage all the way, and the long journey in great comfort was a rousing adventure not beyond the old lady's strength, an event to look forward to and remember. Characteristically each detail of the arrangement was enjoyed, for Grace loved thinking out everything for her mother's comfort and preparing meals for her in the little dressing-room-kitchen that was next to the big compartment of the saloon. In speaking of public work and comparing it to such occupation she would say: 'There is always some one else who can do other things equally well, but no one else can do this particular thing.' And she found compensation in the life she had chosen and never regretted her decision to become a home daughter, though aware of the price she paid.

Her mother apart, however, Grace felt herself to be in surroundings that roused an inward protest when first she returned to live in Cirencester. Oxford had become her spiritual home: its human contacts were stimulating and congenial, while Cirencester cared for none of the things that meant a great deal to her. The little town was then very much cut off from the outer world. It was reached deviously from Oxford either via Swindon and Kemble or by rail to Fairford with a long bicycle ride or a drive by road to follow; there were no buses or cars. It was an agricultural and sporting world where the instinctive response to cultural values was incomprehension. Brains were disliked, especially in women. To many Grace Hadow seemed a queer person who might be seen in the fields without a hat; college made women uncanny, and she was a believer in votes for them. 'You are allowed to choose books for people if you've been at college, possibly even to play a game of tennis', she would say, 'but you are no good for anything else.'

Meanwhile her short visits to Oxford were crammed with lecturing, teaching, and business engagements, but when, in 1909, her godfather-brother was appointed Principal of Armstrong College, Newcastle-on-Tyne, and left Oxford, she felt the loss of the direct personal touch. Friends came to Cirencester for visits, yet on the whole she had little companionship there, and to Cirencester people, she herself may well have seemed donnish and critical, with the incisive eagerness characteristic of her family— she called it the 'Hadow glare'—to frighten them. More than ever at this time her sympathy went out to the unprivileged and the inarticulate. She became engaged in work for women's suffrage, not a hopeful cause in Cirencester where canvassing took you to the odd back yards tucked away behind the streets, or you found yourself addressing village meetings in an attempt to get more than just a few open-mouthed children to listen to a speech on the Green. Yet a local branch of the National Union of Women's Suffrage Societies was started. There was at least one meeting of some proportions in Cirencester in 1912, when Miss Rose Sidgwick from Oxford spoke; there may have been more. Such activity earned Grace unpopularity with the local great; at least she felt that it did, but she was ardent in the cause and worked for it steadily.

When the Conference on Electoral Reform issued its report in 1917 and included a recommendation of Women's Suffrage in some form she wrote, looking back on previous years: 'We shan't know ourselves in any role other than a derided minority. It feels quite odd to think that possibly—even probably—before long people will neither shout with laughter nor throw things at one if one mentions women voting. I am glad to belong to a

MARY LANG HADOW, 1910

From a drawing by L. LESLIE BROOKE

GRACE HADOW

A photograph taken before 1909

generation which has been stoned—not because I like being stoned (it is tiresome, and often messy), but since some women had to go through that to win the thing, it is a bit of luck not to have been out of it entirely. I record it here because it looks as if one of the results of the war was going to be the grant of the parliamentary franchise to women. In years to come it may interest people to realize that before the War numbers of law-abiding and peaceful women like myself, quite inconspicuous members of a political party, got to take being mobbed and insulted as part of the ordinary day's work. I had very little of it—only once was I mobbed—but many of my friends had a good deal. It was just stupidity and one rather hates to recall it now lest it should look as if any sense of injury remained, but as a bit of history it is worth remembering that that—and the outrages perpetrated by militant suffragists, which largely caused the trouble—was happening three years ago. Now, the War has brought us to a peaceful recommendation that at least some women should vote.'

She sent her congratulations to Mrs. Fawcett when the Women's Suffrage clause passed the House of Lords in the Franchise Bill of 1918 with a majority of sixty-nine, and Mrs. Fawcett's reply is one of the few personal communications that she preserved. Mrs. Fawcett was one of her heroines. She would speak almost with reverence of the steady balance of her judgement. The strength and tenacity of purpose through which Mrs. Fawcett never lost sight of her one end, the attainment of the parliamentary franchise for women; and the simplicity and directness of character prompting her to live a life that was both full and sane and rooted in natural human relationships: these qualities were ones that Grace Hadow set before herself as qualities to be attained and held fast.

In later years she came to know Mrs. Fawcett personally as my mother's friend, staying in the house with her and seeing her in private life. She wholly approved of Mrs. Fawcett's leadership in the decision to denounce militancy, and it was with half-humorous reluctance that she felt herself bound to admit in later years that militancy (much as she hated it) had in fact advanced the cause. To one of Grace Hadow's temperament militancy might well have been a temptation had her judgement not been so clearly set against it. For quick decisive action was natural to her, and where she felt issues strongly she would keep nothing back. She remained a law-abiding supporter of the political enfranchisement of women and in this way took her part in committee work, in canvassing, and as speaker when occasion demanded it. It is interesting to speculate how she would have used her vote in those days had she had one. Describing her own political views she dubbed herself an 'individualist anarchist' and she kept clear of political parties.

Her religious opinions had long undergone a period of testing which left her open-mindedly ready to recognize the real thing under many forms and alert about seeing it in these. It would be difficult to describe her attitude to religion as agnostic at any time; it was far too certain of fundamentals for that. If she failed to assent to dogma she had deep and positive convictions which were firmly held and she retained an unfailing reverence for dogma's concerns. A passage from an undated letter to her sister which must have been written about this time gives a glimpse of her mind. 'Has it struck you how little knowledge is needed for love? I suppose no one of us knows one another, and yet we love: just as a tiny child loves its parents without understanding. Perhaps that is why it matters so little that we cannot understand God—understanding has really nothing to do with loving Him. Which would also account for the fact that many saints seem to us to misunderstand Him, and are none the less saints. If I were a poet I should make a song on that—man groping in the dark, and God, not lifting the cloud, but finding him in it and through it. And the text should be: "No man can know, but all men can love."

'I have just been reading the latest attempt to explain Mr. Campbell's "New Theology", so my mind is full of problems and solutions. It must be inevitable that each man should think he has found the key to all mysteries and that his neighbour should never be able to make it fit, but I wish there were a little more peace on earth. The book seems to me great by the force of sheer sincerity; I expected to curse, and I found myself blessing. A non-Catholic never seems to realize the Catholic position (perhaps I don't realize it myself, but anyhow I don't see how a person who believed in the Real Presence could accept Mr. Campbell's creed), but it is interesting to find him and Father Waggett unanimous in pleading for unity of spirit and diversity of form. The magnanimity with which Mr. Campbell says he would not try to convert "even a Roman Catholic" makes me smile, but it is really magnanimous. He must be a fine man and I wish the clergy would read him before they preach at him—I might say instead of preaching at him. I hope Manchester College may invite him to preach to Oxford. I should like to hear him and I never seem to be in London for a Sunday.

'Mother is asleep and I am too lazy to hunt for a book to read, wherefore these maunderings. I should like to get a glimpse of fifty years on. We must be feeling our way towards something, but I wonder what?'

Meanwhile, during the years of retirement in Cirencester, Grace gave what spare time she found to various forms of social work. An offer of her services for parish work was obvious. She submitted it to the vicar's judgement, a fine man, nicknamed 'War',[1] with whose spirit she was necessarily in sympathy, and she worked as far as he thought right for a person whom he trusted and whose qualities he recognized but whose views a High Anglican could not consider sound. On this matter she had told him where she stood. Very soon she had called a flourishing girls' club to life. Her enthusiasm for drama and her recent experience as a producer at Lady Margaret Hall were applied to these girls, and she wrote and stage-managed their first play, *The Knave of Hearts*, acted on 30 April 1911, which her mother describes as 'the result of much hard work and anxious thoughts, and a power able to do much good'. Clearly Mrs. Hadow entered into this venture and sympathized with it. A photograph taken under the drawing-room window of Foss Lodge survives as a reminder of this performance. It displays carefully placed rows of some thirty-five girls; a solid young fairy queen happily conscious of her crown and wand is seated in the centre of the front row with three attendants on either side wearing silver sashes over their chests and their long hair flowing loose like hers. Shepherdesses in neat print frocks, and sandwich men wearing cards from the suit of hearts are behind. At the very back a small inconspicuous head is seen: Grace, rather prim, but arresting as soon as one discovers it for its penetrating intelligence, in contrast to the other happy and placid faces. This girls' club was a new local venture at the time.

Apart from such regular work at the club she accepted invitations as speaker for any meeting that wanted her, mothers' meet-

[1] Canon Robbins.

ings and others, perhaps especially for unpopular causes. I myself heard her preach her first sermon at a small afternoon service in a Nonconformist chapel at Cirencester. These activities made themselves felt. Gradually her fellow citizens began to discover her; it was with surprise and pleasure that she remarked upon it when a local meeting of tradesmen on some public matter elected her to take the chair, a most unusual concession in those days on the part of these men. Her personality asserted itself, work brought friendly contacts, and she grew fresh roots. Early in 1914 she was arranging cultural events through Oxford friends; of a concert at which Madame Roeger Soldat[1] (the great Austrian violinist) played with my sister, Margaret Deneke, Mrs. Hadow records on 23 February 1914: 'The most wonderful music ever played in Cirencester since the beginning of the world.' A year later she notes, on 9 December 1915: 'Dear Grace's birthday. May God bless and guide her in the future as he has done in the past; she is a dear blessing to us all and to many outsiders.' By then Cirencester had claimed her.

Meanwhile her work as lecturer at Lady Margaret Hall engaged her mind. She loved her subject on its merits, and as a teacher had a special power with pupils who were difficult or not yet at their maturity. Her lectures were delivered extempore. She read widely for them, but would often make notes only for main headings or illustrations so that two or three cards seemed to hold what she meant to say. Nevertheless there was careful preparation in thinking them out. Her course on 'Representative Men of English Literature' was enjoyed by successive generations and was one of her most popular ones. 'Introduced by a fascinating survey of their historical setting, figures emerged as real people whose work was the logical and final outcome of their personalities', writes a pupil in recalling these lectures and speaking of their 'vitality, charm and finish'.

Her literary work increased when she gave up residence at the Hall. Besides regular teaching, lecturing, and examining she did

[1] Marie Soldat was the first woman to play Brahms's Violin Concerto. As a child Brahms's attention had been drawn to her and he sent for her to play to his friend Joseph Joachim. After a splendid tea, when asked to play, it was found that the child had left her small violin in the fly outside in the hot sun and when she tried to play the glue gave way. She burst into tears, Joachim offered her his, and the little girl, who was not used to a full size instrument, took it and played Mendelssohn's Violin Concerto perfectly correctly and with spirit, instantly making the adjustment necessary to get the right intervals on the large violin. Joachim was so impressed that at once all scholarships were open to her. (Margaret Deneke.)

a good deal of reviewing, some of it as front-page articles in *The Times Literary Supplement*. She also edited various annotated selections from authors for teaching purposes. One anthology of hers for general readers calls for special mention: *Ideals of Living*, published in 1911 by Sidgwick and Jackson. It is of special interest not only for its own sake but because it illustrates the ideals she valued. The passages chosen bring out agreement within differences in the conviction that wisdom consists in the good life made perfect, for which loving and acting in truth is the guide. 'Thoughts concerning the meaning and purpose of life' are gathered together and chosen 'to represent as many different aspects of life as possible' and illustrating 'points of similarity in the teaching of great men of all ages upon matters of such primary importance as the relative value of things spiritual and temporal or our duty to our neighbours'. The passages range from the Book of the Dead and the Old Testament through Plato, Aristotle, and Epictetus, to the Sermon on the Mount and 1 Corinthians xiii, and onwards to English medieval and modern poets and prose writers. Selection was actually determined by what meant much to Grace herself: the character of him 'that sweareth unto his neighbour and disappointeth him not though it were to his own hindrance', Aristotle's reflection that 'friendship seems to consist rather in loving than in being loved', praise in the Psalms and in Traherne's *Second* and *Third Centuries*, Milton on truth and freedom of speech, George Herbert's *Temple* and *Proverbs*, and other passages where life is seen in familiar, almost homely forms, yet shines in splendour.

She engaged upon her next task also as a labour of love: it was the translation of Dr. Berthold Litzmann's *Life of Clara Schumann*. Her brother had been urged by the youngest daughter of Robert and Clara Schumann to undertake this himself or see that it was well done. His love of Schumann's music, his admiration of Madame Schumann's art and personality, and his own wish to have her life interpreted sympathetically to English readers made it impossible for him to refuse the request. Though his commitments did not allow him to undertake the translation, he promised to write a preface to the life and to persuade his sister to do the rest. 'The task of translation can never be a light one since every language has not only its own peculiar shades of meaning, but also its own peculiar charm—a fragrance which evaporates as soon as the national frontier is crossed', writes Grace Hadow in the translator's preface in 1912. 'This is especially true of the German of Robert Schumann. His delicate, poetic imagination found perfect expression in the language of his hero, Jean Paul, and the endeavour to render his love-letters, and still more his poems, in another tongue is foredoomed to failure; the original words alone fitly express the poet's thought.' It was indeed a difficult task and the more difficult for one steeled to reticence in these ways. It was essential 'to render as far as possible the spirit of the German', but there was sentiment to tone down, and a nice balance to adjust between this and the biographer's fidelity to his subject.

W. H. Hadow's preface is a charming essay, written with warmth and discrimination, and placing Madame Schumann in relation to the music and musicians of her time. Together with the translation it achieves what was intended: a permanent tribute in English to a great artist, whose music established a tradition in our country: 'no one combined all her gifts', he writes; 'none could reconcile such warmth of emotion with such inherent reverence for the chastity of art. She was as incapable as Joachim of trick and artifice; in her playing, as in his, there was an essential nobility which would never stoop to conquer.'[1] The biography contains extracts from the voluminous Schumann correspondence, and the spontaneity, the verve, and the sincerity of Clara Schumann's letters are captured in Grace Hadow's translation; it conveys also their purity of feeling.[2]

She was invited to write on *Chaucer and His Times*[3] for the Home University Library series, a volume which was published in the summer of 1914. Not everyone can succeed in presenting their

---

[1] Fanny Davies, one of Mme Schumann's most distinguished English pupils, was possessed of an amazing power of observation and analysis for the technique of her art. She would tell how as a young girl she decided to choose her teacher by going to hear every great pianist she could, so as to note down their personal interpretation and any details of rhythm, or tempo, or rendering in this or that passage. When she went to hear Mme Schumann with this in view she found no idiosyncrasies to note. Greatly impressed both by the impersonality and the inwardness of this playing she decided she had found her teacher at last. (Margaret Deneke.)

[2] Evidently there was some misunderstanding over proof-reading. The foreign compositor, ignorant of English, slipped in an astounding number of errors which an imposing list of errata does not set right. The misprints seriously mar the book.

[3] The passages from the book, which follow, are reproduced by kind permission of the Oxford University Press.

material in vivid detail within the rigid space allotted to this series, and the attempt involves sacrifices in proportions given to the subject. Her book was unfavourably reviewed for its disregard of the standpoint of scholarly criticism. Nevertheless Chaucer's qualities of mind and character were congenial to her and her little book can claim to communicate the attraction that she felt. The core of what she has to say is in the chapters on humour and on Chaucer's view of men and things; his tolerance, his sympathy with ordinary people, his clear eye for their weaknesses endeared him to her. Characteristic touches here and there bring to the memory her way of taking and expressing things, and in these her voice can be heard. Setting aside the suggestion that Chaucer's married life was presumably unhappy, in view of his references to shrewish wives, she makes the quiet remark: 'When it comes to taking away the character of Philippa Chaucer on the ground that her husband complains in the House of Fame that he is unaccustomed to be awakened gently, it is impossible not to feel that she is receiving unnecessarily harsh treatment.' The Prioress of the Prologue to the *Canterbury Tales* seems 'very much what a fourteenth century Cressida would have been if her friends had placed her in a convent instead of finding her a husband. She has the same daintiness and trimness, and the same superficial tender-heartedness.' Grace Hadow could enter into Cressida, understanding her nature with critical sympathy; 'Cressida is incapable of being swept away by a great passion. She has a cat-like softness and daintiness and charm and a cat's adaptability to circumstances.' Her sketch of this character has personal touches. Here as elsewhere Chaucer's men and women are brought before us vividly, and his power to invest 'the most amazing incidents with an air of homeliness and naturalness' is reflected upon in an individual way. Humour Grace Hadow knew from inside knowledge 'as the faculty which enables us to love while we laugh and to love the better for laughter'. That Chaucer is limited by so-called worldliness she would not concede: 'If he is perhaps over-ready to plunge into the dust and din of life, he never forgets the wonder and the mystery that lie behind the commonplace. . . . The most careless reader can hardly fail to be struck by his wide sympathies, ready humour, and honesty of mind. His idealism, his poetic sensitiveness to the more imaginative side of life are perhaps less often insisted upon, but are no less real. He

is no visionary, afraid to face the facts of life, dwelling in a world
of beauty and delight which has no counterpart on earth, but a
poet who takes no shame in human nature, whose eyes see so
clearly that they are not blinded by evil, who dares to say with his
Creator that the world is good.'

The book on Chaucer was written under pressure; it was the
year of the return of Mrs. Hadow's serious illness, and the sort of
difficulties put in the way are best realized in the recollection of a
friend who saw Grace at that time sitting pen in hand on the
staircase at Foss Lodge because every corner of the house was
taken up by something more immediately important.

The war gave a new turn to her thoughts for books. Together
with L. Leslie Brooke[1] she brought out a tiny slim pocket anthology, *At the Front*, which was beautifully spaced and printed and
was sold for the benefit of the Red Cross. Designed for men on
active service it may well have given pleasure and comfort to
many a soldier. By 1916 she was once more enjoying herself with
a hero after her heart, when she made selections from Sir Walter
Raleigh[2] and wrote an introduction to them. The passages illus-
trate his personality and are chosen with delicate discrimination.
Her preface brings before us vividly the historical circumstances as
they affected him, his character in its gallantry, its dash, its steady
courage under failure, its tenderness, and it shows his life of brilliant adventure, of hardship, and ill luck. Further thoughts of books
remained schemes; possibly her interest in character and customs
might have led her to write a book very much her own in future
years of retirement had she lived longer; her steady interest in this
subject is seen also in her broadcasts on 'Wayfaring in Olden Days'
and 'Exploration at Home' (for the B.B.C. in 1928). At the time
when she resigned her lectureship at Lady Margaret Hall in 1917
her pen turned to articles or booklets connected with new work
which claimed her and were written as occasion arose. Some
appeared in magazines or educational journals; the greater part
are anonymous contributions to the literature of Women's Institutes and other organizations concerned with adult education.

[1] L. Leslie Brooke. Artist; illustrator of *Johnny Crow's Garden* and other
children's books. Born 1862 (son of Leonard D. Brooke, of Oxton, Birkenhead);
married (1894) Sybil, daughter of the Rev. Stopford Brooke; died 1940.
[2] Published by the Clarendon Press.

CHAPTER VI

BETWEEN CIRENCESTER AND OXFORD
1914–1917

THE war set its mark upon Grace Hadow; it weighed on her mind, and she felt it deeply in its moral issues and in its challenge to human nature. Her lectures for the Michaelmas Term of 1914 were to include Carlyle; she finds them 'turning into Bernhardi instead: what an amazing book', she adds, 'and most amazing of all the man has a streak of idealism'. The heroic impulse that swept the younger generation of 1914 was hers too, and she rallied to the defence of the moral and spiritual values that were at stake. The invasion of Belgium had branded the enemy, yet she was eager to see those values assert themselves wherever they could be traced. Chivalry, just pride, and courage appealed to her, whether in friend or foe, and she kept her sense of fairness and of justice at a time when it was very hard to do this, but her passions were as deeply roused as any one's by German ruthlessness. At the end of a letter to me she remarks: 'By the way have I to regard Frau Soldat (the great Austrian violinist) as an alien enemy, because I can't!' She abhorred the creed of hatred in all its forms and the senselessness of war, yet deep down in her there was a mixture of combativeness and spirituality that would have made the finest type of soldier.

It was a grief that women were not called upon to make the supreme sacrifice and it was hard to bear that she was not free to do war work near the front. Air raids, when they came, seemed an opportunity to get near sharing something of the danger from which men were protecting women and children. On the front page of a war diary which she kept between 1914 and 1919 she pasted two pictures of St. George: Mantegna's and Dürer's engraving where the dragon lies reduced to insignificance between the horse's legs and the saint raises himself in his stirrups to look 'for fresh dragons to kill'. The old lines are inscribed below:

> Of them that died in Thermopylae
> Glorious was their fortune: fair is the fate.
> For a tomb, they have an altar,
> For lamentation, Memory
> And for pity, praise. (Simonides, A.D. 1914)

In this her attitude is sufficiently indicated. She faced the war and all that it meant fully, compelling herself to realize it and transcend it as far as might be. That first Christmas of 1914 she was fascinated by the fraternizing of our men with Saxons and Bavarians; though the angels of Mons touched her with their wings, she was sceptical and slightly shamefaced over them; but the chief impression that was soon burnt in upon her mind was of the iron heel of Prussia.

By October 1914 Grace Hadow, who had thought that the war might never touch their neighbourhood visibly as it had touched Oxford, was concerned in many forms of local war-work. A new strength and independence seemed to come to her, or perhaps qualities shone out that were ever present, but were hitherto less clearly seen by those outside her own immediate circles.

She was soon taking part in arrangements for Belgian refugees. Great goodwill went into preparations for their arrival: 'On Monday to 26, Black Jack Street which has been fitted up for refugees. One working woman had scrubbed it out, others had scoured pots and pans. Every scrap of furniture has been given. While I was there . . . Mrs. Chamberlain (our housemaid's aunt) came in with a bunch of chrysanthemums for the house and promised a sack of potatoes later. The village women are raising a levy for relief work. The Liberal Association asked its members for 1*d.* a week. I heard some of the secretaries saying they had been offered 6*d.* by some of their working members.

'Our neighbour, Mr. Lawson, asked his wife to pack some of his clothes and send them to the Belgians. Among the things he put out she found a brand-new suit which she persuaded him to put back in his drawer. He went downstairs after the altercation, picked up the paper and saw the news of the fall of Antwerp— and at once he went back and told her to pack that suit.'

So writes Grace Hadow on 22 October 1914, and a week later: 'This afternoon Mrs. Trotman asked me to come and help sort out twenty-three refugees who were to be divided between Ashcroft and Black Jack Street. Five were lost on the way, and one man arrived unannounced, so it turned into nineteen. They are of a better class than we have had before—all seem to talk French and the women wear hats. Their luggage is horribly pathetic—bundles obviously done up in quilts pulled off their beds in a hurry. One couple from Antwerp started from Belgium with a daughter of twenty-three and an old mother of seventy-three but got separated from both and have no clue as to where they may be: "Quelle jolie histoire, n'est-ce pas?" I heard the father say.

'I tried to talk to a very nice woman from Antwerp, and our two broken Frenches made out that she was much touched by "les Anglais" while I stumbled out our pride in Belgium. They look so haggard, poor souls.'

Gradually a picture is formed of those Belgians into whose lives Grace entered: the rougher ones at the workhouse 'completely baffled by night clothes' which they wore over their day things if at all; the shoemaker, too, who came back to the workhouse 'mad drunk—with a knife': after having been treated by 'kindly disposed fools so that it took two men to tackle him', he and his children were returned to headquarters. There was a 'pair of smiling giants who make bricks, and who are here with "mama" and their sister'; there were also the 'nice young clerk called Lanvers' from whom Grace had Flemish lessons while she tried to get his fourteen-year-old brother taken at the Grammar School; and then the 'nice butcher who had gone to fetch a cart in which to escape with his family and goods when the Germans came and looted his safe with all his money' . . . 'One can see how he hates charity'. There were well-to-do ones, who had lost everything. A man told 'with great pride of their house in Malines and the garden where he would walk for a couple of hours at a time looking now at this, now at that and thinking that his neighbour's over the wall was not so well cared for. . . . Now they do not know if the house in which they spent twenty-one years is standing or not.' They got separated during their escape with long anxiety about getting together again. 'It seems horrible to write down the stories of the refugees, but they do make one realize war as nothing else does.'

As the refugees got to know Grace Hadow they told of what they had seen and suffered, and the callous cruelty of the enemy to non-combatants was borne in upon her: there were two nuns who had seen grievous distress over and above their own.

'I called on the nuns this evening. Only Sœur Catherine was in, but I talked with her for three quarters of an hour. She told me that their Convent at one time sheltered three hundred wounded Belgian soldiers and as they talked to each other of the things they had seen the sister would cry "Ce n'est pas possible!" only to receive the answer "Je l'ai vu, ma sœur." The sisters had with them one child whose nerves had been shattered by the sight of her little brother tied to a German horse and dragged to death. One night the Convent bell rang and on opening the door they found fifty refugees, carrying their children and their poor little packages—among them "un monsieur" who had been owner of several chateaux. They had absolutely nothing left. The sisters came over with a number of Belgian wounded. There was also a wounded, dying Uhlan—a Protestant. The Belgians, mad with rage, wanted to throw him overboard, but there were some Englishmen there, one of them a doctor, who stood up to the furious crowd, "No," he said, "Germans do things like that, but Belgians and Englishmen do not", and the crowd subsided.' Further visits are reported: 'I saw the nuns again, Sœur Germaine told me the reason why so many Belgian families are divided. At Louvain the Germans took 3,000 inhabitants to the city gates. They separated the men from the women, and sent them off to Germany, and then they deliberately separated the women from the children and *sent the children away by themselves*.'

In December 1914 an army division was sent to Cirencester, which to its own unbounded surprise was turned into a garrison town. Soldiers were billeted upon the inhabitants wherever room could be found, and although for Mrs. Hadow's sake it was not possible to take soldiers at Foss Lodge, Grace turned over to them her own study, a former studio adjacent to the house as 'a tiny private reading room'. . . . 'A sergeant (looking about 20) came over from the Apsley Hall to inspect the Studio. He says he'll like to read my books. I wonder.' Soon the sergeant began to feel at home with her: 'My friend the sergeant shows an instinctive inclination to take off his hat to me. Remembering that this is unprofessional he nods. I think he was in a shop three months ago.'

Grace had a flair for discovering what would be of use to the men and of acting at once when a need was seen. To equip them for France she offered to teach them elementary French and got some graded classes started. 'I went to take an elementary French class tonight and found it a little difficult: two of the men were Glasgow graduates who had learned French for six or seven years, two or three were middle-aged Tommies who knew no word of

it, and one was an educated gentleman whom I took for an officer
till I saw the corporal's stripe. It was quite impossible to mix
them. I have promised to get someone to take a conversation
class for those who know French and only real beginners are to
come to me . . . but Corporal Pickering has put his name down
for a book. He says that when he tries to talk French it comes out
Malay. My colliers were more suited to me.'

She made many friends among the soldiers and kept in touch
with no small number. An entire album of postcards in the
queerest taste, sent her from France, remains to record it. From
these contacts she collected her impressions of the war seen from
the soldier's point of view.

To those who knew her the War Diary will recall Grace
Hadow's eager speaking. The book brings a good many interesting little stories, sidelights on men and matters that flit by. Sometimes these come from her brother and from others who were in
the thick of directing affairs in one way or another. At other times
they come from friends who had special knowledge.

'Today has been curiously typical', she writes on 6 May 1915,
'of the various points at which the War touches the average person
who has no special job in connexion with it:

'(1) I spent an hour at the Red Cross Hospital making splint
straps.

'(2) Heard from Sennelager that the parcels had arrived and
sent off cigarettes and food for the prisoners.

'(3) Received several contributions for a "Gloucestershire" bed
in the Serbian Hospital and saw about getting an appeal printed.

'(4) Made arrangements for the Belgian Repatriation meeting
on Monday.

'(5) Heard from a Belgian Corporal from the trenches in
Flanders.

'(6) Heard from one of the Camerons who is in hospital with
pneumonia.

'(7) Heard from Mildred Vernon Harcourt from an R.A.M.C.
Hospital in Boulogne.'

To comment on these points where war touches the 'average
person', Sennelager—one of those inhumane German prison
camps—implied a personal relation on the part of Grace Hadow
to men imprisoned there, especially to her correspondent Corporal
Hughes, who was captured early in the war and kept first at

Sennelager, then at Soltau. On the theme of prison camps she might have written a book. However, she chose rather to get Hughes himself on his return to put down what happened to him when a prisoner and what he did: a bare account of facts hardly filling a slim penny note-book—without commentary or recrimination, entirely artless yet telling by its very simplicity. Her interest in these particular men did much to keep up their spirits and she managed to think of things to send them that were just right: 'Hughes writes that the boxing gloves are in constant use. The English prisoners give exhibits of boxing to the huge delight of the Belgians and the French and give lessons to anyone who likes to learn. He adds that boots are most welcome as the camp is in a bog and the boots the men have rot at once. Of all the books I have sent him only one has been confiscated—a cookery book' (April 1916). Hughes's steady refusal to work for the Germans got him into trouble, but he stood firm.

Another enterprise for prisoners that Grace Hadow pursued with great energy was procuring blankets. She herself was much impressed with the result of the appeal she organized for scraps of wool to make these: 'I put an appeal for odds and ends of wool, wherewith to knit blankets for prisoners, in the *Daily Graphic*. I wished I had weighed what has come—and still comes in—19 to 20 parcels at a time. Wool from every part of the United Kingdom. I distribute sacksfull of it and still it overflows a large clothes basket: all this in odd half balls and scraps left over from knitting. I have already sent off 14 "blankets" and the lightest weighs over 2 lbs. I wonder if the lady who offered us "10 minutes a week" for war work is knitting?'

Grace Hadow was also concerned in the local register of those willing to do war work. On 19 June 1915, 'The High Steward called a Town Meeting at Cirencester to discuss local "National Service" and it was decided to make use of the existing Relief Committee as a nucleus and to authorize the Relief Committee to form a register of every adult in the Town who is willing to do War-work. The problem will be to find work', she notes; 'I have suggested following Gloucester's lead of last year and organizing fruit bottling either for ourselves (if there is a likelihood of distress in winter) or to send to prisoners of war—according to *The Times* their unvarying diet at every meal is black bread and thick soup, and my men at Sennelager seem to like fruit.'

The war entered into daily life on all sides; it also cut deeply into social traditions. Most striking was its temporary effect on the status of women which came to be measured more directly in terms of their work. This development Grace watched closely.

For Dr. Elsie Inglis she had a great admiration, seeing her for the great woman that she was, with a mind unruffled and a spirit tempered by the obstacles which she encountered on the way to her ideal of a life of service as a woman doctor. In her quietness and confidence in pursuit of a single aim Grace Hadow found inspiration, as she also found it in Mrs. Fawcett. She followed the fate of the Scottish Women's Hospitals at Royaumont and in Serbia with steady interest and was present when Miss Hutchison on her return home told, in the quad of Oriel College, how she brought back the Union Jack under her blouse in the retreat from Serbia. She rejoiced in Dr. Rosalie Jobson's report how she and her associates, like Dr. Elsie Inglis, after being rejected by our own authorities, had been accepted in France where their surgery met the great need. The story of the struggle of women doctors to win through and of their success in the war had her almost passionate sympathy. She took a keen interest in the new occupations which were opening for women as ticket collectors or clerks on the G.W.R. in Oxford, as bus- or tram-conductors, in industry, and in professions. These were felt as an achievement in the long story of women's work. Her own membership of the local War Agricultural Committee was to lead her to find a new vocation in constructive work on behalf of country women: 'A meeting of the War Agricultural Committee to-day' (she notes on 24 January 1916). 'The Board of Agriculture is asking for a canvass of women in every parish in England to ask for volunteers to work on the land. We met about a dozen farmers and discussed matters. Some had tried women and would have gone bankrupt if they'd stayed a week longer, some always worked a part of their farms with female labour and found it a success. All agreed that "women be funny". A Sub-committee has been appointed to deal with the matter.'

Soon Grace was speaking at war agricultural meetings in different parts of the county, and she found 'both farmers and women are far readier to respond than I expected'. Some women were banding themselves together to cultivate the gardens and allotments of men at the Front or to run co-operative poultry farms.

On 28 February 1916 she records briefly, 'I've just been elected a member of the Gloucestershire Chamber of Agriculture. A very odd effect of the War on an Oxford teacher of English literature.'

A little article of hers written in the late autumn of that year for the *Common Cause* (published by the National Union of Women's Suffrage Societies) so well embodies this combination of agriculture and of literature that I shall quote it in full. It also shows her point of view. Though feminist, in the sense of championing women's work, it is not so in any sense of hostility to men

'*Women at the Plough*

'A typical October day: a pale blue sky, across which the strong West wind drives huddled masses of cloud so that lights and shadows flicker and change continuously over the open rolling country. The air is full of the smell of autumn—that indescribable wholesome fragrance which seems of the very essence of earth—the hedgerows are heavy with huge festoons of "old man's beard" and briony; there are blackberries everywhere, and here and there flames a bush of scarlet hips. The sun is hot enough for spectators to bask on the grey stone walls, and very soon the walls are black with them, for here is something new in our part—a demonstration of women on the land. We are agricultural folk; even the shopkeepers in the little towns often have a bit of land as well, and most of us know something of what farm work really means. We have scant sympathy with those who fear honest sunburn or hardened hands; we know that hay-making is hot and dusty work, whatever the poets may make of it. Our boys "mess about" on the farm almost as soon as they can walk, and you may often see a proud baby of five or six perched on the back of a patient cart-horse riding it to water on a summer evening. Before compulsory education forced us to send our children to learn "oonderments" in school, many a boy was leading horses at eight years old. Even today there are experienced hands of thirteen and fourteen in professional loose velveteen coats and corduroys standing about watching with critical eyes what "they women be goin' to do".

'It is a kindly audience, sympathetic and interested, but it is not an easy one to face, for it is very largely composed of experts, from the oldest inhabitant, who sits chuckling on a big stone and wheezes out that "we shan't want no more chaps or lads soon", to the village women themselves, many of whom know from experience what a hard day in the rick-yard means. In the big field ten furrows are marked out, and soon ten teams come jingling and swinging, their own ploughmen in charge. By each furrow stand competitors—girls and women of all sorts and kinds, brought together by their own desire to work for their country where work is needed. One little group is gay with blue overalls and brightly coloured 'kerchiefs, others are in knickerbockers and long coats, plain serviceable working kit in these soft fallows sticky with yesterday's rain. The village women wear pale blue and pink prints. But it is hard work ploughing on heavy land and the ploughs are set deep. There is one thin slip of a child of fourteen who is almost swung off her feet as the plough turns, and one blue overall finds her plough-share buried deep in mud, where the crowd has cut up the ground by the gate. The rightful owners of the teams watch with undisguised anxiety, and at critical moments cannot forbear stretching out a helping hand (one can see the plough women wish they wouldn't, but there is a kindliness in it which is irresistible) or calling a familiar "c'mover" in tones that Ned or Dobbin are accustomed to and therefore understand.

'Other women are spreading manure, some cleaning roots, some drilling, others harnessing teams and leading the waggons through gates and round obstacles. But next to the ploughing, the crowds most enjoy watching the rick-yard. Here half a dozen women are preparing straw for the thatchers—"yealming" as we call it—and at the word "Go" they pull at the wet straw, give it a curious swing in the air to straighten it, and pile it criss-cross in neat bundles at a surprising pace. After this comes thatching, and the crowd cheers warmly as an old lady of seventy-one (in a sun-bonnet of her own making) takes her "scratch" (a forked stick holding a large and very heavy "yealm") on her shoulder, and with absolute sure-footedness climbs up a high ladder to the top of a rick, and proceeds to thatch as coolly as if she were twenty. Already she has won a first prize for manure-spreading, and her green and red armlet (which shows she has worked over a month on the land) bears a special badge, "Give I because I be over age, and be drawin' my old age pension". The village is subscribing for a silver brooch as a mark of gratitude for the farm work she has done this summer.

'On the whole the farmers—and there must be more than one hundred of them present—are well satisfied. The "women's work" (though as one shrewd old farmer says, "If you're wise, you'll never say what's women's work and what's men's"), i.e. manure-spreading and root pulling and cleaning and "yealming" was done "as it ought to be" (high praise from our cautious experts).

'The work with the horses was plucky and promising. It is no use pretending that girls who have begun farm-work this year can take the places of men who have been at it all their lives: "'Tis an art as has to be learned. When a man's been at it since he was quite a little chap

'tis second nature to him, and he don't have to think how to do it";
but they have proved conclusively (a) that not all women are afraid of
horses (as I have heard stated even by farm women), (b) that they can
very quickly be turned into efficient undercarters and farm hands.
No doubt educated women, in this as in other professions, learn
rapidly because they have been trained to use their brains at the same
time as their hands, and in some cases they have proved themselves
capable of taking full responsibility of a farm. In this as in so many
other instances, it is not a case of man *versus* woman, but of individuals
and of opportunity for training. Some work is so heavy that few
women could tackle it properly, but those who have tried farm work
know how quickly it hardens the muscles, and our thatcher of seventy-
one is good evidence of the healthiness of an out-door life.

'Farmers are shy of employing women in many cases, not only
because of practical difficulties with regard to housing, and training:
"We've no time to go round nursery-maiding" is a common point.
But there is no doubt that the work of women on the land is doing
much to break down a high wall of prejudice, and in this—as in so
many cases—the mutual understanding and respect born of working
side by side is furthering the common cause of men and women, and
helping towards an amicable settlement of at least one labour problem
after the war.'

G. E. H.

'Women of all sorts and kinds, brought together by their own
desire to work for their country where work is needed', that
motive expressed also the impulse from which the Women's
Institutes were to grow.

Whether Grace Hadow instantly foresaw the educational possibilities of Institutes or not it is hard to tell; certainly she cannot have foreseen the large-scale development of the movement
that has happened since the War of 1914–18, nor her own big
share in it. It is curious that she does not enter the formation of
the Cirencester Women's Institute in the war diary. Perhaps it is
because it was just one incident among many which she merely
forgot to record (there is no entry for that day) or possibly the old
instinct of slipping away from any credit that might be assigned to
herself is responsible. Mrs. Hadow's journal states: 'July 10, 1916:
The Woman's Institute established. Grace president and chief
speaker.'

Grace Hadow continued her connexion with this first Institute
of her own and was known there in later years as a person and not

merely as a legend. During her last years at Cirencester it must have brought to her a pledged body of adherents and a home platform of her own. But she would never have thought of herself in that way. The first mention of Women's Institutes in her war diary is on 25 February 1917: 'Quite an interesting meeting at Sapperton yesterday. A campaign is being held to form Women's Institutes throughout the country and I went to start one there. We had an exhibition of war-food—really delicious barley bread and oat cake and parkin, and an excellent address on rations from the sister of a neighbouring vicar.'

By 2 April in the same year she is speaking of having helped to found the Cirencester and District Food Production Committee as a last job in Cirencester and with a view to organizing the increased production of vegetables and fruit in cottage gardens and to co-operative marketing later on. It was at the time of anxiety about the nation's food supply, when Institutes were founded to help with this. After remarking on opposition from some farmers, who, being more prosperous than ever before, saw no reason for fostering food production, she speaks of the helpfulness of other farmers and of many conversions among them to employing women carters, and she continues: 'We have founded seventeen Women's Institutes in surrounding villages and the women really are eager to try new methods and to experiment with War breads &c., &c. The movement ought to do a great deal not only to promote thrift but to educate country women and to improve conditions of village life.' By the spring of 1917 she had gauged the educational and social possibilities of the movement for countrywomen.

In the spring of that year her mother died. With her death the home at Cirencester lost its meaning; the war was then at a critical and dangerous stage. She resigned her lectureship at L.M.H. and decided to look for full-time war work.

The job that offered came as a surprise to friends who were accustomed to think of Grace Hadow in an educational and literary connexion: she was appointed director of a subsection of the Ministry of Munitions.

CHAPTER VII

MINISTRY OF MUNITIONS

1917–1919

THE work to which Grace Hadow was appointed took her to a new sphere and drew forth powers of her mind and character that have remained unforgettable to her immediate colleagues. She was invited to be head of a subsection of the Welfare Department of the Ministry of Munitions. This section was concerned with the health and happiness of women munition workers, employed in private establishments as well as in national factories all over the country, outside working hours. 'Notwithstanding her protests she was persuaded to accept the post', writes Dr. Collis, her chief. 'Vainly did she declare that her only métier was educational and literary; how brilliant her success is only known to those with whom she worked.'

Welfare work was not yet universally accepted as an essential to the efficient conduct of industry, and social services were comparatively speaking in their infancy. The Department offered an opportunity for new lines of approach to social maladjustments. It had come into being soon after the Ministry of Munitions was set up in 1915, as a result of research into the health of munition workers and into the causation of industrial fatigue. Bad factory conditions and inadequate recreation were found to be responsible as well as over-long hours without a weekly day of rest; and to remedy these and other adverse influences Sir Seebohm Rowntree had been invited to supervise the new Department and to give it the benefit of his experience as a pioneer in welfare in his great factory at York. Enthusiasts had joined him such as Dr. Douglas Newton (later Lord Eltisley), R. R. Hyde (subsequently director of the Industrial Welfare Society), and Lord Dunluce (the late Lord Antrim). When the work expanded Sir Seebohm Rowntree retired, since he could only give part of his time, and Dr. E. L. Collis (now an emeritus professor) took charge. He was then a civil servant, a medical inspector of factories, and an active member of the Health of Munition Workers Committee which had indirectly helped to start the Department. Dr. E. L. Collis was Grace's immediate chief and worked very closely with her; he was ready to put at her service his wide experience and technical knowledge, and she thought highly of him. The late Mr. Humbert Wolfe, perhaps more widely known as a poet than as a civil servant, became secretary to the Department.

A vast variety of matters were the Department's concern:[1] lodgings for workers, their housing conditions outside the factory, transit, crèches, maternity homes, clubs. Various subsections were set up to deal with various aspects of the work, and these necessarily interlocked, so that smooth and efficient working depended upon co-operation between the sections, yet the departmentalized administration of a huge Ministry obviously brings the danger to those who work in it of seeing little beyond the detail which is all important in itself. The Department was doing experimental work that had nevertheless to fit in with the machinery of other departments. During its short existence it was subjected to successive reconstructions. Grace's arrival coincided with a difficult moment of expansion or transition between the complete civil servant whose actions were constrained by a lifetime of peace traditions and the complete amateur in public affairs who wished to push his own thing through without reference to anything else. She was able to be a happy medium and her colleagues responded.

The work of the Department was then in the middle of its development and most of the personnel was fixed. Miss A. G. Philip, ex-chief woman-inspector to the Board of Education, who held a responsible post in her section, writes: 'It is difficult now

[1] A note in Grace Hadow's War Diary in the autumn of 1917 gives an amusing list of the variety of functions supposed to be covered by Welfare. 'Recent Letters at the Ministry of Munitions:

(1) An unknown woman giving an indefinite address asks us to stop the hammering in the Munition factory opposite her house as the noise keeps her husband awake.

(2) A man whose wife has deserted him asks us to provide some-one to look after his children.

(3) A lady asks us to buy her billiard table.

(4) A woman from Seven Kings wants to know where to leave her baby while she goes out to work.

(5) A woman in Glasgow asks us to arrange suitable hours at which she can visit her child in Hospital.

(6) Leslie Potter's mama writes to tell us that he has broken six clocks and watches "though he told the dilution officer he was mending them" and makes such a noise that she constantly has to change her lodgings because of the neighbours' complaints. Will we please deal with—and reform—him?

(7) A house painter writes to complain that he has been asked to kill vermin in a hostel "which my Sercierty do not allow"; gives as a reference the Prime Minister and denounces his Manager as a "Professional Octrobus".'

(1941) to remember what phase of that development was in pro
gress when Grace Hadow took over the leadership of one of the
sections. There is however no difficulty in remembering the immediate response of the whole section to the charm of her clear,
fine, buoyant personality. There cannot have been gathered
together in any department such a strangely assorted team as the
one she took over. The men included an eminent general,[1] a young
peer, a poet, who was extremely and prosaically efficient, and a
number of permanent civil servants. Amongst the women were
university lecturers, teachers, Home Office officials and a beautiful
lady of fashion whose knowledge of affairs proved highly valuable.
This queer crowd became, under Grace Hadow's leadership, one
of the best working teams I have ever seen. Her friendly confidence in all of us, her wit and cheerfulness, her entire lack of
personal vanity or official prejudice, her single, steady, courageous
aim of the goal we had in view—these were the qualities that
bound us all together and made the work of those years (1917–
1918) a peculiarly happy memory.'

The Department is long dispersed. After the War of 1914–18
the extra-mural subsection was absorbed partly by the Ministry of
Health, partly by the Home Office, partly by Local Authorities,
and when in recent years a more terrible war overshadowed the
last one, reviving the same social problem at home, much of the
experience of this first Welfare Department had been forgotten
and had to be gone through again. At the time extra-mural welfare
had to meet temporary needs and to safeguard the conditions
of women's labour now for the first time made mobile. It had to
improvise practical and sympathetic treatment which involved
consideration as much of the psychological as of the physical
requirements of workers, and in meeting these needs it struck upon

---

[1] 'From the war point of view one of the most interesting things I have come
across in the first week at the Ministry', writes Grace, 'is a very eminent General
who recently had the whole Southern Command; being now superannuated he has
come most cheerfully and simply to do subordinate office work. He comes up to ask
for time off to attend Court Martials as simply as any clerk.' The late General Sir
Alfred Edward Codrington, G.C.V.O., K.C.B., told me his work was principally to
visit factories in any part of England where munitions were being made. When
bad conditions or difficulties were reported he would be sent, and he recalled: 'Miss
Hadow used to say "we must send off the Guard" and off I went to many places.'
Sometimes such a visit resulted in a struggle with authorities to get improvements
made. 'Generally I have the impression of a strenuous fight by our department
under Miss Hadow against the apathy of bureaucracy. But I feel that under her
leadership we did a great deal of good.'

social problems as they related to working-class lives as a whole. In less than two years it could not provide lasting solutions to all the problems which had arisen, but the foundations were laid for very important developments in social welfare later on. The Department operated in a sphere that was already covered partly by forces of local government, partly by voluntary organizations. In order to fill in the gaps left by existing agencies the extra-mural department developed co-operation between statutory authorities and voluntary organizations, and it was here particularly that Grace Hadow was to gather insight which proved of value in the future. She also discovered new powers of her own in administration. The problems with which her section dealt called for unconventional treatment and gave scope for resourcefulness.

One of her official duties was to receive reports from a staff of extra-mural workers each with her own district, and some of these record how well she knew what help to give in encouragement, in good suggestions, in ready sympathy—also in amusement. Hers was not a mind to miss the humour of diverting incidents or situations, and her imaginative insight stood her in good stead. For the rest she profited by the training in the powers, the restrictions, and the ways of a Government Department, and though she remained a rebel against officialdom, she learnt a good deal about public affairs. One of the means of her own devising for furthering co-operation within the Department was a residential conference which was arranged at Lady Margaret Hall, Oxford, for several subsections in the summer of 1918. The personal contacts established by living and conferring together in a pleasant place were felt at the time 'to have made departmental jealousies difficult'. The programme was drawn up with a view to giving members in each subsection a better idea of how their work fitted in with that of other subsections as well as giving them an opportunity to learn something of the scope of what was being planned and achieved by the Ministry as a whole. And there was provided a remarkable occasion for seeing this last in historical perspective. Grace had succeeded in persuading Sir Hugh Bell, the great iron-master and humane employer of a previous generation, to give an address on the relation between the employer and the employed as he saw it after fifty years' experience. Tall, alert, a truly venerable figure, he contended that the economic point of view for that relation was not inhumane. He was a heretic in that assembly since he disbelieved in Government intervention, and yet his wide knowledge and his personality reinforced arguments with which his hearers were disposed to disagree. The challenge was highly stimulating. The weighty statement of a divergent view within agreement upon the same end seemed to mark a stepping-stone in social history. There could hardly have been a happier choice of an exponent of the older idea of the relation between employer and employed.[1]

Meanwhile in the country as a whole the employer's ideas of what was necessary for the worker were being revolutionized, and the worker was acquiring a new independence and status. Grace gained personal experience of the problems involved in this development. She visited industrial centres, and on one important visit, when she was sent to Barrow to advise and report on local difficulties, there is incidental evidence[2] that she made a marked impression there on those concerned and that her advice was accepted. There may have been other occasions of the kind that were never recorded unless it were in office files. She visited factories, addressed meetings of munition workers, took part in educational activities for workers. A remark in a letter of hers, dated 18 November 1917, describes one of her lectures: 'Parenthetically it may interest you—it interested me a good deal, and surprised me almost equally—to know that a lecture on Nature Poetry (with no lantern slides—no nothing to help it down) drew an audience of 500 munition workers—men and women—on Friday night and I never talked to a more responsive one. They were quite a rough type, and my heart was in my boots when I began, especially as I had been told the employer's point of view—expressed with some force—was that no sane person could expect factory hands to listen to stuff like that. And they came to such an extent that there was no standing room. How's that for the working man and woman after a hard day's work!'

Grace's sympathy and affection went out towards the munition workers about whose lives she was then thinking a great deal.

[1] 'Sir Hugh Bell, who died in 1931, was chairman of Bell Bros., the Tees-side firm of iron-masters which had been started by his father in 1844. With a breadth of vision rare among his contemporaries he saw what the relations of master and men might and should be, and declared himself to be "always on the side of the men". His ready sympathy, his love of children and of animals, joined to a depth of wisdom both in business and in daily life, won for Sir Hugh a cherished place in the wide circle of his friends.'

[2] Reference in a letter of her brother's.

They were never merely a class of people to be dealt with in a mass, but men and women living strenuous lives, often in hardship and danger, and themselves as much subjected to the tension of war as the rest of the world. On 13 July 1918 there was an impressive service in St. Paul's for munition workers, which was attended by the King and Queen, when the nave was packed with men and women from the Arsenal. 'Looking from the choir on that great mass of men was curiously moving', she writes, and 'the Last Post made me think of the 200 killed and wounded at the Arsenal a week ago and their comrades who were back at work next day. The Lord Mayor attended in state, and the Bishop covered with orders and medals and somewhere, I suppose, the King and Queen. But it was the congregation that counted.'

With the constant tension of the war situation at home and abroad, disillusionment crept in. The heroic impulse which Grace had so strongly shared in 1914 was not stifled, but war came to be seen more clearly as a testing time of all human relations and there seemed a good chance that what is best in these relations would be set at naught by what was taking place. Everything was in the balance and it seemed impossible to estimate what the future would bring. How could the world be built up again? Early in 1918 such thoughts were passing through her mind even while she was still engaged in full work at the Ministry with its urgent practical problems. 'It is a curiously and increasingly restless time', she writes in January 1918. 'At first most people thought the war would soon be over and things would be much as before. Now we all realize they can never be the same again and no one knows what the difference will be. It gives sometimes a sense of vast growth and possibilities—sometimes of vast insecurity. Will there be a revolution all over Europe? Is there going to be a socialist world? What part is Ireland to play? and India? Is there going to be a great awakening of village life? Are the men at the front—with the energy and faith of youth and the experience of old men—going to make a new thing of civic, industrial and political life? Will war have so brutalized them that we shall have a bloody revolution? or will it have taught them discipline and a horror of violence? What of all this new world of women—women police, women porters, women engineers, women signallers, women drivers, and above all women voters? Where are we all going? It is like being hurried along in a fog—and the pace quickens. Every nation grows increasingly impatient of war. I sometimes wonder if the best hope for a lasting peace does not lie in finding with modern warfare victory is impossible and the whole thing is bound to be a nightmare of suffering which achieves nothing—nothing which can go into history books as a gain.'

In October 1918 work in London was interrupted by a journey to America for which Grace was 'lent' (for two months) by the Ministry to the Y.W.C.A. as one of a party of women sent to address meetings and to serve as a mission to exchange ideas on welfare; for the American Y.M. and Y.W.C.A. had been made responsible for all welfare work at home and abroad by the American Government. As far as Grace was concerned this expedition was marked throughout by the queer sense of unreality that we associate with nightmare or a dream that runs along the lines of ordinary life but never quite fits into them. Much of this was due to the shadow of war which tinged familiar circumstances with strangeness; much came from the fact that nothing turned out as it was planned. There was a rather grim crossing in the *Olympic*, camouflaged as the *Sheldrake*; her animated account of it describes now groups of subdued people compelled to be passive since they could do nothing to meet danger except obey orders, now these same people as tweedledums and tweedledees in life-belts, and now again it is lit up by glimpses of beauty of sky or sea, or a distant iceberg, or stately grey transports silently passing.

The Ambassador, Mr. Page, was on board, crossing to his own country mortally ill; a U-boat lay waiting in search for them; there was a great storm, but the momentous news reached them in mid-ocean by wireless that Germany had asked for an armistice.

News of the actual armistice (signed at the 11th hour, on the 11th day of the 11th month (1918)) came to Grace in Oklahoma City, where she was awakened at 2.30 in the morning by noise, pistol shots, and voice after voice shouting 'Victory'. Motors tore round hooting as they went, huge flags streamed in the wind, and a tumult of shouting, singing, and shooting went on all day and into the following night. A procession formed itself carrying the flags of the Allies; a big drum beat incessantly. At 3.30 p.m. the tumult was still going on; motors still hooted, dragging tin pans behind them; people beat tin lids and shovels, blew whistles and screamed, waved flags, wore paper caps: 'joining in I've just met a staid elderly woman walking round the hotel ringing a dinner bell—and one thinks of Europe', she writes. At 11 p.m. they were still at it. Meanwhile in London Lloyd George adjourned Parliament with the suggestion that all members should go to St. Margaret's, Westminster; there was 'some processing all the week and pandemonium Saturday night'. The tour projected for the party of Englishwomen could not be carried out, partly because a virulent type of Spanish influenza was raging and in most States public meetings were prohibited, partly because the American Government decided to start a big drive for gaining the support and interest of the public in the war effort of America and the Allies, and to concentrate upon this for the time being. For this Grace was offered the opportunity to go as speaker to the West, and she took it as too exceptional a chance to be missed.

She was accompanied by an American chaperone who had lived for eighteen years in the South, and she and Madame Bernard travelled to Texas and Oklahoma to represent England and France. One may infer that Grace Hadow's wit and power of description and of telling stories made themselves felt on this strange journey as well as her liking for people and things indigenous and with a flavour. She met with response in her attempts to establish contacts and felt and noted these impersonally as instances of the growing understanding between England and America. She was claimed to describe air raids and tell war stories, and when Grace said anything that her official chaperone approved she would look at the rest of the company and exclaim 'I tell you our Englishwoman is not slow'. There were continuous meetings and speeches; sometimes Grace and Madame Bernard between them were speaking six times a day and travelling all night; another time they counted twenty-one speeches in two days. The audiences were very varied: 'Victory boys and girls', also half-Spanish and Mexican audiences, coloured people, audiences of mixed European origin. In the remoter parts of Oklahoma State she found 'cheery, kindly folk': Indians 'in queer long rickety carts, sometimes piled high with snow-white cotton, and real Buffalo Bill cow-boys, loose limbed, hard-faced young fellows in open shirts and broad-brimmed hats, riding with absolutely straight legs and perched up on high Spanish saddles'. And she was told there would be a procession to her meeting with a band 'that had not practised much together, though some of the ladies were acquainted with their instruments'. Farmers, cowboys, Indians, more or less the entire populace, 'swarmed into a rough barn proudly labelled "Empress Theatre" which was packed chiefly with men. When the meeting was over person after person came up and said, "The biggest thing coming out of this war is the friendship between America and England".' In a drug store soon afterwards she was bombarded with questions, and some eager arguers stayed till a farmer pushed in—'now give me a chance, you've had her for half an hour'—and proceeded to discuss with considerable intelligence the relative powers of President Wilson and the King and finally parted from her the best of friends, urging her to read the *Stockbreeders' Gazette*.

In Oklahoma City Grace took the opportunity of attending service in a negro church. 'A very interesting experience this morning (November 10th). I wanted to the blank amazement of all my kind hostesses here to go to a coloured church and—rather to my embarrassment—some kind white folk (entirely unknown to me) volunteered to take me. We drove down to a very poor quarter of the town and after some difficulty (no white had any idea where a coloured church might be) found a little red-brick church at the corner of a street. Here we were met by "John", my host's coloured man (and a direct descendant of President Polk of the U.S.) who led us up to a seat of honour in front. For four weeks no churches have been allowed to hold services and to-day, the first day the ban was lifted, the little place was packed. For music there was a piano, violin and flute and, as they played a voluntary, there entered the strangest procession I ever saw; from both sides of the raised platform where the pulpit stood, came a stream of Negresses wearing short white surplices and college caps. They did not march, they danced a solemn ritual dance, crossing over in the middle and then climbing up the platform and sitting on a raised dais at each side. The Minister, an extraordinarily handsome and powerful Negro (one of the finest and tallest men I ever saw) in a long, black gown, sat in the centre with two Elders—one coal black; the other almost white— beside him. Behind us sat a row of amazing old women in white caps, who were referred to as the Board of Stewardesses. The service was extraordinarily moving. There was a great deal of singing—bad, emotional hymns, but sung with a passion of fervour. Two of the Negresses had quite lovely voices—one a very pure soprano, and one a contralto—and the Minister himself had a wonderful bass, very sweet and flexible, and of great depth and strength. He spoke a good deal of the losses during the epidemic, but chiefly of the passionate joy of being together again to worship God. Every now and then he would cry, "Do you remember, Christian, how it says . . ." and then his great voice would break into some hymn and the choir and the congregation would take it up. The sincerity was beyond question. His eyes filled with tears as he spoke, and the Congregation would sway and sob and ejaculate emphatic "Yes, Sirs" at frequent intervals. Now and then would come a hysterical scream and I saw one girl frantically waving a pair of hands clad in immaculate black kid above her head. You couldn't laugh, you couldn't feel it ridiculous. Those people were in the presence of God. At the end of the sermon—it ended with a fervent appeal to sinners to come forward and join the Church—the Minister came down and shook hands with the new Church members and told them what Sunday school to join, and then asked me to give them a "message across the sea" (what he actually said was, "We have here among us a splendid woman from across the seas who will now deliver a message", and I had to get up). I had heard that, among other things, the Germans had tried to make the negroes feel that this was a white man's war and that it was not fair that their sons should be taken, so I just said a few simple words as to what war meant and how proud we and they should be that our men were fighting side by side to do away with such horrors and to uphold righteousness and ended with the words of the old coloured woman whose only boy was sent to France the other day and who said to him as she bade him goodbye: "Remember, my son, Heaven is as near the battlefield as it is near to us right here".'

During a time in New York, when first she reached U.S.A., Grace had the opportunity of real exchange of ideas with thoughtful individuals and of getting information too on American welfare. Here it seemed that Americans were going through the same experiences that we had gone through in the earlier years of the war and were feeling their way to solutions in which our experience might be useful; however, as yet they were not profiting by our mistakes. The tour proved worth while in ways that had not been thought of in the first place. Grace herself acquired much greater insight into America and its problems than when she stayed at Bryn Mawr as a young teacher. The warm-heartedness of Americans again appealed to her, as did their enthusiasm and response to ideals as well as their generosity and quickness of mind.

She travelled home in a 'funny little boat', the *Grampian*, which was slow and steady. Two days of heavy storm took the ship far out of its course, but after eleven days' voyage she reached port.

She came home in December 1918 to the unsettlement that pervaded the period of demobilization, a difficult time when the tension of war was replaced by a baffling sense of instability. There was labour unrest which looked as if it might be serious, there were incessant deputations and processions in the provinces, there were 'peaceful mutinies' in England of soldiers refusing to work because they were not demobilized, there was the threat of a police strike, and a good many actual strikes took place. The big railway strike was delayed till the autumn, but the coming year was a restless time and, for her own part, Grace Hadow had to face holding on in the extra-mural Department while bit by bit it was unwound and its functions were transferred as far as they survived. There could be little satisfaction in the work under these circumstances, and it may well have seemed like having built on shifting sand. Instinctively her mind was sent back to dwell on where true values lay. 'It is always sad to close any chapter', she writes to one of the extra-mural officers[1] who was leaving because the Department was being disbanded, 'but I think that I can feel that all the very difficult and strenuous work of welfare was fully justified and that our works will live after us though they will probably never be associated with our names. There is no doubt of the tremendous impetus given to the improvement of working and living conditions during the war and I think we can feel proud to have carried our stone and have laid a foundation on which other people will build. Personally I have very happy recollections with the welfare section and not least of the extra-mural officers who in many ways had the hardest task of all and whose unfailing pluck and energy accomplished so much in the way of stirring up civic consciences.'

Meeting the returned prisoners of war, with whom she had kept in touch, was a refreshment in spirit: one in particular from

[1] Mrs. Knight-Coutts.

Cirencester had worked her three little mats in 1916 and carried them about him from camp to camp and found it a 'bit of a job to keep them clean', as well he might when one recalls those camps or realizes what it meant. Then, there was special joy in the return of the most faithful of all her soldier correspondents, Captain Hughes, whom she induced to write down an account of his experiences during his four years' imprisonment in Germany.

Meanwhile her brother had been invited in July 1918 by H. A. L. Fisher, then President of the Board of Education, to organize a scheme for army education which took him to France behind the lines for some months as Director of Education to the Y.M.C.A. and then home for further development and organization of this work with Lord Gorell, for the Army Education Corps at the War Office. His scheme was worked out with an idea of bridging over the return to civilian life for those serving in the army, and of attempting to organize a sort of army university. Young officers out in France could attend courses in their spare time and come back to the University to finish in a shorter time than three or four years. The scheme provided courses also for non-officers and non-university men. It was described from the first as 'training in citizenship rather than vocational', and was expanded to suit different sorts of men covering a regular general education throughout service and a final year in England with very little military duty and a real grounding in the work a man meant to go on with. By May 1919 the Trade Unions had accepted it, and there was high promise in it, though like other educational reforms it was not fully carried through in the end. However, Grace and her brother could at this time discuss their common interest in adult education and in citizenship taken in the fullest and widest sense. While he was working at the War Office and she was at the Ministry, they set up house together in London for some months and once more had the joy and advantage of one another's companionship.

In spite of her awareness of distressing unsettlement at home and of 'sceptre and crown' 'tumbling down' in Europe, Grace set her mind on seeing hopeful signs for the future. Girls who had learned skilled jobs had now realized that there was satisfaction in such work. Writing of a conference in March 1919 she says: 'It came out that many women who either had never worked before or had been in the lower grades of domestic service have learned a certain pride since they entered munitions. One girl said, "You see, four of us were the only girls allowed to set our own tools in the shop. We're used to swank a bit. I don't mind cooking, but if I cook I want to train and be a first-rate one, not just an ordinary general." That spirit is worth encouraging.'

And she set great store by the enfranchisement of women as a positive achievement hastened on by the war and by the new opportunities for the work of women which full citizenship brought with it. She followed the steps of this and was present at the ovation to Mrs. Fawcett in music and speeches at Queen's Hall on 18 March 1918 and again on December 9 when Lloyd George spoke: 'the first time in history that a Prime Minister has addressed a mass meeting of women on the eve of an election.' It was disappointing that in this first election only Countess Markievicz was elected and, as a Sinn Feiner, did not take her seat.

Grace had a great belief in the future of women's work in public service and her close touch with Women's Institutes was even then showing her a new opening for this and a sphere for its development; her own experience among munition workers and in the Ministry and her brother's experience in the Army and the War Office had strengthened her belief in adult education and had given her an insight into its organization and administration. Her faith in human nature was unshaken in spite of all the war had shown her of its weakness and folly and of the damage it can do by its delusions, and she believed in the people who were to have more responsibility in shaping society than they had hitherto had. The key to building up a better future seemed to be found in adult education and in the work of women.

Before Peace Day her brother had left the War Office and was back at Newcastle and she herself had returned to 51 Harley House, where Edgie's children were invited to see the Peace celebrations: 'The children came up', she writes, speaking of 19 July 1919, 'and we all went to see the Procession. London is beautiful in flags and there was something extraordinarily moving in that great procession and still more in the monument erected at Whitehall, very simple and plain, with a scarlet wreath each side, a few standards and the inscription: "To the Glorious Dead." Fireworks in Hyde Park in the evening, great jewelled serpents and wonderful chrysanthemums of fire lit up the sky for miles round. It rained a little and the bursting rockets behind the clouds were incredibly beautiful. Then at eleven came the signal which was to light up bonfires throughout England. It was all the strangest mixture of rejoicing and tears—that sky of rain and glory was oddly apt.'

Looking back on the five years of 1914–19 in the attempt to see what they meant to Grace Hadow it is noticeable that she rose to the greatness of the time and shared it. She faced fully what the war meant, and faced it in its implications for individuals and for the daily life of many sorts of people; she became aware of how deeply it cut into the social traditions of England and put an end to a phase of society. She sought out men and women in various conditions of life who were uprooted or directly affected by the war: Belgian refugees, country people of all kinds, munition workers, employers, individuals, the many people in the Ministry itself. Her experience of men was widened. It was also deepened since she saw many in circumstances when traditional reserve gave way. With the impulse towards unity that galvanized English people when war came, her instincts for team-work, always strong, were strengthened and became more comprehensive. Without any sacrifice of her own strong convictions she cultivated a trained power of working happily with people whose ideas and tastes were unlike her own. There was much to do in shaping life after the war and no doubt her way would become clear. Inwardly her heart was fixed on impersonal issues. Her home ties were not weakened, and she retained the strength of feeling that was always hers, but she now felt it a hindrance to the deepest purposes of life to cling too much to external things, even to persons; personal ambition, deliberately set aside in former years, had no longer to be reckoned with as a motive.

CHAPTER VIII

BARNETT HOUSE, OXFORD

1920–1929

GRACE HADOW had enlarged her life during the war. Henceforth she must, if she would express herself, take full and conscious part in some form of social service. What opening for this would there be when the war was over? She had enjoyed administration and felt that she was built for it. Would there be further opportunity for a responsible share in such work? It was never her way to indulge in plans or in speculation about her own future, but she had the building of a better England very much at heart and it is clear in retrospect that her instinct must have prompted her to such questions. Her experience in the Welfare Section of the Ministry of Munitions had proved to her the value of social services and the need for them; there could be no doubt that the immense gain they brought, since the war, to less privileged sections of society must be maintained, yet if the reconstructed England was to be worthy of England's tradition there must develop side by side with these services responsible citizenship. Such thoughts had been borne in upon her while at the Ministry, and she felt it in her to make a contribution to such an end. Nevertheless, work in a Government department in the ordinary peace-time course of things had little attraction for her.

Overtures were made to her with regard to the secretaryship of Barnett House, Oxford, an institution which had not yet found itself but was possessed of a latent principle of growth. The House had been founded in June 1914 as a memorial to Canon Barnett[1] and was conceived as a centre of information on social and economic questions, its functions being to collect a library for these studies, to provide lectures on special aspects of social and economic matters, and to furnish a training course for social service. Further development was envisaged without being specified. The war had checked it, and one of the prime movers in the foundation of the House, Sidney Ball,[2] Fellow of St. John's

---

[1] Founder of Toynbee Hall Settlement, London.

[2] The idea for a room in Oxford which was to house books on social studies as a memorial to Canon Barnett originated with the Rev. G. K. A. Bell. Professor Adams

College, had died meanwhile. With his experience in adult education and his knowledge of the working classes, he had been expected to take a leading part in the development of the House, sponsoring its studies in Oxford and urging their importance, for Oxford in 1914 was still pre-eminently a university town and not an industrial city; economic questions had not acquired the prominence which has been theirs since, and the University did not as yet provide for their study through the Honour School of Philosophy, Politics, and Economics.

However, interest in these matters was spreading, and the House promised to supply a lack in Oxford. As to how far Barnett House within this perspective alone would have appealed to Grace Hadow may be open to question. Had the secretaryship been a strictly defined post with a good salary in a settled and prosperous institution she would probably not have been tempted by it. But the House was not endowed, its development was problematical and would have to be shaped according to circumstances; it offered neither a position nor a safe berth but a most interesting opportunity for a person of enterprise and vision. Further, one prime mover in its foundation had a clear idea of a particular direction in which the House might be developed: Dr. W. G. S. Adams (later Warden of All Souls), then Gladstone Professor of Political Theory and Institutions in Oxford, who had worked in Ireland with the great Irish leader of the rural life movement, Sir Horace Plunkett, and was fired with the ideal of 'better farming, better business, better living'. Before the war his mind had been engaged with the thought of adapting it to England, and to this end and to the ideal of social co-operation he was to give for many successive years the best part of his time and energy that could be spared from the University. In

took it up enthusiastically and built upon it, approaching Mr. Cartwright (secretary of the W.E.A.) and Mr. Sidney Ball. The decision to start Barnett House was taken in 1913 in Sidney Ball's room at St. John's College, Oxford, the same room in which years before Canon Barnett had first propounded his plan for settlements, and there had taken part—to name the chief—Professor W. G. S. Adams (afterwards Warden of All Souls), Mr. Sidney Ball, the Master of Balliol (A. L. Smith), the Rev. G. K. A. Bell (now Bishop), Dr. A. J. Carlyle (later Canon), Mr. (now Sir David) Ross, and Mr. E. Whitley (of Trinity College). Mr. Whitley generously provided a loan which enabled the founders to buy the gabled, red-brick house at the corner of Broad Street and the Turl (now Parker's bookshop) where Barnett House started. A list of subscribers was issued and the Council formed; Mrs. Barnett became a Council member and a subscriber.

January 1919 Professor Adams had decided to return from
10 Downing Street in favour of academic work, but he had retained an enthusiasm for voluntary social service that was com-
mensurate with Grace Hadow's own. In the event there was to be
the closest co-operation between them. There was a preliminary
discussion with regard to the secretaryship of Barnett House in
which he put it to her that 'a soul was needed' there, that 'windows
could be opened there', and that the right person was to have
a free hand; and he recalls how rapidly she caught on to a suggestion of rural work that would fit in with the purpose of the House
and 'ran away with it', building it up in her mind, seeing a way
at once by which Women's Institutes could take a share with
other voluntary organizations. He then felt 'the plan had clicked'.

Such a vista for the future might well attract Grace Hadow.
Almost everything had to be constructed, and she herself was
invited to do it; the fact that the development of the House
was speculative as yet must have been an additional inducement;
a contributory motive for acceptance no doubt lay in the fact that
this secretaryship would naturally settle her in Oxford in the
home of her friends to whom her presence meant much. During
recent months she had been chafing with inward exasperation, and
her work had come to an end just at the moment when there was
everything to do; after a strenuous journey in pursuit of it she
had reached an impassable barrier beyond which lay the Promised
Land in sight. The way to a sound future pointed—she was sure
—to adult education as a means of developing responsible citizens;
here was an opportunity at hand of directing it into new channels
—channels whose waters she knew very well indeed. The Council of Barnett House were looking for a secretary 'who could
shoulder the development of the House and conduct all business
connected with the work and studies of the House'. They were
ready to accept a lead.

On 31 October 1919 the Council appointed Grace Hadow
their secretary as from January 1920, on a half-time basis, leaving
her time to write if she so desired, and in March 1920 they
accepted 'Professor Adams's scheme' which was 'to place the
facilities of the House at the disposal of villages within 30 miles
of Oxford and this by establishing in Barnett House an advisory
body to assist Librarians in villages with information on social
and economic questions and further by an experiment in close

co-operation with certain voluntary organizations[1] to assist in meeting the growing demand in villages for lectures'. The Council accepted the scheme; two years later, when it had been tried as an experiment, 'rural development' was made part of the regular policy of the House.

The main distinction of Grace Hadow's secretaryship lay here; the rural development undertaken was creative; it was pioneer work and contributed greatly to making the reputation of Barnett House as an institution which fosters experiments and co-operation in social service.

Prospects for adult education in Oxfordshire were none too favourable in 1920. In the present state of consent it is not altogether easy to re-create the mental atmosphere of those days. Signs of encouragement were few for a plan that built upon the interest taken by villagers in good books or in thinking about philosophical, economic, or humane subjects. Village libraries were moribund—at the best it was possible to play a game of billiards there; mostly reading-rooms were rich in dust and dank in smell, the furniture scant and angular; for reading matter perhaps a shelf of discarded books, a few old magazines, or nothing whatever. Women were not supposed to need such a place. Incredible as it may now seem, the Oxfordshire County Council had refused the offer of a Carnegie grant for starting a County Library that would ultimately be paid for from the rates, and the refusal was based on the sincere and straightforward conviction that 'Oxfordshire people don't want to read'. Grace Hadow, however, had not spent her young days in the heart of the country in vain; she had a humorous understanding for that point of view and also had an intimate knowledge of what it feels like to want opportunities and be debarred. She resolved that the inarticulate wish of those villagers who wanted an easy access to books should be helped to become an articulate body of opinion : 'We must prove that Oxfordshire people do want to read.'

The first step was to get in touch with individuals and organizations who were interested in adult education and themselves already taking part in it, and to enlist their help and sympathy for the Barnett House scheme.[2] Further, in some villages there

---

[1] The Workers' Educational Association, The Red Triangle Federation (Y.M.C.A.), and the Women's Institutes.

[2] There was a small travelling library of a dozen boxes of about 100 books each, which Mr. Griffiths and Mr. Warrilow, then working for the Red Triangle Federa-

were local lending libraries with books that were never changed and rarely added to, and among the librarians of these were the few who believed in reading and who knew the country people who desired to read. The Barnett House facilities were offered to these, and they welcomed help. By gifts and purchase a separate lending library for villagers was collected at Barnett House and in default of any other place it was lodged in the secretary's room. Country readers found their way in, the Barnett House Librarian was as ready to recommend biography and travel as remoter subjects; she won their confidence and understood their needs and the lecture scheme furthered the Library. A dilapidated black Ford van (a war veteran) belonging to the Y.M.C.A. and driven by Mr. A. H. Griffiths (himself a pioneer in rural adult education) took books and lecturers to groups of villages, till supplemented by a snubnosed Morris car (named 'Andrew' after Carnegie) driven mainly by Grace Hadow herself and finally replaced by a grey van especially constructed for the purpose and bearing the letters O.R.C.C.[1] in a monogram inset in a circle.

Where lectures were held all those attended on whose support any communal effort in a village relied, and audiences covered a wide range of talents and interests and might include a distinguished Indian civil servant or the Director of Education himself, or other well-read people, usually the vicar, the schoolmaster, perhaps the manager of a co-operative store, perhaps a station master with advanced views, an enlightened farmer, as well as staunch supporters of the Women's Institute or tradespeople or farm-hands and perhaps the older schoolchildren. Grace Hadow herself was in her element as one of the lecturers, and the courses led to personal relations with many sorts of people. The lecturers gave their services voluntarily on subjects ranging from County History to Local Government, or Ideals of Living to Shakespeare, and extending to European and Colonial History and scientific matter.

From among the lecturers and others promoting the Barnett House scheme there grew a team eager to see it succeed. On 8 October 1920 Grace Hadow called together representatives

tion, had collected from the Y.M.C.A. War Libraries, and these were passed round among the ten or twelve villages where live clubs had been formed. The Y.M.C.A. made a gift of all their stock, and selections from those books formed the nucleus for the County Scheme.

[1] Oxfordshire Rural Community Council.

of the Y.M.C.A.,[1] the Village Clubs Association,[2] the Workers' Educational Association,[3] and the Women's Institutes[4] 'to consider co-operation in social and educational matters and to prevent reduplicating or checkmating one another's efforts'. The simple idea commended itself to those who met, and soon the committee expanded its membership and changed its name to Council, becoming a consultative body of voluntary societies which was attended also by officials of the statutory authorities. Applications for grants from the Local Authority to pay for classes passed through it and were made simultaneously by each voluntary society co-operating. In such co-operation the Community Council followed the pattern of the National Council of Social Service to which it became affiliated; it was, however, the first rural council of its kind, and therefore of rural community councils Dr. W. G. S. Adams[5] claims Grace Hadow as 'pious founder'.

The Council could also offer practical advantages, since together with Barnett House it became the recognized channel by which grants of money were applied for and obtained from the Plunkett Trust and later from the Carnegie Trustees for work in rural adult education. Grants from public funds are neither lightly given nor lightly got, and if Sir Horace Plunkett and Professor Adams were able to provide the key to some public chests it fell to Grace Hadow to provide evidence for the trustees of work done and to urge on and inspire workers. Part of the Community Council's early task was to educate its own members and the general rural public in the working of the machinery by which public grants for social services were administered and obtained and to make known what services were available. The Health Report of the O.R.C.C.[6] proved a very effective piece of educational propaganda in this way, giving practical information on health services. Another task was to encourage and preserve

[1] Mr. A. H. Griffiths, Mr. H. Warrilow, Mr. A. Lett, and Mr. W. (later Alderman) Hyde for the Y.M.C.A.

[2] Mr. J. Nugent Harris, Mr. H. Lacey, Commander Kettlewell for the Village Clubs Association.

[3] Mr. (now Professor) N. F. Ashby (South Eastern Branch), Mr. E. S. Cartwright (Tutorial classes), Miss H. C. Deneke (University Branch) for the Workers' Educational Association.

[4] Mrs. Hobbs (President), Mrs. Burge (Committee member) for the Oxfordshire Federation of Women's Institutes.

[5] Warden of All Souls till 1945; Chairman of the N.C.C.S. since 1919.

[6] Compiled largely under the direction of Councillor W. (later Alderman) Hyde.

inherited skill. Rural industries[1] were encouraged and developed, especially among blacksmiths whose trade was disappearing with the horses, and here results remained striking and tangible: in recent days Oxfordshire blacksmiths have been able to point to fine pieces of workmanship in wrought-iron gates, or fire-irons, or other objects made from artistic designs.[2] A pioneer wireless set, given by Sir Horace Plunkett, would travel round on the top of the van, and Mr. Griffiths demonstrated the marvels of this new discovery to villagers in days before there were wireless programmes.

Music and drama were helped with Carnegie grants, and through schools and festivals a standard was set; good music was brought also into the villages themselves and talent in acting was fostered and good plays were provided. In initiating all this development Grace Hadow played a notable part and everyone felt it.

It would be going too far to record in detail all that was done and the names of all who made a real contribution to the development of adult education and of social services in Oxfordshire. In a multitude of people who played a part Grace Hadow remained a central figure, and it was through her enthusiasm and quick resourcefulness that the scheme itself took shape, while her power to inspire others helped to make it effective. 'We are trying to build up a finer and better England and to do so on a sure foundation of mutual helpfulness, self-respect and extension of knowledge. Isn't that worth working for?' So she wrote at the time.

There were set-backs, however; and not everything on which Grace Hadow spent much thought and trouble and time was crowned with success.

Plans for educational work among men and boys in the county went awry, and just when both seemed within reach, funds and the right person to do the work failed. There was great encouragement, however, at difficult moments in the personal interest which Sir Horace Plunkett took in rural development. He had been invited by the Council of Barnett House to give the first Sidney Ball Memorial Lecture, which was delivered on 1 Decem-

---

[1] Under the direction of the Rural Industries Bureau and organized by Mr. A. H. Griffiths as chief officer.

[2] Since 1939 more especially they have done impressive work in repairs and renewals of agricultural machinery urgently needed during the war.

ber 1920, and he chose for his subject 'Oxford and the Rural Problem', making an appeal to Oxford for 'leadership in thought on the threefold problem in its entirety', i.e. the problem of better farming, better business, and better living. Some time before, to ensure the continuation of his life's work, he had founded and endowed the Plunkett Trust for Rural Development and had consulted Professor Adams; in the Trust Deed which gave the trustees power to co-operate with any institutions within the British Empire or the U.S.A. there were especially mentioned for Oxford the School of Rural Economy, the Institute of Agricultural Economics, and Barnett House.[1] For this last Sir Horace Plunkett accepted 'the Barnett House scheme and saw in it a means of bringing home to country people the ideal of better living by educating the villagers themselves in the broad principle of co-operation' so that they themselves 'no longer dependent on the initiative and enthusiasm of one or two people could attain to making rural life as full of stimulus and as attractive as it might be'.[2]

Sir Horace had been fired with the idea of education in the broad principle of co-operation which inspired Grace Hadow, and he came to recognize in her a kindred spirit. His thought had been in advance of his time and of the co-operators in Ireland, where schemes of his own had suffered because the idea of co-operation was not understood. His ideal of 'better farming, better business, and better living', however, stood firm, and it was analogous to the ideal of betterment of rural life which Grace Hadow was helping to work out in the more restricted world of Women's Institutes. Even then she was taking her share in interpreting this ideal to mean disinterested co-operation for the benefit of the community, improvement in the standard of living, and a more liberal education. She had seen how simple meetings of country-women to pursue their common interests were focusing the needs of the moment and in so doing were affording an opportunity both for encouraging individual talent—be it for housecrafts or the arts—and also for training in citizenship. Sir Horace Plunkett, 'old and weary and yet with the flame of service still bright', saw embodied in Grace Hadow qualities of mind and spirit for which he had lived, and their association in a common

[1] Founded in 1913, 1909, and 1914 respectively.
[2] Quoted from the Sidney Ball Memorial Lecture (Oxford University Press).

ideal of living developed into a friendship by which his impersonal hopes and schemes became vivid and attainable once more.

In June 1921 Sir Horace speaks of her coming to Ireland: 'I should like you to know the Plunkett House people now you are going to make a success of the Foundation the end of which is there'; and at a time when carrying the rural work through was an uphill struggle he wrote: 'You are on the right road where I went wrong, it is only a question of pegging away. You and your team must win. Macte tua virtute puella.' Grace had the incidental but delightful satisfaction of bringing refreshment of spirit and a new hope of success, in his old age and after disappointment, to one of the finest leaders in social reform: 'It is silly egotism I suppose', he writes to her on 31 July 1924 in thanking her for her share in a conference, 'to talk of my own gratification at seeing my life's work which always relied on the efforts of my fellow workers, seeming to bear fruit. No one knows as well as you do how much the most difficult part of the rural problem is that for which you have made such sacrifices. Happily we shall have a verbatim report of your admirable speech to-day, so your weary watching through those eight sessions and your final summing up of the argument which correlates Better Living and Better Business will hearten many another worker for a new rural civilization.'

By then some results of the 'pegging away' which he recommended could be recorded. In 1923 the Oxfordshire County Council adopted the Public Libraries Act on the motion of Councillor (later Alderman) Hyde. This came as the climax of a campaign which had been arduous and not without dust and heat; however, the Barnett House scheme had proved that with the co-operation of voluntary societies the Library could be run cheaply and could be paid for with a farthing rate, and councillors as a body had become convinced of the demand for the Library. There were by then some fifty libraries in the county; village librarians, taught by conferences, had become a self-conscious and vocal body; conferences for rural teachers had helped in this and these had become part of the Director of Education's educational policy; the readers themselves knew their mind, and among the general Oxfordshire public a slightly hostile indifference had turned into friendliness. The Women's Institutes had thrown their weight into the campaign. Some had surprised their local councillor by questioning him on Library policy and roused him by the quite unexpected experience of finding voters interested in the Council's doings; as a body they had canvassed for the election of a woman candidate[1] to the County Council, who was pledged to the Library scheme and got in. A new spirit had arisen, and proof of the need for a County Library had been fully established. The Village Library collected at Barnett House was taken over by the County Council under the Carnegie scheme, and the Librarian, Miss Mackintosh, passed on to be employed by the County Council as their first County Librarian.

The courses of experimental lectures in Oxfordshire also had their bearing on future developments. They carried their sheaf towards proving the need for an established service and so towards founding the Committee in June 1925 of the Extra-Mural Delegacy for Oxford University which serves Oxon., Bucks., and Berks.[2] Here too a smooth transition was effected. Mr. Warrilow, who was inspired by Grace's work and as organizer of the lectures had done much to build up the 'rural university', became first organizer-tutor to the Delegacy.[3] The fixed idea that country people required no education outside purely practical things had been shaken. A new interest in rural education arose and gradually the subject became fashionable; for already the tide of national interest in rural matters was setting in.

In imponderable essentials there was also lasting gain from the Oxfordshire Rural Community Council. People engaged in similar work but for separate voluntary societies profited from meeting and exchanging ideas and found that they could help one another; in some instances it was noticeable how cordiality supervened as they came out from caves of mistrustful isolation and how fellowship developed where there had been armed neutrality. Certainly much prejudice was broken down.

Meanwhile Grace Hadow herself became more and more recognized as an authority on adult education. A resolution from the Executive Committee of the O.R.C.C. pointing out how unsuited the Board's regulations were to country circumstances resulted in the appointment of the Board of Education's Advisory

---

[1] Mrs. Kettlewell. [2] The University Extension Delegacy had existed since 1885.
[3] Mr. Warrilow had been appointed by the Y.M.C.A. Council and supported throughout as Educational Secretary to the Red Triangle Federation. Nevertheless, with rare generosity, the Y.M.C.A. allowed his services to be given to this community movement in a completely disinterested way.

Committee on Rural Adult Education of which she became a member; and she was meanwhile also urging rural adult education on various national bodies, the Oxfordshire experiment having broken new ground. Gradually the county acquired a status in the official world of rural adult education, and this fact reacted on public opinion in the county itself. Subscribers to the O.R.C.C. remained few. Nevertheless they formed a democratic council which elected its executive officers. And when Squire Ashhurst (then Chairman of the County Council) consented to stand as President of the O.R.C.C. a landmark was reached which may be taken to indicate the absorption of the O.R.C.C. into the tradition of voluntary public service. It was a sign of that amalgamation which was hoped for between what was best in the old order and what is best in the new. In the villages themselves the O.R.C.C. had its effect in giving an impetus to local co-operation, especially through the excellent constitution which the National Council of Social Service provided and provides for the management of a village hall. With changes of population and as villages grow in a changing society, it is possible that local social councils may gain a new importance. The living tradition of voluntary social services must not die, and it will be vital to make sure of this in shaping the future.

Grace Hadow had become a member of the Executive Committee of the National Council of Social Service, which was founded in 1919 to promote the idea of community service and of team-work between voluntary organizations and public authorities. 'Then as now', writes Major Lionel Ellis (first Secretary of the N.C.S.S.), 'many were hoping to build a better world in which co-operation rather than competition should be the governing principle. Grace Hadow was one of the first to see how this principle could be applied to the countryside'; and he tells how she was an original member of a committee appointed by the N.C.S.S. to deal with rural policy, which had 'many meetings and few good ideas until she gave them an account of an experiment in Oxfordshire which resulted in a conference called by the N.C.S.S. at St. John's College, Oxford. This became the starting-point for the National Movement to form Rural Community Councils in every County. It was a small but distinguished gathering,[1] for it included notably Sir Horace Plunkett, Sir Daniel

---

[1] Among others: Professor W. G. S. Adams (later Warden of All Souls), Mr.

Hall, national leaders of voluntary societies, representatives of the Ministry of Agriculture and of the Carnegie Trustees: but it was Grace Hadow with her deep understanding of village life and her clear vision of how that life could be made richer and fuller who led the conference from generalizations to practical proposals. She helped largely with the drafting of the conference's conclusions in a paper which secured not only the co-operation of the chief voluntary organizations concerned with village life but also led the Carnegie Trustees to give generous financial help which made possible all subsequent development of Rural Community Councils. Without the example of the original Oxfordshire experiment (which was Grace Hadow's creation) and without the subsequent leadership which she gave the R.C.C. movement through the N.C.S.S. I doubt whether that movement would ever have existed. From its inception till the time of her death she played a leading part in the National Council's work as a member of the Executive and of the Rural Committee, bringing to all discussions an unquenchable enthusiasm, a fine mind, and a sensitive appreciation of country life. She had in abundance the gifts of the true leader—conviction, energy, understanding. She was a beautiful speaker—easily the best woman speaker we had—and combined a moving seriousness with great wit. She held her head high as she walked and faced difficulties undismayed and with a saving sense of humour. I never knew her to be downcast or downhearted. English village life owes a greater debt than is realised to Grace Hadow and we who had the honour of working with her owe her far more than we can express in words.'

The Barnett House scheme in Oxfordshire meant doing in practice and in detail what could be reinforced by co-operation through the National Council of Social Service on a national scale. In 1923 Grace Hadow was appointed to serve on the Rural Industries Bureau, remaining a member till 1936, and her effective membership helped to promote in higher quarters the marked success of the development of rural industries under Mr. A. H. Griffiths's direction in Oxon., Bucks., and Berks. The N.C.S.S. had appointed her to start Community Councils in other parts of

(now Dr.) Charles Orwin, Lady Denman of the National Federation of Women's Institutes, Sir Henry Rew (Chairman of the Agricultural Wages Board), Mr. Vaughan Nash of the Development Commission, Mr. Alan Dobson of the Ministry of Agriculture (now Secretary to the Fisheries), Mr. George Dallas of the Agricultural Wages Union, Sir John Ross, and Lt.-Col. Mitchell of the Carnegie Trust.

the country: voluntary help replaced her in Barnett House at times when she was absent, and she could resign the portion of her salary equivalent to what she was paid by the N.C.S.S. This brought documentary proof that, since the rural work was financed through grants from public funds, Barnett House, by undertaking the scheme, was financially rather to the good. It was a fact which gave her great satisfaction, especially since Mrs. Barnett did not appreciate the pioneer work that was being done. Mrs. Barnett's own plans for the House were emphatically different. However, Grace Hadow's vision and personality carried the day and the rural work proceeded. Meanwhile Mrs. Barnett's schemes were given every reasonable chance and the Secretary did in fact take a good deal of trouble over them, but they proved unworkable.[1] Though their views were opposed, in their mutual relation over Barnett House Mrs. Barnett and Grace Hadow were able to derive amusement from one another.

While circumstances favoured rural educational development and offered the greatest opportunities through the Secretary's personal gifts, the other work of Barnett House was also developed and the House became well known as an institution which stands for the promotion of social studies and for the principle of co-operation in social service. Whoever wrote or called there for information was helped and answered—and the Secretary was often amused by the wide range of questions that came. The Library grew quickly and became notable especially as a students' library for its collection of blue books; investigations were carried through on subjects bearing on social development; the courses of lectures on special aspects of social and economic matters were of interest, and especially valuable also before the school of agricultural economics was consolidated and before the Honour School of Philosophy, Politics, and Economics became established. The University has recognized the Barnett House training course for social service, but for further integration with the University the road was not open. Much work was done to extend public interest and knowledge of local government; many conferences were arranged under the aegis of the House in social reconstruction of the hour. Co-operation between voluntary societies to promote services provided by statutory authorities remained the

---

[1] They involved a big appeal for money, which was separately organized but which failed.

keynote, and in this combination of forces Grace Hadow saw the modern equivalent of the fine tradition of voluntary public service which has marked our national life. Here she was up-held and further inspired by the broad-based historical insight and the large-hearted human and social sympathy of George Adams. In 1929 she resigned the Secretaryship of Barnett House on her appointment as Principal to the Society of Oxford Home Students. Dr. A. J. Carlyle, one of the founders of the House and a promi-nent member of the Council, then wrote to her in words that summed up the regard in which she was held and what she had done for the House. She remained a member of Barnett House Council till her death.

29 Holywell,
Nov. 20, 1928.

My dear Miss Hadow,

I do not know how to congratulate you on your being appointed as Principal to the Home Students without condoling with the Council of Barnett House in the prospect.

For I don't know what the House is to do without you—it is really you who have built it up—all the serious work which has been done—and have made it far more effective than we could ever have hoped. For, besides other things, your admirable work for the County Rural Organization has given it much greater significance than we expected. It is really impossible to measure what you have done for the House and the work.

I think the Home Students are singularly fortunate in having obtained your help and I have no doubt that you will find the work most interesting and that you will give it a great develop-ment, as great as you have done to Barnett House.

With the best wishes.
Yours sincerely,
A. J. Carlyle.

An article of hers on 'Rural Adult Education'[1] is subjoined as illustrating her approach to the subject and her way of ex-pressing herself.

[1] Reproduced from a typescript copy found among her papers. I have been unable to discover if it was ever published in a journal or elsewhere.

THE ADULT EDUCATION MOVEMENT AND RURAL LOCAL GOVERNMENT

(*or—an alternative title*—THE VILLAGE THINKS)

In the latest of Oxford novels, *Laurel and Straw*, Dawner, the more experienced Rhodes Scholar, gives to a new-comer, whose passionate desire to take a course in 'banking and business efficiency' seems likely to be thwarted, the advice: 'Don't let work worry you. We all came up here to work. We remain to be educated.' It is a platitude to say that what the average Oxford undergraduate needs is the education of life itself: that a large part of what the University can most usefully teach him is contained in no books and cannot be learned by the most diligent attendance at lectures: that intercourse with men and women of experience widely different from his own, and friendship with those whose shibboleths he has been taught to regard as anathema form at least as important a part of his education as an enquiry into the philosophy of M. Henri Bergson or a study of 'The Statistical Verification of Social and Economic Theory'. What is less often realized, or at all events less often stated, is that the boy or girl whose formal education ceased at fourteen, who has graduated, or is qualifying for a degree, at the university of life, is apt to be as lopsided as the boy whose whole experience has been a sheltered home and a first-rate public school. In either case an exceptional person will contrive to develop all round in spite of difficulties, but not many of us have the staying power and enthusiasm of Thomas Cooper, 'shoemaker, musician, journalist, and poet, who by incredible labour and at the cost of destroying his health taught himself the elements of Latin, Greek, French, Mathematics, and English Literature', or the dramatic sympathy which enables us to understand a point of view wholly different from our own. At the bottom of class warfare lies the frame of mind which says: 'Those people . . .' whether the phrase indicates a brutal and ignorant proletariat, bloated capitalists, or an effete aristocracy. So long as we regard any section of the community as something apart from ourselves we are certain to misunderstand and—intentionally or unintentionally—to misrepresent it. 'That's where old gentlemen comes down from Saturday to Monday', was an Oxford cabby's summary of the function of one of the most eminent of Oxford colleges. 'The village women would never care for poetry', says an equally ignorant lady of quality. There is no means of convincing either that they have not finally summed up the conclusion of the whole matter, except by bringing them into personal touch with those for whose activities and tastes they so lightly answer, bringing them together not to do each other good or consciously to educate each other, but through some common interest.

I well remember attending an early meeting of the W.E.A. in Oxford, so early a one that those mystic letters were unintelligible and I asked my neighbour for what purpose we were met. She looked at me coldly: 'It is to bring the workers into touch with the University', she said; and I was left wondering by what right a university don with eight hours work behind him and another two or three before bed-time, was deprived of the title 'worker'. 'I never knew before that ladies worked', was the comment of a parlourmaid newly come to the house of a woman whose wealth enabled her to give much public service. And besides such memories rise those of the old gentlemen who tell you that all that is needed to cure industrial unrest is 'eight hours a day with a plank and a wheelbarrow'.

It is the familiar story of Disraeli's two nations, and the difficulty that one nation has in understanding another, but at least in these nations within our own boundaries we have certain traditions and instincts in common, certain habits of mind which belong to us as Englishmen.

The movement for adult education in villages affords an opportunity for approach which is worth considering. In the words of the Final Report presented by the Adult Education Committee of the Ministry of Reconstruction in 1919, 'The main purpose of education is to fit a man for life, and therefore in a civilized community to fit him for his place as a member of that community.' And again, 'The whole process must be the development of the individual in his relation to the community.' Now in a very large number of cases while a man has some dim idea of his position nationally, while he realizes his rights as a voter in a parliamentary election, he thinks little if at all of his direct responsibility towards the locality in which he lives, unless this is presented to him as part of a duty to Conservative, Liberal or Labour. A local government election in a city is usually the occasion for an exhibition of party political feeling, but the election once over, how many of the electors know or care what action their representatives take, unless it is such as to involve a rise in the rates? In rural areas the interest taken is even less. District Councils are associated in our minds with roads and sometimes with a housing scheme; in their other capacity as Guardians of the poor they have for some of us a more tragic familiarity. The Parish Council and the County Council might almost as well be non-existent for all we know or care. Few of us could say what powers they have or why they were created. And yet in a village every detail of life is such common property, we are all so conscious of every local problem whether it be the nuisance of refuse dumped in the village ditch, or the distance Mrs. Jones's children have to walk to school, that local government in itself (though not in name, often not in formal application) is a very live thing.

An average village of some four hundred to a thousand inhabitants contains a considerable variety of interests. There are the squire and his family, who may be in residence for most of the year, or may only come for the hunting. There is a little group of farmers, the elder, as a rule, men of a certain shrewdness and narrowness, with little imagination, kind hearts, and an impatience of book-learning bred partly of well-meant endeavours on the part of theorists to find them short cuts to prosperity. There is possibly a hard-worked village doctor, the only man in the place with some knowledge of science. There is the schoolmaster, and in these days there are possibly one or two week-enders or artists, beings of another world who may or may not become part of the village life, and there are agricultural labourers and their families. The list is by no means exhaustive, but even so it indicates a very wide range of interests, education, and experience; while at the same time in no one group or class are there sufficient individuals to run any village activity alone. If there is a choral society, a cricket club, a Women's Institute, it will include representatives of several, if not all, classes, and whereas in a town the tendency is for people of the same social experience to gravitate towards each other, the actual size of the village population makes this in many cases impossible in the country, unless you propose to keep yourself to yourself to an extent which precludes you from all share in corporate action.

Adult education in rural areas is therefore fortunate in that it rests on a foundation in itself educational. It is an admirable and most useful thing to get a university graduate, trained in the subtleties of the latest economic theory, to discuss international finance with a group of wage-earners. It is valuable both for lecturer and class. But it is quite as valuable to get together, not of set purpose but in the natural course of events, a number of men and women of widely differing education and experience, who know each other, as we in villages do know one another, but who hitherto have never met to evolve and to compare ideas. As I write, there comes into my mind a village where for ten weeks last winter a class met to discuss such questions as 'The Rights and Responsibilities of Citizenship', 'The Individual and the Community', 'The Citizen in Business'. There were the vicar, the squire and his wife, the station-master, one or two small shop-keepers and their wives, and a number of young farm hands. The average attendance through those winter nights was twenty-six, and the discussion was most lively. I have no doubt that if the squire or the parson had asked one or two of the other men up for a smoke and a talk that they would have come—and probably would have felt extremely shy and tongue-tied: inevitably there would have been a sense of deliberate desire to bridge a gulf. But in the class there was none of that. No doubt a certain number of the members came, at all events in the first instance, less because they wanted to come than out of a public-spirited desire to help the thing along, but that might just as well be true of the elderly farm labourer turning out again after a hard day, as of the squire hurrying back from a meeting and putting off his dinner. Members were drawn together by a common interest in something outside themselves, the fact that one of them could speak from experience of service on the County Council, another from the religious point of view, a third from his personal knowledge of trade, and a fourth from his—or her— experience of the relation between wages and prices, made everyone realize that they had something of importance to contribute to the discussion, while the books brought out by the lecturer gave oppor- tunity for study and stimulated thought between the meetings. In such discussion, on neutral ground, of history, literature, economics, political science, and what you will, lies an opportunity for that civic education on which the Report of 1919 lays stress. It is difficult to go beyond the principles of F. D. Maurice: Adult Education is 'not merely to be a system of instruction, but a way of life shared by teachers and students . . . a bond of intercourse'. Maurice is speaking of such institutions as the People's College, but in village life the opportunity lies at our door without the artificiality inseparable from any institution. Colleges are excellent—for higher, in the sense of more scholarly, education—they are essential: but the mass of adults will never pass through any College, and even if they did, College can only provide one part of education. The Adult Education movement is concerned with all classes and all types. In the village it has scope for an experiment of peculiar interest and peculiar promise. We hear much of the limitations and restrictions of country life. Here is something in which it offers peculiar opportunities.

It may be said that the village I have referred to above must have unusual advantages, that such a class could not be formed elsewhere. Here are a few examples taken from the printed report of the Delegacy of Extra-Mural Studies of the University of Oxford for 1925–26:

Ascot-under-Wychwood (Oxon., pop. 365). A course of sixteen lectures on 'The History of Western Civilization'; average attendance 12; fifteenth year of lectures.

Carterton (Oxon., pop. approx. 500). Twelve lectures on 'The History of the Eighteenth and Nineteenth Centuries'; average attendance 32; second year of lectures.

Ellesborough (Bucks., pop. 500). Eight lectures on 'English Social and Economic History'; average attendance 18; fourth year of lectures.

Subjects on which other courses were given in other villages include: 'The History of Exploration', 'Mind and Conduct in Everyday Life', 'Shakespeare', 'The History of Democracy'.

Experience is the same in other counties, and especially in Nottinghamshire and Gloucestershire, where resident tutors for rural work have been appointed in connection with the local Rural Community Councils. The surprising thing is the extent of the demand. To those accustomed to city audiences at popular lectures the average attendances may sound small, but when you consider the distances that have to be walked through wet and muddy lanes after a day's work in the open air, and that in nine cases out of ten the class is held in a poorly lighted school-room where the members have to sit cramped in desks made for children, the fact that so large a number of people attend regularly and pay—out of their scanty wages—for the privilege of coming, speaks volumes for their interest and enthusiasm. A class which has been in existence for fifteen years stands for something in the life of the village. It matters nothing if the subjects they meet to discuss are Shakespeare and the musical glasses or economic theory: the main point is that they meet and in meeting almost insensibly acquire the habit of putting thought into words, the custom of speaking freely before each other, the ability to differ without undue heat, which are essential if democracy is to have any real meaning, or local government is to be more than the occasional election of a Parish Council which never meets, and if it did meet would be prevented by the electors from taking any action.

Villagers are human beings. It is advisable to state that emphatically in an age which threatens to regard us as a picturesque survival needing the protection of numerous beneficent associations to prevent it from becoming extinct. The sane method of dealing with any problem is surely to start with what is there and to see what seems the natural line of development. I welcome the advent of motor buses and even of motor cycles, I hope to see electric power in use in every village in England and Wales, but I do not believe that the contribution of rural England to our national life lies in any form of urbanization, but rather in developing on definitely rural lines, essentially rural qualities. The recent movement for adult education in rural areas has a special interest of its own, and seems likely to prove of permanent value in our national life, because it springs out of village conditions as they actually are. Under all diversity lies our common local patriotism, our common local needs, our intimate knowledge of each other. Insincerity is futile in a place where everyone knows all about you and your father and your grandfather, where even if, like the gentleman whose memorial tablet stands in Ely Cathedral, you live with 'inflexible constancy' for the better part of a century, you will never out-live your past. It has often been said that it is just these conditions which have led to narrowness of outlook, selfishness, a domestic tendency to gossip and ill-temper, but if there is any truth in this accusation, it is due to the accidental, not the fundamental conditions of country life. Education has been stunted, men and women have been cut off from the larger world. With improved means of communication, with the advent of motor transport, of rural libraries, or wireless, the old restrictions are disappearing, but the old traditions of village unity remain, and if the movement for Adult Education can follow the lines of this tradition, it may do much to make the English Village of today a vital factor in modern democracy.

Grace E. Hadow

Barnett House

Oxford.

CHAPTER IX

PRINCIPAL TO THE SOCIETY OF OXFORD HOME STUDENTS

1929–1940

'THE Society of Oxford Home Students may be said to be the origin of women members of the University. A little group of women, several of them themselves to become famous, desired to attend the lectures given by their husbands or their friends, and on a certain memorable day Mrs. Creighton and two or three brave friends boldly ventured into a lecture given by Mr. (afterwards Bishop) Creighton. From this small beginning arose a movement for the admission of women to the University, but the two first women's colleges, Lady Margaret Hall and Somerville, had too few students to make it possible for them to provide separately for their own educational needs. There therefore came into existence the Association for the Education of Women, which arranged lectures for the members of the two colleges and also for the larger body of other women living in Oxford for University education. Gradually the Colleges St. Hugh's and St. Hilda's were added, but the Home Students has remained the largest body, although in these days only a minority of its members are actually living in their own homes.' In these words Grace Hadow summarized the intricate story of the origin of the Society of Oxford Home Students for the purposes of an appeal for endowment which was issued in 1936.

The Society's name—now no longer appropriate and changed to St. Anne's—enshrined the distinguishing point in conditions of residence for these undergraduates as compared to those at the colleges. Originating in the obvious convenience for Oxford residents and some of their imported relatives to combine the advantages of attending lectures provided by the Association for the Education of Women with living at home, the special conditions of residence in private houses were also fostered by the first Principal as an ideal of living on its merits, and in subsequent years they stood the test of experience and proved their value in fact. When in 1910 the University appointed by statute a Delegacy for Women Students to make rules as to the recognition of

Women's Societies and their registration, the Society of Oxford Home Students, though not constituted by the University, was recognized equally with the women's colleges as already existing, and its governing body came under the control of the Delegacy. At that same date Mrs. Arthur Johnson, Principal since 1893, was reappointed Principal of the Society by decree of Convocation, the first appointment of a woman by the University.

By admission of women to the University in 1920, the Delegacy for Women Students became superfluous. The four women's colleges gradually established their own forms of government and sought Royal Charters, and in 1921 the Delegacy for Oxford Home Students was constituted, with the Vice-Chancellor as *ex-officio* Chairman, while the University Chest became responsible for holding what assets there were. In 1927 the Statute was further amended to provide for the election of representative tutors as Delegates. In this way the Society acquired a special standing as part of the University.

Meanwhile, in the years of its existence since 1879 the Society had evolved a character of its own and had become conscious of itself as a 'structure spiritual, social, and educational', consisting of a body of students past and present, in the making of whose corporate ideal plain living and high thinking played its part. The ideal characterized a great tradition in the Victorian upper middle classes and it had been continued as a rule of life in successive interpretations. Mrs. Arthur Johnson stood for it in terms of gracious family hospitality and of beauty in the home; herself a vivid figure, compact of instincts artistic, chivalrous, pertinacious, kindly, and individualistic, she stood out as one of the leaders in the early days of women's education in Oxford. The second Principal, Miss Burrows, who took office with the appointment of the Oxford Home Students' Delegacy in 1921, lived for the same ideal in her own selfless way, maintaining close touch with students and working for the appointment of a regular staff of tutors.

By now there had come into prominence in the affairs of the Society Annie Rogers, formerly Secretary to the Association for the Education of Women, in which capacity she had for many years watched Congregation with an eagle eye for the rights of women in Oxford. A classical scholar, and a woman of shrewd judgement, she was beloved by her pupils who knew her best, and by those friends who refused to be borne down by her forceful concentration on University politics. Her interest in the doings and habits of individual members of the University amounted to an intellectual passion. She knew exactly who served on which board or council, and it amused her to be able to calculate and note 'so and so will now be at such and such a meeting'; she would mark him down for his share in deliberations, and in this way she felt called upon to be a keeper of her fellows' conscience. The peace-loving might fear her zest and the discreet her relentless questions; and it is likely that her manipulations roused opposition as much as they gained support for her. However, she liked to have all the cards on the table in the game of University politics, and she was a person to reckon with. By 1929 she had long become a noted character in Oxford and was taken as part of the scheme of things. Remarkable in herself, individualistic to a high degree and mentally alive, she was arresting in her vitality and in her pronouncements, a person whose acquaintance one would regret to have missed.

With the passing of the Association for the Education of Women she had begun to turn her more especial attention to the evolution of the O.H.S. within the University, and the Society undoubtedly owed her gratitude for good work done on their behalf and especially perhaps in their finance. Numbers had grown rapidly to their present limit of 220 normal undergraduates, the administrative and tutorial system had been established, but accommodation was altogether inadequate and finance remained a difficult problem. In the Jubilee year of the Society, 1929, when a new Principal was to be appointed, the story of the O.H.S. had reached a critical point; numbers had outgrown the original conception, especially since the war of 1914–18, education in the country at large had undergone considerable changes, and within the Society itself important decisions were due with regard to future development. There was need for direction, policy, and leader-ship. Not unnaturally some anxiety prevailed about securing the right person and, in the usual Oxford fashion, the appointment had been surrounded by searching critical talk. Would this suggested Principal, Grace Hadow, who was known to have a decided personality and many outside interests, ride roughshod over the Society's cherished traditions? Could she be trusted to preserve its distinctive character? Would she wish to dominate? Would she want to undertake too many extraneous things? Would she be

Bassano

GRACE HADOW, 1938

Faire sans Dire

SOCIETAS MVLIERVM
OXONIAE ☙ PRIVATIM
STVDENTIVM

BOOK-PLATE

drawn by L. LESLIE BROOKE *and presented by*
GRACE HADOW

interested in young people? Her first address to the assembled J.C.R. dispelled all doubt; indeed she soon won the Society's confidence.

She seemed especially constituted for this, the most difficult of Oxford principalships. The head of a residential college has advantages at her disposal that do not accrue to this Principal. College buildings and college grounds may be encumbered with debt, nevertheless they are an outward and visible sign of corporate life and a substantial or potential asset. Further, the very fact of living together under one roof or within easy access sharing buildings, grounds, chapel, meals, and amenities makes it possible to collect members of the college at short notice for any purpose. Organization is in that way simplified, while individuals or groups of people find it easy to see as much or as little of one another as they please. The Principal of the O.H.S. (St. Anne's), on the other hand, is responsible for 220 undergraduates living in scattered households; in addition to getting to know them within the eight weeks of each academic term she must be in personal touch with the hostesses in whose households they live and who are responsible also for carrying out the University regulations about residence. The balance between cohesion and divergence in the different elements of such a society is not easy to strike and is hard to maintain.

Close touch between the Principal and her students and their hostesses was a living tradition in the O.H.S. in spite of the large increase in numbers. It fell to Grace Hadow to uphold this tradition and build upon it, then to guide the Society in further steps for developing community of life in ways best suited to its character, and, by her wisdom and personal effectiveness, and by the weight that she carried also on important bodies outside the Society, to contribute considerably towards raising its status.

Grace Hadow was a great Principal. She accepted and revered the living part of the traditions that she inherited, yet she interpreted them within the light of present circumstances and laid a foundation for development on firm, clear lines. Everyone who had worked with her had found that she could make them feel that what they were doing was the one worth-while thing in the world just then. And there was a radiance about her personality that was intensified by the wide range of her interests, and by the fact that she belonged also to a world outside. Her own spirit seemed to put dynamic energy into the work of the Society. In the ten years of her principalship she became recognized as an outstanding figure in the University. For the last few years she was a member of the Hebdomadal Council, while her work as Councillor of Barnett House and on the Extra-mural Delegacy continued. She also remained on the Advisory Council of the B.B.C., on the Adult Education Committee of the Board of Education, and on the Executives of the National Council of Social Service and of the National Federation of Women's Institutes. This list by no means exhausts the committees on which she was serving at the time of her death, and mostly she served on a committee as if it were her only one. In a headship, however, where her personality had free play, her gifts as administrator and educator could have fullest scope, and this came to her in the years when she reached her own highest maturity and when her varied interests and contacts seemed to converge.

If her work outside the Society made demands upon her time and energy she brought back with her a wealth of contacts and width of outlook which were of high value to her work as Principal, and this was soon felt by members of the O.H.S.: 'students, old students, Tutors, and staff, all rejoiced in and were proud of her'.[1] At the very first Gaudy which she attended her speech captured the whole Society. She soon won their affection, as she could hardly fail to do. Her work as Principal was to involve dealing with complex personal relations. In carrying out her object of leading the Society to a new stage of development and improving its standing in Oxford and outside, she took infinite trouble to give individuals their due and to take into fullest consideration the points of view of those who were indigenous to the O.H.S. or who had wholly identified themselves with the traditions of the Society. And perhaps this applies in a special sense to Annie Rogers, whose proverbial strong-mindedness could hardly be quelled but some of whose tactics called for reversal. In the past Grace had shared her brother's amused exasperation at numerous notes which she addressed upon occasion to members of the University to instruct them in their duty, and she would console herself at moments when she found Miss Rogers difficult by thinking of her as 'the Duchess in Alice' and would thus enjoy her. Meanwhile her approach, now humorous,

[1] R. F. Butler in *The Ship*.

now serious, but steadily generous and considerate, won its way at long last when this stern critic of hers became a friendly one. 'Grace Hadow was a woman of the world', said one who knew her as Principal, adding—after a moment's breath—'the world God so loved'. Her personality developed in greater freedom of expression and greater width of sympathy through exercising responsibility for many individuals, dealing with them, acting on their behalf, and yet steering the course of the Society as a community.

'Many and varied were the problems brought before the Principal to be solved with unhesitating judgement and individuality', writes R. F. Butler, then Vice-Principal of the O.H.S., in recording her impressions, and she speaks of the Principal's room as being 'like herself, sunny if austere, orderly, artistic, alive with flowers and with efficient activities. On its telephone were transacted affairs of County and National importance, to its door came streams of students, old students, hostesses, and seekers after knowledge of every kind. For each there was a welcome and individual kindness, an incredibly rapid solution of difficulties and always smiles and laughter. Her radiant personality pervaded all it touched.'

Perhaps the most spectacular development of the O.H.S. which happened during the principalship of Grace Hadow was the erection of the present Library Building (now known as Hartland House) and the provision of new offices and common rooms in Musgrave House.

The problem of finance weighed—and still weighs—heavily on the Society, for its very character puts a check upon the expansion of its financial reserves. Residential colleges can supplement their income by letting their buildings to conferences during vacation; what profit there is from boarding fees necessarily goes to individual hostels and hostesses among the O.H.S. Tutorial fees and the Common Room fees can do little more than cover cost; the only financial hope seems to rest in grants and in endowment, and to obtain grants means making persistent representations to authorities rarely eager to be convinced. The Delegacy of the O.H.S. being a University body, the Principal bore her share in representing that the University's non-collegiate daughters have as good a claim upon its generosity as the University's non-collegiate sons. Some measure of success was obtained.

Except for some small benefactions St. Anne's Society is unendowed. However, a generous donor, Mrs. Hartland, was prepared to pledge a magnificent gift of money for a building, the execution of which hung fire owing to difficulties in securing a site and in carrying through complex negotiations. Mrs. Hartland meanwhile was beginning to lose patience; her gift originated in the generous self-expression of one who wished to afford to others opportunities which she had been denied. Naturally she wanted to see work begun, and it fell to Grace Hadow to overcome obstacles and get this done. Imaginative understanding of the donor's interest and intentions, obligation towards the O.H.S. together roused her human and administrative powers. Negotiations called for realistic planning, judgement, and consummate tact. They were carried through successively.

It was late in the day for securing a site in Oxford. However, with the co-operation of all the interests concerned the present site between Woodstock and Banbury Roads was finally obtained. It included Springfield St. Mary and the house formerly Mrs. T. H. Green's. At the same time a legacy from Mrs. Musgrave of the lease of a private house in South Parks Road made available in the present 'Musgrave House' pleasant, sunny quarters for Common Rooms and offices, and also a good garden. These would serve till at some future date the new buildings could be completed. Sir Giles Scott provided the design in an impressive building comprising Tutors' and Principal's rooms, Common Rooms, Library, and Lecture Rooms. No more than a torso could be erected. The Library stands now as an earnest of future achievement, but stands on a freehold site in an excellent position and built not in brick but in grey stone as a contribution to Oxford architecture. It was a triumph of patient negotiation and persistent effort to secure the site and make sure of the first essential conditions for the magnificent buildings which it is hoped to erect when finances allow at some time in the future, and it was a great pleasure to the Principal to obtain the services of Sir Giles Scott, whose work in Liverpool and Oxford she much admired. At the evening party when Oxford came in large numbers to be introduced to the building, their frank surprise at the fact that the O.H.S. should possess a Library and Lecture Rooms as good as the colleges was expressed to her without reserve, much to her amusement and gratification. Looking festive and decorated with flowers arranged by the Principal herself, the building seemed to have stolen a march upon outsiders as if it had been erected overnight.

The opening of the Library on 16 July 1938 was a great day for her; she threw herself into the preparations for it with all the old ardour and was alive to the significance of the event as well as to amusing incidents. Underneath the quietness and dignity of the hostess, who could not let herself be absorbed in any one conversation, there were the old high spirits now attuned to the right word for each guest or the pointed remark of the moment as it flashed upon her. Standing in the new Lecture Hall, in pale grey silk, she looked distinguished that evening, as indeed she could when becomingly and carefully dressed. But undoubtedly the most striking impression that will be retained of her appearance is in academic dress which she wore at the inaugural ceremony in the afternoon. This set off her face to best advantage in its clear outline and in the radiance it often had when listening or alert. The photograph of her head and shoulders taken by Bassano shows this: her face lit up from within, taking in everything. It is an excellent picture and true to life. The inaugural ceremony was planned for members of the Society only. She then spoke little, but had reserved for herself the theme: 'This is a day of thanks and of thankfulness', which came from her heart and came in measured expression to each and all concerned in the building and its purpose.

The ceremony itself was to centre in Mrs. Hartland and was planned with expressive ritual, culminating in the formal presentation of a silver master key by the Vice-Chancellor to Mrs. Hartland: 'At any time of the day you may come into any room and we hope you will', he assured her, explaining that the key opened not merely the front but every other door as well. There were speeches by the Vice-Chancellor,[1] by Sir Giles Scott, by Mrs. Hartland herself and by the Chairman of the Delegacy,[2] who presided, and after thanking Sir Giles Scott for his work in a building that added to Oxford's fine architecture, spoke of the long journey on which the Principal was about to set forth. 'Indeed if she went to all the places to which she has been invited she would have to be numbered among those women whose faces launched a thousand ships; as it is she is merely looking in at Australia and New

---

[1] Dr. A. D. Lindsay, Master of Balliol.
[2] Dr. (now Sir) Cyril Norwood, President of St. John's.

Zealand and then undertaking a long lecture tour in the United States.'

This tour, it was hoped, would raise money for the endowment of the Library. The links of the O.H.S. with America were many, since the society numbered a good many Americans among their old members. Even at that very time the Principal was lecturing on features of English life and character at the American Summer School then in Oxford and she hoped, by her visit to the U.S.A. to strengthen not only the links which bound the O.H.S. to America but to start a workable arrangement for interchange of Oxford and American women students, perhaps on lines not dissimilar to the scheme for Rhodes Scholars, though on a very modest scale.

Between the inaugural ceremony and the evening party of 16 July there was a moment in which I could be taken aside and shown personally where especially good ideas about the building had succeeded; and in mounting the stone staircase Grace paused to speak quietly of how she felt satisfied that all had been done for 'after my time' when, with the freehold site and the buildings so far planned, her successor could go ahead with all essentials secured. Endowment for upkeep, however, remained a present anxiety; it had been possible to transfer money from the Annie Rogers bequest for immediate running expenses as long as no repairs need be undertaken, but there was nothing to fall back upon, and here there was something yet to do.

Asking for money was an art in which Grace Hadow was not gifted—she knew her nature would not bend to it—but a lecture tour for fees must bring in some money, since a generous American old student was paying her journey, and it might after all lead to some gift: so she hoped, though characteristically she had already coupled with it wider schemes and in the event was to find herself caught in others.

During the ten years of her principalship various circumstances contributed to make even more than the lion's share in dealings and transactions for the O.H.S. fall to Grace Hadow herself. It was a moment of transition when delegation was difficult and sometimes impossible. With members of the Senior Common Room her relations were of the happiest. The Society was developing in the direction of giving to Tutors a share in its government, and with such a movement the Principal was in full sympathy.

However, staff-meeting apart, there had been little occasion to draw the Tutors together; the Principal instituted weekly lunches in her house to which all Tutors had a standing invitation and could come and go as they pleased. In its hospitality and friendliness this invitation was much appreciated and it proved exceedingly fruitful in bringing members of the S.C.R. into close touch with one another and giving them a corporate sense which once realized has remained. The Principal herself worked towards improving Tutors' stipends, which dated from a time when voluntary service was hoped for and when it was not generally accepted that educated women earned their living. She believed in the tutorial system of Oxford, interpreting it in the sense of her own day as an opportunity for friendship between an older and a younger generation.

The residential system of the O.H.S., by which undergraduates lived in private families, had been modified by the provision of two hostels: St. Frideswide's, Cherwell Edge, for Roman Catholic students, and Springfield St. Mary, founded by the Anglican Wantage Sisterhood. Under Grace Hadow's principalship these hostels grew and were developed, and two more Roman Catholic hostels were established, one to allow the nuns of the enclosed order of the Sacred Heart to come to Oxford, the other to house nun students of all orders. In addition, there were eleven 'approved' houses taking four or more students and twelve 'authorized' houses taking three or less. Residence in the larger hostels she regarded as having the advantage of the small college which existed in the days of her own generation and which made a claim upon the public spirit of each member, this advantage being supplemented among the O.H.S. by membership of the much larger community in respect of Common Rooms, clubs, games, the Library, meetings, and the terminal service at the University Church of St. Mary's. This last the Principal valued and never missed. It is likely that she envisaged further development of the residential system in the direction of hostels, though in such a matter she was content to move at the pace set by older members of the Society. Meanwhile she recognized that some undergraduates benefited by living with a hostess who took a personal interest in them and she enjoyed finding the right hostess for the right undergraduate. For the Roman Catholic communities her principalship came at a critical moment in their struggle to obtain better education than had been open to them. The need for this was urgent, their difficulties in getting the opportunity were considerable; yet it was essential for regeneration and for making Roman Catholic lay education adequate, and it was to meet this situation that the two additional Roman Catholic communities were added to supplement Cherwell Edge. This expansion demanded of the Principal more thought and care for their special problems than would otherwise have been the case. Her nuns were keenly aware that she had done much for them and she was in close sympathy with their needs.

She dealt with undergraduates in individual ways. Respect for the integrity of the individual and sensitive consideration of his or her needs were characteristic of her. If she had been urged to pick out one single thing as of greatest importance in her office as Principal she would have said 'Dealing with the young'. She thoroughly enjoyed young people and had little difficulty in making them feel it her constant aim to come into touch with them all. On occasions when the whole Society were assembled she was able as an arresting and forceful speaker to establish a living relation with them at one meeting. However, she also invented ways of seeing and entertaining them in small groups and had many devices for this: motor rides to the country when she went to visit a Women's Institute or drives on a spring evening to some copse or lane to hear nightingales sing or, when the blackout came, walks round Oxford to see the buildings by moonlight. She kept in touch with them too after they had gone down and with students of past generations whom she met at the Gaudies, and she also gave close and constant attention to the question of finding suitable posts for members of the O.H.S., a matter in which her many connexions enabled her to explore new avenues. On all sides her personality was felt and enjoyed. 'What struck me most in G.E.H.'s handling of her responsibilities as Principal', writes Helen Darbishire,[1] 'was her generous humanity which kept her mind as well as her heart always open to the inner individual needs of each student. She understood Black Sheep of almost every type, and though she had an austere moral standard she would never allow routine discipline or accepted codes to override her own intuitive sense of the best way to deal with an individual in trouble.' The Principal knew young

[1] Principal of Somerville College till 1945.

people's enthusiasms and could share many of them and be amused at others. A vivid picture of her dealings with them and of how she saw their problems is contained in an address which she prepared for a special audience of the National Council of Mental Hygiene. In free personal expression it shows what she planned for them as well as her faith in the younger generation and her hopes for their future, and what she expected from an Oxford education. Much as she owed to this last herself, she did not think it to be the best and only education for every intelligent girl, and she felt that the common idea that all should aim at obtaining it was based on misunderstanding and called for adjustment.

As trustees of learning universities must foster trained powers of criticism; intellectual independence and freedom for individual thought are rock-bottom conditions. Grace Hadow knew and recognized that a university education, to preserve its character, must be governed by the standard that true learning sets. She believed in Oxford's way of demanding from those being trained both precise and specialized knowledge and the power to estimate that knowledge as well as to use it; she set a high estimate upon a training both in taking and in testing evidence. She stressed the importance of precision of thought and of expression and set a high value upon discussion at its best. And she concurred that the end of it all is the 'fashioning of good members of society and developing fitness for the world'. This last, not with a view to establishing a millennium for a number of people in ways such as she and others might think best—though an endeavour to secure such a millennium might result from such an education— but with a view to training a right judgement in all things. A mind so trained should understand truth without fear or favour, and be able rightly to rule and to obey. She was too well aware of good men and true all over the world and at all times to be ready to claim that it must necessarily be an Oxford education which induces a right sense of proportion or a power to put first things first. Nevertheless she would have claimed with other Oxford educationists that an Oxford education in its demands on knowledge and on judgement should cure Oxford's sons and daughters from yielding to the temptation to take short cuts in intellectual things. She would also have subscribed to the view that having such an education with all its attendant privileges the sons and daughters of Oxford should be left with a sense of obligation, urging: What am I to make of it? What can I do in return?

The following paper is reprinted, by kind permission, from the *Journal of the National Council of Mental Hygiene,* October 1936, in which were published addresses given at this Council's Mental Health Conference on 'Education for Living'. Following upon a session entitled 'Moulding the Mind: Eight to Fourteen', Grace Hadow's address was one of three at the session entitled 'The Finished Product.'

'It is a commonplace that except for Royalty and Brides few of us rank as news unless we happen to be unfortunate or criminal. If we drive our cars with reasonable care and safety no one is in the least interested; if we crash into a shop window we shall probably be awarded a headline in the local paper and may even find ourselves in the list of road accidents in *The Times.* This tendency to get a thrill out of the darker side of life no doubt has its compensations. Before such an audience as this I should not venture to express an opinion on the subject, but I mention it at the outset of this paper because unless one is setting out to advocate some special method of education it is inevitable that one's tendency is to dwell on difficulties and elaborate failures rather than to praise. I do not think that this is because we are more interested in failure than in success as such but because we feel education to be a matter of such importance that we want to make it as nearly perfect as may be and therefore we fasten on what is wrong in the hope of putting it right. I should like to say quite deliberately that the majority of girls who came up to me from secondary schools are healthy-minded wholesome young people and that any exceptions I may mention later are exceptions.

'Broadly speaking I should say that the girls who come up to Oxford have a real desire to make the most of it. Home Students differ from others in that they live in comparatively small communities (hostels which hold 6 to 30 undergraduates) or in twos and threes in private families. A large number of our Entrance candidates are also trying for admission to one or more of the residential colleges and I sometimes ask them if they have any preference for the one kind of life or the other. A considerable proportion like the community life: there is always great competition to get into the larger hostels: they like the comradeship, the noise, the amenities of college life. On the other hand a certain number of girls—particularly those who have been at boarding schools—say: "I have lived in a community for 8 or 10 years, and I'm tired of it. I want something different." There is no doubt that girls find the responsibility as prefect, and still more as head girl, something that is a strain and occasionally there is a marked reaction when first they obtain their freedom. I do not mean that they plunge into wild excesses: their daringness does not usually amount to more than a sudden outbreak of lipstick and unpleasantly scarlet nails and a tendency to cut lectures, but for some girls I have no doubt at all that their first term in Oxford releases a real tension. I have sometimes re-read at Christmas the testimonials which are written by Head Mistresses when candidates were admitted and have compared this succession of serious-minded girls with a keen sense of public duty with the irresponsible young first-year students whom I see at dances and sherry parties. Here I realize I am dealing with a very real difficulty. From the point of view of the girl herself, I think it would nearly always be beneficial for her to have a break between school and the university.

'The change from schoolgirl to university woman is a very marked one, and for many people it is too abrupt. A girl has been at a boarding school where even under the free and most modern methods she has been carefully guarded and sheltered. Her work has been to a great extent mapped out for her. She has lived entirely among women and girls and has associated chiefly with people of her own age. I submit that unless her home conditions are bad it is good for a girl of this sort to have a few months at home, not under the more or less exciting conditions of being home for the holidays, but living with her parents and having the greater freedom that normal home life should give to a girl of 17 or 18, and, if it is possible for her also to spend six months abroad, so much the better: it will broaden her mind and teach her to stand on her own feet. For the girl who has been to a day-school it is even more advisable that there should be a break before she comes up to the university. If she has never lived away from home, she is often miserably homesick when first she finds herself in completely new surroundings, and I have known girls wretched because they have found little details of manners and behaviour differed from those to which they were accustomed.

'I fully realize however that there are two great obstacles in the way of this break. The one is that it means the loss to the school of some of the best of their girls just when they are of a standing and an age to be most useful and to make their influence felt. The other is that most unfortunately a girl's ability to come to the university often depends upon her obtaining a scholarship from her Local Education Authority and this grant depends upon the result of the July examination. If some way could be found of obviating this it would be the greatest blessing both to the girls and the university authorities. At present an unhappy candidate often finds herself taking the Entrance examinations for Cambridge, to two sets of Oxford Colleges, for one or two London colleges in the Spring, and in July of the same year has to take another big examination on the result of which depends her whole career. It is a cruel anxiety for her and it leaves the College uncertain whether their vacancy is filled or not.

'One word more about another delicate and difficult matter. I wish we could get out of our own heads and the heads of other people that a university education is a mark of special distinction and something that every intelligent girl should aim at. I believe in a university education —if I did not, I should not have dedicated so large a part of my life to its service—and for certain people I think it gives the best training not only for this or that profession but for life. On the whole I think Oxford turns out not only good doctors and lawyers and teachers and Members of Parliament, but good wives and mothers and citizens. But I am quite certain that it is not the best training for all intelligent girls: some of them would do far better at less specialized universities; some if they went straight from school to Colleges of Domestic Science or Horticulture or Froebel or Secretarial Training.

'I wish that Head Mistresses would pass a self-denying ordinance that for the next five years they would make no mention in their reports of entrance won to the universities, or at all events would lay no stress upon these successes. The present tendency is to judge the worth of a school by the number of girls it can send to the university and the result is inevitably a temptation to push on a girl who shows promise in the hope of getting her to Oxford and Cambridge regardless of the fact that these may not be the places for her. This is, naturally, especially true of the type of school which perhaps sends up only one girl in four or five years. Again and again I have seen those who have been the clever girl of their school, who have been taught to a point which just makes them good enough for admission and who on the strength of that are given school scholarships or other grants and sent to Oxford. There, instead of being regarded as the brilliant girl of their year, one of whom everyone is proud, they find themselves possibly among the weakest of a number of students who have been picked from schools all over the country: the disillusionment is very bitter, and in some cases the strain to keep up and not to disgrace the school is very great. If as happens, a girl of this sort fails in Pass Moderations and has to go down at the end of her first year, the disappointment is intense for her and her family and her school, and one cannot help feeling that the whole thing has been a waste due to the desire to fit everyone into this bed of Procrustes. If only we could see education as a whole—land work, domestic science, scholarships all as facets of the same thing, all equally worth while, we should spare some misfits and much unnecessary anguish.

'Part, and a most important part, of university training is learning to hear all opinions attacked and defended. Possibly this comes as more of a shock to girls than to boys. I do not know. Certainly now, as always, young people of both sexes tend to be swept away by enthusiasm for this or that cause. In their first term undergraduates are beset by people wanting them to join this or that club or society, to denounce this, or to advocate that. I should say that in Oxford, as elsewhere, the two things that interested young people most were politics and religion, and to many of them it certainly does come as a shock to hear convictions challenged which they have always taken for granted. Very few Entrance candidates show much evidence of thinking for themselves. It is true that there are not many schools which would send up candidates, such as those whose papers I once saw, who being asked to criticise the *Vicar of Wakefield*, wrote: "*The Vicar of Wakefield* has nine faults" and then proceeded neatly to tabulate them: but we all learn to avoid setting questions on such subjects as the Chinese Exhibition because we know we shall get a reply not what the candidate really saw and liked or disliked, but what she can remember of what somebody told her she ought to like or dislike. It is the old story of the mob in *Sylvie and Bruno* with their cry of "Less bread, more taxes". You may think I am exaggerating this laziness of mind, but even those who win their way to Oxford are capable of a lack of thought which is sometimes staggering.

'One of the weaknesses in school training is lack of precision in thought and expression. We are so anxious to make lessons interesting and to encourage girls to enjoy the spirit of what they study that we forget that "If terms are not correctly defined words will not harmonize with things", and that "The wise man is never reckless in his choice of words"; there is a fine recklessness in the choice which many of our candidates make of words and an ignorance of grammar which leads to confusion of thought. For such people to find themselves in a world which still maintains the tradition of argument as one of the best intellectual games, which expects everyone to be able to give a reason for the faith which they hold, or to be ready to defend a faith which they do not hold, is not only bewildering but sometimes devastating. Inevitably it means for some people a period of distress and upheaval, though for many it leads to clearer thought and more firmly based convictions. I have known cases of undergraduates simultaneously joining the Fascist and October Clubs on the very admirable ground that they want to hear both sides, but it by no means follows that they understand either, and with all the modern outcry against "sloppiness" and sentimentality I can see no sign that the present generation thinks more clearly and accurately than the past.

'One thing however is certain: the interests of the present generation are world-wide. It is always possible to get a large audience of young people to listen to a talk on the League of Nations and while I have spoken—perhaps a little lightly—of the irresponsibility of people in their first year, I should say that on the whole the tone of Oxford was one of conscious responsibility as citizens. I am not thinking of those who join the Social Service Union or spend part of their vacations at Settlement Weeks but of the large numbers who fill the Town Hall to listen to Sir Arthur Salter on Sanctions or a Cabinet Minister on India and throng St. Mary's on a Sunday night. It was impossible not to be struck by the comments of girls of all kinds on Professor Gilbert Murray's lecture on the Italian-Abyssinian dispute: "It was such a comfort to hear Professor Murray taking such a decided line, because one knows he is always just." When once that first shock of hearing all things attacked and defended has been got over, young Oxford passionately desires to be just, although since it is young, justice often seems a simpler matter to them than it does to us who are older.

'This questioning of all things necessarily includes a questioning of rules and regulations. Just after the War there was a tendency to kick against every sort of restriction. We older people encouraged a great deal of foolish talk about the crass stupidity and selfishness of the elderly and the rights of youth. Youth has its rights, but these do not— or should not—include the right to burn its own and other people's fingers at the fire of life. If one reads the books written now by certain of the people who were at Oxford about 1920, it is impossible not to be struck by their conscientious and earnest desire to be shocking, the efforts with which they drag in totally unnecessary allusions to illegitimate babies simply because they are illegitimate, or to lavatories simply because they are lavatories. I see no sign whatever of this in the present generation: they are much less self-conscious. Like the young of every generation they want to experiment for themselves; they want adventure and they are not always ready to accept the wisdom of their elders —if these things were not so I should feel very anxious about the future of the race—but two things stand out conspicuously, their sense of justice and their sense of citizenship. They will discuss things very frankly, and I have known a girl, after the error of her ways has been pointed out to her, say thoughtfully, "Yes, I think that is very sensible", not with any idea of being patronizing or impertinent, because she— rightly—thought it of importance that she realized where she had gone wrong and was honest enough to confess it, without any emotionalism about it.

'Since by its peculiar constitution my society contains both girls living at home and those living under ordinary College conditions, it may be of interest to compare the two. First as to girls who come up from boarding schools or day schools. Here it is necessary to remember that on the whole those who come from day schools tend to come from poorer homes. In many cases they are State scholars, and in quite a number of instances they have few or no advantages in the way of books or talk at home. Such girls sometimes find their first term at Oxford a great strain, and I think they often benefit considerably by living as a member of the family with only one or two other girls in the house and with a hostess who takes a personal interest in them. They have all the advantages of being members of a large community as far as Clubs and Societies and Games are concerned without being overwhelmed by a crowd of strangers.

'A few of the girls from the better type of boarding school also benefit by being placed in the family of an Oxford don, where they meet older men and women as a matter of course, and hear things discussed from a grown-up point of view. I have known students who learned to appreciate this greatly, though in some cases they had at first been disappointed at not getting into a residential college. On the other hand there are girls who resent being mothered, and I am sometimes amused at the determination with which I have known most blameless and excellent students keep their parents from contact with me, not because they are afraid of disclosures on either side but because they want to feel their own independence and don't want to be talked over. I regret anything which keeps me from knowing parents or headmistresses, but I have a good deal of respect for the attitude of mind. If at the end of three years these girls are to go out into the world and earn their own living or manage their husband's houses, Oxford must help them to learn how to manage their own lives, and it is neither deceit nor ingratitude which makes them not so much impatient of advice as anxious to choose for themselves the person whom they will consult and the time when they will approach them.

'Girls actually living in their own homes are in a slightly different category. Without doubt I think it is on the whole usually more difficult for them to concentrate on their work since inevitably there are claims on their time and their thought which are not made on a boarder and do not arise at all in the case of a girl living in a College, though even here all human relationships are not severed and I have known a girl put to quite as much strain by a nervy and difficult friend as by an inconsiderate mother. In dealing with women one has to face the fact that claims will be made on them which are not made on their brothers. A boy is not sent for in the middle of term to go home and nurse his mother nor to look after the household for a week while she is in hospital: a girl is. A boy is not expected to run the house if he is living at home and his mother goes away or falls ill: a girl is. Naturally claims of this sort arise more frequently when a girl is living at home than when it is a case of sending for her, to say nothing of the fact that her leave of absence will be limited. Again it is more difficult to exercise discipline over a girl living at home and injudicious parents can foster idleness. With all these drawbacks however there are certain advantages.

'The girl who had been at a very pleasant and comfortable school, has passed direct from that to the still more pleasant and to some extent artificial life of a College, in some cases leaves the university still very much of a child, having had very little contact with life, and just as it is often easier for a child to get over homesickness and settle down if it goes away from home fairly early, so it is sometimes easier for a girl when she goes out into the world if she has had some training in the give and take of life. Everything naturally depends upon the home. Not infrequently, in the case of Home-Students, the girls have been away to boarding schools and come home for their university career. For the self-centred, the shy girl, the good mixer, community life is often the best, and it is not uncommon for a student who has lived at home or with a hostess for her first two years to ask permission to go into a Hostel for her last year, but it is also not uncommon for those who have been in Hostels to move out in their last year for the sake of the greater quiet. After all it is only in the Women's Colleges that undergraduates expect to have rooms in college throughout their university career. Practically all Oxford men are in lodgings for at least one year.

'To sum up: It seems to me that the key-note of Oxford is the desire to know, to utter, and to argue freely: that, as mercifully is always the case, the young have a desire for adventure, for experiment, for independence, and that this generation having grown up in an atmosphere of change and development has a real desire not only to enjoy life to the full, but to take a hand in reshaping the world.'

CHAPTER X

HOLIDAYS, I

HOLIDAYS meant a great deal to Grace Hadow: go-as-you please days with no binding engagements, no perpetual drain upon her time, sympathy, or faculty for drafting documents, and no letters; she had an infinite capacity for enjoying them, and judged it the essence of a holiday to do the very opposite of what one usually does. Those were days when her sense of romance had scope: 'You can't both have adventure and be comfortable', she would say; a spice of risk or danger was necessary for the fullest enjoyment of a holiday and surroundings where everything was as different as possible from home. Most of all she loved mountain climbing. This was something of a thwarted passion since a promise to her mother prevented her from going on with it after the trial trip in her youth with General Bruce. She was between forty and fifty when she took to it seriously. Most people's zest would have been quelled by a disposition to mountain sickness. It very nearly killed her on one big climb. However, climbing satisfied two very strong instincts: one for the exhilaration in risks, the other for forethought and efficiency in equipment just for the purpose in hand. Her climbing was probably more a matter of endurance and moral control than of exceptional skill, but her guides knew they could depend entirely upon her courage and strength of will, and all in all she achieved a considerable number of major climbs, never allowing herself to think she was a 'real climber' but getting great happiness from it all.[1] Her stories give a vivid impression of much bad weather, of rejoicing in exposure to lightning (especially when carrying an ice-axe), of progress by inches across *arêtes* or *gendarmes*; she would humorously realize the absurdity of taking so much trouble to produce one's own discomfort, but also enjoyed the refreshment of spirit that there is in nature's lonely places, and knew what it is like to be poised in mid air concentrating every faculty on foot- or hand-hold, and how impressions of dawn, of sunrise, of walls of ice, or

---

[1] Among other peaks she climbed the Fletschhorn (several times), the Zinal Rothorn, the Lauterbrunnen-Breithorn, the Matterhorn, the Finsteraarhorn, the Dent-Blanche.

snow, or granite then sink unconsciously into one's being in an unforgettable way. She had a keen sense for loveliness in wild scenery and in landscape—especially for long views and for sharp contrasts.

Her first holiday abroad since the war (soon after she became Secretary of Barnett House) was spent with her brother in the Puy de Dôme district in France. Some of her letters in August 1920 to my mother and me breathe the holiday mood when her surroundings became animated with pleasing fancy and every moment was consciously enjoyed.

Aug. 10, 1920.   Hotel de l'Univers,
                                                           Clermont Ferrand.

I love to think of you seeing beautiful things and packing every minute with all the enjoyment it can hold. . . . Did you ever read a strange story by Algernon Blackwood of a town he came to in France, where all the people were really cats, and held witches' revels at night? I think this must be the same place—only converted: they are very good cats. The whole place swarms with them, sleek, grey, demure, and I think this accounts for the strange silence of it all. When you look down on Clermont— which is a good sizeable place—you hear no sound, you see no smoke from any chimney, not even from the factories, and when you come back, before every door and in every window is curled a soft grey pussy. Little fluffy dogs obviously brought up by cats also abound, but real dogs are few, are muzzled, and as a rule driven about in cabs and motor cars—presumably so as to be out of the cats' way.

Lena tells me you like your Hotel. This one appears to be largely run by a smiling boy with a broom and a stout fatherly waiter, exactly like the Verger at Ciceter Church. Madame sits in the Hall and turns over the pages of a large book, but I have not yet discovered that anything results from this. In a crisis she screams up a speaking tube and the smiling boy appears and takes charge. I caught him trying on my neighbour's hat as he did the rooms yesterday. I wonder if he wears mine. It is a simple-minded place, I think. Another thing that strikes me is their inordinate pride in having gas. House after house announces proudly: 'Gaz à tous les étages.' I presume they are flats, but nothing else indicates this and I feel inclined to pencil in : 'We have electric light.'

Enchantment grew when she stepped into the Middle Ages at Le Puy with its steep streets and ancient buildings, its flashes of colour, and its vivacious people with whom she is anxious to get into touch:

Aug. 15, 1920.   Grand Hotel des Ambassadeurs,
                                                        Le Puy.

. . . You would love this place. It is exactly like the town of a French story book—the Hotel stands back from the street in a courtyard and the moment our bus emerged from the tunnel which leads from the street, out came smiling folk to welcome us as if we were their long lost friends. Everyone smiles and chats and is interested in a stranger (obviously strangers are rare) and I wish you had heard the peal of laughter with which our chamber maid greeted Harry's enquiry as to whether there was a lift: 'Il n'en est pas dans le Puy.' Now we have seen the town I realize the humour of the question. A 17th century house seems rather modern: one Church is eighth century, the Cathedral eleventh century, and the streets are for the most part nothing but steps, though occasionally one proudly opens out enough to allow an ox cart to wind along it. At every corner sit rows of old women (and sometimes of boys and girls) making the most exquisite lace. I never saw a place so given over to one industry—and today is high festival. All those nice muslin mob caps have either black or bright coloured ribbons round them, and the effect with the coloured lace pillows and pins with gay pink and blue heads, is extraordinarily jolly. There is a big fair today, and my window looks straight on to a square with a fountain in the centre and broad stone steps leading up to the street above. On the steps are fascinating pots—brown, green and blue—and furniture which I long to be able to take home. I saw a really beautiful chest of drawers, and a big cupboard which your Mother would have loved : both quite simple but with that wonderful colour that only comes with age. Did you see many of the peasant head-dresses at Clermont? The streets are full of them here, and very gay they look and very natural in these streets. The really swagger thing is to have gold ornaments in your cap, and a long gold chain hanging in festoons across a black silk bodice, and then a black or blue apron. But I expect you saw them for yourself. It is funny to see these very dignified peasant women (and they are charmingly dignified) herding small pink pigs with umbrellas— but the herding is most necessary since these absurd streetlets are choked with pigs and large alderney coloured cows. The favourite way of taking pigs home appears to be on a leash, and naturally every pig gets entangled with every other and winds his own cord firmly round his own hind leg.

The town is guarded by the most gigantic statue of the Virgin and Child—made of guns taken at Sebastopol, of all amazing materials. Every now and then, apropos of nothing, a great rock suddenly shoots up 300 or 400 feet quite sheer, and on these extraordinary needles are perched Church or colossal statue. The result is certainly odd. On Sunday there is to be a great procession to carry the Miraculous Virgin (in the Cathedral) through the town, and in these queer up and down streets it ought to be a beautiful sight. . . .

Tell your mother, with my love, that the chocolate was the greatest comfort this morning. We had to get up at 4.30 a.m. and our first chance of a meal was at noon : we did succeed in getting a tiny cup of very bad coffee at a sort of workman's shelter by the line about 9, but that was literally our only chance of anything at all. The chocolate proved grateful and comforting. . . .

August 19, 1920.   Le Puy.

. . . We went for an excursion you would have loved, today; at least you would have loved the main part—I am not sure about getting there and back. We got up at 6, had coffee in a funny grubby little café; and then set out in the queerest and most ram-shackle of auto-buses packed to bursting with a cheerful chattering crowd. We managed to get the two seats next the driver; but even so a smiling fisherman sat on Harry's feet all the way. Then we bumped and rattled up into the mountains. The driver shared my chocolate and told me lurid stories of recent murder on the road and was generally friendly. Finally he dumped us in a pine forest with no house in sight, waved his hand, said he'd be back at 6 o'clock and left us. We wandered on—like Hänsel and Gretel —till we came to a tiny lonely inn by the side of a lake—the crater of a volcano, nearly 3 miles round; an almost perfect circle with pine forest to the edge all round, and neither outlet nor inlet. The

queer thing about it is that it is higher in Summer than in Winter.
From 8.30 a.m. to 6 p.m. we roamed about the forest—a forest of
thick tall pines, carpeted with the softest and greenest moss against
which gleamed masses of wild strawberries. Every now and
again came a clearing, purple with heather, and then we looked
right away over the Cevennes. I expected to find a Witches' house
at every turn, it was so still and so old, and the trees were festooned
with gray lichen till they looked like old old trolls. I never saw
trees so thick—mile after mile of them uncleared and most impressive. We got lost once or twice. But it was the 'quietest' day
I ever spent.

. . . Le Puy is like living in the 13th century. The shops are
little dark cellars: the streets are flights of steps—so narrow
neighbours could easily shake hands across. Almost every house
has some quaint or beautiful carving or moulding, and every
little square (paved and crooked) has its fountain. Literally every
street of the old town takes one to the great flight of steps which
leads from the open street straight up to the High Altar of the
Cathedral. Unluckily they have blocked up the West end now,
and floored the Cathedral though the steps are still there underneath, but is extraordinarily impressive all the same—the great
wide flight up through the great porch, over 100 steps. We go on
Tuesday to a village in the hills, with the attractive name of La
Chaise Dieu.

Tell M. G. S. I am glad she is not here to mock my valiant
plunges into conversation. I get along quite well when they don't
burst into heroics over the War—then a perpetual repetition of
a polite 'Oui' seems bald—but I shake hands at intervals. I am
probably adding to the belief that all the English are mad, but
we are at least friendly.

It was in 1922 that she began mountain climbing in Switzerland
once more under the direction of Alice Bruce, who was known in
many a high valley as 'Fräulein Generalin' and who enjoyed her
friend's delight in the new world into which she was introducing
her. Writing from the Lötschental, 18 August 1922, she discovers
with pleasure how human life is lived above the snow line:

Aug. 18, 1922.   Hotel Nesthorn, Lötschental.

To say I am proud of being used as an antidote to nightmares
is a very mild way of putting it. Here is a nice story, not of mine

but of another member of our party. A number of them were
going up to a Hut for the night, a dangerous bit of glacier where
a guide had been killed the year before. As they went their guide
dropped the lantern which went hopping, hopping down the
glacier till at last it disappeared into a crevasse. They struggled on
without it with some difficulty, and were very glad to get to the
Hut. To their surprise it was locked, and when they knocked
with their ice axes no one answered. The prospect of being locked
out for the night in the snow was not cheerful and they hammered
louder. Still no reply. At last their guides went round shouting
to the guardian by name and finally he opened the door. He had
seen a mysterious light bounding along the glacier and made sure
it was the ghost of the guide who had been killed; when later,
out of the dark an ice axe knocked at the door, it was altogether
too much for him. He had no intention of letting that knocker in.

We climbed up about 3,000 ft. to one of those fascinating huts
that has no guardian but is like a mixture of a fairy story and a
doll's house. We went in and found everything ready and wood
for burning, cups, and pots, a kettle, a spare rope and ice axe, and
even a few books and some huge boots with felt soles. We filled
the kettle from the glacier stream, lighted a fire (which smoked so
that the tears streamed down our cheeks), and made ourselves
tea. Then we washed up, put money for what we had had in
a box, left a pot of tea (poured off the leaves), the remains of our
sandwiches, and a kettle half full of boiling water for the next
man. It was like baiting a mouse trap. Hardly had we gone when
we saw two men come down from the mountain and go into the
Hut. We thought how pleased they would be to find a meal all
ready and waiting, and we thought so the more when about two-
thirds of the way down we got caught in a terrific thunderstorm.
In two minutes we were soaked to the skin, our boots full of water,
hail cutting our faces. Up higher it would have been difficult to
get across some of the slopes, and we thought of our two mice (and
two more peasant women who were going up as we went down)
drinking our tea and getting the benefit of a fire which had ceased
to smoke when we left.

We found the Hotel much agitated and interested, especially
as one of us arrived first, and the other two later, and they made
sure some of us at any rate had got struck and the others had
callously left the remains. Yesterday we did a baby climb up

a little 10,000 footer and got a wonderful view of Mont Blanc and the whole Weisshorn range. Our guide had been in the Papal guard and entertained us with discussions on the characters of the various Popes.

In 1923 she was preparing to take climbing seriously, having secured a long holiday. The first part was to be spent with members of the home party at Bérisal and with Alice Bruce, getting into training, when ill luck crossed these plans, and she found herself at Evolena lamed by a poisoned foot wasting nearly three weeks, but providentially saved from permanent injury by an efficient young Swiss doctor: an accident that she describes very characteristically:

Aug. 7, 1923.   Grand Hotel, Evolena, Valais.

You don't mind a funny story when you know beforehand it has a happy ending, do you? This really is funny, and it is already having a happy ending. I wasn't quite sure on Saturday and Sunday if my silly foot had really suddenly got much worse or if I was just fussing, so I left it to Fate to decide if I should see the doctor again or not. Fate (as it turned out most kindly) decided not: once I ran into him (at 10 o'clock at night) in the road in the dark, when obviously I couldn't ask him professional questions; and yesterday the whole Bérisal Hotel looked for him in vain before we started (he was seeing to the hay) and I caught sight of him as we were in the carriage setting out for the station, heavy luggage sent off already, room given up &c. As if I had seen him either I shouldn't have been allowed to travel, or I should have got blood poisoning (I'm not quite sure from the amusing little man here whether that would have implied a permanently stiff ankle or the loss of my foot or both—he likes to pile it on) it was a mercy I did not. As it was we had an easy journey here and I sat and guarded luggage whenever we had to change. It ended with an amazing drive of two hours along a road so narrow that if we met anything one of us had to back, through wild gorges to this plateau. Here I lie in bed with French windows opening on to a wide terrace, and directly beyond the most lovely view of snow peaks and glacier: at Bérisal (though I like the place itself much better) my window looked only on to a wall of pine trees. This is almost like sleeping out of doors. By the time we got here it did seem as if it might be sensible to do something. Luckily there turned out to be an Hotel doctor: a sturdy, powerfully built young man with no English but a sense of humour. He came and looked at my foot and then explained cheerily that unless something drastic was done at once—well I really should become like Herod. Then the amusing part began. I provided entertainment for the entire Hotel staff. From the amount of things it appeared to be necessary to bring into my room you'd have thought it a major operation at least, and as I sat helpless one excitable and kindly person after another would burst in, look fixedly at my unfortunate foot for a time, ejaculate: 'Eh ciel! ça fait du mal!' and go out again. The chamber-maid is much impressed with the fortitude of the English (tiresome of her as after that I naturally have to say nothing ever hurts). 'If the Swiss get a pain in their finger or a bruise,' she said, 'they say "Mon dieu! je vais au ciel!" but the English always "C'est rien".' As a matter of fact I am getting the cheapest possible reputation for heroism, I should never have dreamed it possible an abscess could get so bad and hurt so little. But it probably means another week more or less on my back.

I like my square doctor—who bows like a Japanese. He gave me a shock last night by saying—rather sternly—as we parted for the night: 'Morgen wenn Sie aufstehen, müssen Sie baden.' I felt slightly insulted. Could it be that his patients were not in the habit of bathing? Then he went on: 'Für eine Stunde', and my bewilderment increased. Why on earth should I spend an hour over my bath. However it suddenly dawned on me—it only means I have to sit for an hour at a time with my foot in a bath of camomile tea, the nasty one—it was with the utmost difficulty the Hotel could produce any vessel large enough to hold my foot.

You'll never again be able to say I don't talk about my health. . . .

My days are much occupied. I begin to understand how busy you always are when you are in bed. Mine begin with an absolutely heavenly sunrise. The great mountains begin to stand out against a pale sky and then the snow shows first dead white, then warmer, and then one peak becomes flame-colour; and one just holds ones breath and sees God walk in the Garden. It is like being blessed at the beginning of each day.

At 7 my cheerful chambermaid bursts in with my breakfast, after which I am at home to odd callers till 10.30 or 11. All our rooms open on to the Terrace so it is easy to run in and out.

Round about 11 the chef sends me up a foot bath of literally boiling camomile tea, and I spend ¾ hour saying firmly 'That is too hot'. No one believes me and they all tell me not to make a fuss: 'You soon get used to it'—I'd like to see them keep a finger in it (I grow vindictive). I get up and dress and sit with my foot in this stuff for an hour (I've learnt to put on a dress quite comfortably without moving). Then my nice young ogre comes and dresses my foot and grins and says 'Sie sind zufrieden?' and I say 'very but please hurry this up'. Yesterday I was allowed down to lunch and hopped down a little late. After lunch I lie on the couch they have put for me on the terrace till about 5 when the bath and foot dressing are repeated. That takes till dinner, and after dinner we play cards till bed time.

My ogre (he is exactly my idea of a young benevolent ogre and will never be a fashionable physician—bless him) was away for the night last night, so my room smells more like a hospital than ever as he left me all his paraphernalia to do my own dressing. 'Kommen Sie morgen wieder?' said I, 'Ja' in his deepest voice and with his griniest grin 'Ich will Sie nicht verlassen'. I felt like Naomi and Ruth. Did I tell you he is coming to England next month and has invited himself to see us? That young man will lose nothing for want of a little resolution.

The jolly part of all this is that Lena—who was longing to see Arolla but would not have left me to look after her mother if I'd been allright, went up with Miss Bruce for a night yesterday. They will have had a glorious 3 hour walk in the early morning and were going to play on the glacier in the evening. Then today they were to take lunch to a very beautiful lake a little way off the path on the way down, and I suppose Lena will turn up this evening. My difficulty is to prevent Mrs. Deneke waiting on me hand and foot—which is one way of looking after her.

I can't tell a bit when I shall get up there. They can't let the silly thing heal yet and I can't walk till it does and meanwhile I've lost every vestige of training—tut! tut! . . .

Aug. 24, 1923.   Hotel Mont Collon. Arolla.

I take back all my complaints of Providence. It gave me an absolutely perfect day yesterday—and I walked for 17½ hours, so I made the most of it. I started with a guide at 2.30 a.m. and did first a pass, then a glacier, he said as we were already so high, it seemed a pity not to do a second of the big fellows while we were about it, so we did a second mountain (I forgot to say we had thrown in a ridge and some baby gendarmes on the way) and crossed on to another glacier, then up to a hut perched on the cliff, and then down about 150 miles of glacier, getting home at 8 p.m. to find Miss Bruce beginning to wonder where we were. I couldn't get the guide I like best and the man I had though very nice gets nervous and excited in a tight place. For instance— knowing he had a complete novice to deal with—it seemed to me unwise of him as we started up a long ice slope, which implied an hour's solid step cutting, to inform me that if either of us slipped, we were both bound to be killed as he could not possibly hold me alone. And once, when I sat on nothing in particular on the face of a precipice trying to pretend to myself I wasn't frightened, he leaned over the edge and murmured 'C'est dégoûtant'. What really bothered me however was his habit of shouting at me all the time when I was in difficulties as so often I was. I could not understand what he said and if he'd left me alone I could have found my way in time. All the same he was a really nice fellow and against his nervousness must be set the fact that he told me with pride that many guides would have refused to do what he had done without a second. I fell into more crevasses than I should have thought possible in one day and was hauled out like a fish: few things are less conducive to dignity than being hauled on your face along wet snow. We had one very beautiful and quite easy bit—but right at the top of our first mountain with a huge corniche on our right and a sheer ice slope on our left and just room to cut steps between them, the guide keeping as near the corniche as possible so that he felt every step and each time his ice axe went in up to the head. I am still a very bad climber, but I am getting better, and I was very proud when the guide offered to take me up the show difficult mountain of this district. We leave tomorrow if it is fine, so I shan't have time this year.

By 1924 she had found her first guide at Simplon Dorf in Anton Dorsaz, former President of the local commune, a well-known local farmer and cheese merchant who had been with her in the Lötschental in 1922, and she set out on serious climbing with him. They went up his favourite Fletschhorn in the worst weather for fifty years; which she reports in a letter to her brother:

'Saas Fee, Aug. 15, 1924. . . . I am off on a 5 days tour alone with a guide (one of the best): the first time I have ever been flung entirely on my own resources among a people who have not one word of English. I don't know whether to say my luck is good or bad. I meant to do one of the really big things from here and the weather puts that out of the question: on the other hand at the bottom of a foolish heart has lurked a desire to be for once on the mountains in the kind of storm of which one reads. Well, I've done it. My guide is fearfully proud because none of the guides here will believe that he "allein mit einer Dame" did the Fletschhorn on Wednesday. Apparently all the parties that set out to do anything from here turned back. We got to the top allright, and had—at an outside estimate—three minutes there. I never conceived that one could be in such a storm without being frozen and I wasn't even cold. I had to keep breathing the icicles from my hat because they hung over my eyes: my hair was full of ice: we were caked with ice from head to foot; and within a very short time the steps we had cut coming up were completely obliterated. To be candid I didn't a bit like going down a very steep ice slope unable to wear glasses because they instantly got crusted with ice, and so unable to see whether I was in the step or not; whereas the rocks—which Dorsaz said were really dangerous—I thoroughly enjoyed. By the time we got on to the arête there was such a gale that he made me do bits of it sitting lest I should be blown over. In one place the rock was so rotten that he told me he thought it would be impossible next year, and one could hear stone avalanches rolling down all round one. You couldn't see more than a yard or two. I don't know why I wasn't scared, but I think the wind excites one too much. I also had another experience that I've rather wanted. You had to stand on a sharp peak and jump up to a rock—with nothing all round you— a higher jump than I could well do. The first time I missed, and as Dorsaz put it, "die Frau tanzt an dem Seile" but the second time I thought I did it rather neatly for an elderly maiden lady. But I have learned that to hang on the rope over a precipice makes me sympathize deeply with the martyrs who were sawn asunder. It hurts horribly—however it would have hurt a great deal more without. We got back soaked to the skin and having been unable to stop for any food for the last 7 hours to be greeted at the tiny mountain hotel by three nice Frenchmen—real experts—who had done one of the smaller peaks and who hung out of the window and shouted "Quel courage" in their nice encouraging French way. Two men came in later who had lost their way over a pass and my guide had to get their rope off with pincers it was too frozen to move. I am now swelling with pride because Dorsaz says that if I came next year he will take me up a side of these fellows that no woman has yet done. I shall never be a good climber, but at least I got there and I love it.'

That same year when climbing on the lower slopes of the Weissmies, the Nebelmeer below seemed 'not the usual beautiful rippling level expanse of cloud, but a raging sea with billows 40 to 50 feet high: quite gorgeous and quite wicked'—it turned out to be a fifteen-hour walk and the last eight in unbroken rain except for an interval of 'nearly an hour when we plunged into a mountain hut and the reign of King Alfred, where a kind peasant woman made us a roaring fire of logs, and we took off such clothes as we could and she baked them while we sat and steamed. The only chimney was a hole in the roof. There was only one room, and the only light and air (apart from chinks in the walls) came from the door. She ground coffee and gave us lovely cups of hot coffee into which she wanted to ladle butter (I drew the line at that) and I had difficulty when we left in making her accept anything. One of the children—to whom I had given chocolate—followed us for miles like a mountain kid, and embarrassed me by offering me wet cold whortleberries: a nice child.

'We got to Simplon Dorf (two hours below this) about 6.30 with water running out of every part of us. There I telephoned to the Kulm to ask them to have a hot bath ready for me and some dinner (I'd had two sandwiches and some prunes since 2.45 a.m. and I was hungry) and went into the Hotel to get some coffee while Dorsaz went to find me some kind of conveyance. I didn't feel I could face another two hours of road with a wet knapsack to carry. Certainly the Swiss are a friendly race. I wasn't stopping at that Hotel—I made pools wherever I sat down—I spent about a franc: but nothing on earth would induce them to let me go on as I was. They built up a wood fire and made me drink hot coffee by it, and then "Madame" took me off and gave me a complete outfit of her own clothes and a big coat to drive up in (I think she probably saved my life). By the time I had changed the Wagen was ready, Dorsaz turned up and wrapped me up in his huge

SAAS FEE

winter over-coat, my sopping things were put on the floor and off we went. It was one of the queer continental carriages rather like an old-fashioned bathing machine with a hood and was drawn by an enormous horse wearing a large mackintosh. We walked until it grew dark, and then having no lights—we trotted past the blackest pine trees you can imagine and under wonderfully grim mountains. I got in at 9 p.m.—and enjoyed both bath and dinner and am not ½*d.* the worse.'

The ascent of 'that fellow', the Fletschhorn, by the side no woman had done was accomplished the next year. It involved camping for the night on the open mountain side, and descending to Saas Fee, and it almost cost her her life from an attack of mountain sickness.

'It has been a very queer time. I know you haven't nerves, so I don't mind telling you the true story, but it is for you alone. I am thoroughly ashamed of it—though I don't quite see how I could have helped it. In any case I am perfectly all right now and never likely to go through anything similar again. Briefly I think I have been nearer dying than ever before—not dramatically over a precipice, but just simply, plainly of exhaustion. It is quite interesting for once to know what it is like.

'On Monday we went up to the bivouac. It was like acting the sacrifice of Isaac: Dorsaz carrying a faggot on his back, the 14-year old Peter carrying blankets, and myself. Dorsaz sent me on ahead, and I shall never forget that walk with the mountains absolutely to oneself and the purple evening light. We camped in a sheepfold under the rocks where Dorsaz lit a blazing fire, and Peter stirred the soup with a stick since we'd forgotten a spoon.

'Then we adjourned to the "Schlafzimmer" where Dorsaz had spread a large blanket on the rock: we took our knapsacks for pillows, and lay down side by side, Dorsaz coming round and tucking us up. Unluckily for me Peter—who was in the middle—unconsciously and naturally collected all the blankets during the night and I got no sleep and got pretty cold (one couldn't take the blankets off a child) which I think may account for next day. However I was quite all right in the morning when I got up about 2 and we lighted the fire again and drank hot sweet coffee stirred by a grimy pocket-knife (I kept thinking how Robin would enjoy it all). Then we put Peter back to bed again and started. I've never started so high in the dark. It really is thrilling to walk on the edge of blackness, with a tiny star of light in front. We went over loose moraine and then up a quite magnificent glacier, very steep and getting in and out of huge crevasses ("Step as lightly as you can" said Dorsaz anxiously as I scrambled down on to a snow bridge well down over a bottomless pit). As we went up, dawn broke. Below us stretched mile after mile of "Nebelmeer" great purple peaks rising out of it and flame colour behind. And then suddenly the whole snow on which we were turned pink. We'd just got to the really dangerous part—falling stones—when I got taken ill. I thought it was nothing and would pass and we wanted to get over the bad rock so we went on, and then when we just had to go through with it, I really got rather bad. I won't harrow you with details, but it was sheer waste to try and eat, and that kind of effort with no food does for you, and the slower you get, the longer you are without food. The net result was that I had 21 hours living on occasional sips of wine or brandy varied by a few lumps of sugar. The actual climbing was great fun, but whenever I had such a jolly bit that I forgot to be ill, it meant such physical effort that I collapsed afterwards. There was one really nice place when you let yourself down over a sheer precipice till you had no foothold at all, and then have to swing by your fingers across a rock to a foot hold you can't see and which is so far that you feel as if your fingers couldn't hold. I didn't quite understand the first time and luckily missed my swing. I say "luckily" because as I swung back I saw neatly on a ledge of rock my little pot of cold cream which must have squeezed out of my breeches pocket as I went over the edge. It just enabled me to retrieve it before I did my final swing. We did the whole long and very interesting climb, and then started down. It should take us about 3 hours, and it took 9 and I did it partly crawling and partly sitting and partly on legs which got less and less under control. At intervals I just had to lie where I was till it was possible to crawl on another few yards. It got dark and you can guess what it is like to go down a steep hill over boulders in the dark when you can barely stand. Finally I just came to the end of things. We knew there was a hut about ¾ hour away and I besought Dorsaz to wrap me up in all the warm things we had and leave me under a rock while he went on and got food. I knew he must be dog-tired and very anxious (he told me next day and more than once I looked as if I were dying!) and I saw no sense in his being more uncomfortable than necessary.

I thought he could come back and fetch me later. However, nothing would induce him to leave me, so I lay happily on the track till I could pull myself together. I don't believe I should ever have done it, only I was determined Dorsaz should not spend the night out knowing he would give me all the warm things. We got to the Hut finally at 12.30 to find it shut (which they are never supposed to be) and almost the worst moment was when Dorsaz said: "I can make no one hear." However, it was all right in the end. The guardian and his wife came down and made us hot tea, and I got a room to myself with lots of blankets and the windows open. Next morning I breakfasted off hot soup in bed and stayed in bed till 11.30 when I started on the 3 hour walk here. I found I was a bit shaky but quite allright. Then we met a search party coming to look for our remains. The entire countryside was thrilled—and it all knows how sick I was!! I've done my climb no woman has done before—but I can't boast of it. Luckily the weather did not break till we got in. We could see tremendous showers all round but got only a few flakes of snow.

'Yours ever
'G. E. H.

'I hope to be able to climb again as soon as the weather smiles.'[1]

Grace was extraordinarily wiry and capable of feats of endurance; she was happiest on rock, but had a capacity for going on undaunted for long distances uphill or across snow slopes and moraines, much as she exclaims about disliking that medium for walking. When she was sixty she could feel 'rather pleased with myself physically', walking up to a hut carrying a sack in 2 hours, instead of the regulation 2½, then 'starting at 4.45 across grass, about an hour, to plug up loose moraine of soft slippery small stones sliding from under one's feet at every step and about as steep as it could be', to 'merciful big boulders and easy glacier' and 1½ hours of 'abominable steep snows, across narrow ice with a sheer drop one side and a steep fall of ice into another crevasse on the other, and having to jump on a narrow ledge of ice on the opposite side below and then climb up an ice wall curving above my head'—this a walk of twelve hours from which she returned 'fresh as paint'. The moment she 'loved'—'I really do enjoy rock'

---

[1] Soon after, she climbed the Südlenzspitze and the Nadelhorn 'under excellent conditions'.

—was when they came to the top of a chimney and she saw she had to drop through a hole down a very steep snow wall 'apparently into infinity'. The guide seized her arm, 'Ayez confiance en moi, Madame' and hurled them both over the edge. 'We just shot down—it was heavenly.' Then there were the impressions of light and ice: 'I know nothing so solemn as that moment before sunrise when the glaciers above look extraordinarily other-worldly, gray and menacing, and the mountains stand out against a pale sky' had been her observation on starting on this walk across the grass with dawn breaking. Another morning, and this at Saas Fee at 4, she 'went out into one of the most wonderful sights I've ever seen. The moon nearly full, and in every direction it shone on glacier and hanging glaciers and great snow peaks. To thread one's way among the crevasses was like walking through a half heavenly, half infernal fairy land. The moon shone into great caves of ice, looking as if they went down into the centre of the world, and the ice glittered under our feet. We walked up steep snow and ice for $3\frac{1}{2}$ hours till we reached the top of an 11,000 ft. pass from which one sees the whole great range of mountains behind Zermatt. Then, after a short rest, just for fun we went up a snow peak close by.' . . . Coming down for several hours 'very steep snow and ice and across some of the most magnificent crevasses I've ever seen, shading from pure white to the most vivid blue and hung with icicles.' . . . 'I seem to have been living for weeks among ice-caves and snow fields and precipices. Miss Skipworth and I did a solid fortnight of climbing, including 3 high snow passes and 2 first class peaks; my longest day was 19 hours (it should have been 17 only, but I was tired and slow). A peak nearly always means 2 days: one to go up to the Hut and one to climb it: and so does a high pass if you don't mean to rush it. . . .'

'I think my most wonderful time was doing the Dent Blanche. You go up from Arolla—a 4 hours steep walk—just along a shady path, then over snow, and then a little rock scramble till you find the Berthol Hut perched like a huge bird on a cliff. All round lie huge snow fields out of which rise great jagged peaks—the Dent Blanche, the Matterhorn, the Bouquetins—and one gets there just as sunrise is beginning to turn the peaks pink and orange. It was so late in the season that I'd the Hut to myself—the only drawback to this being that the guides shared my room instead of sleeping in the loft, so that I could not have even a chink of window open. Next morning we left about 2.30 a.m. in the moonlight and had a 3½ hour walk across the glacier before we came to the mountain itself. It is fun to climb with some really difficult rock. We got down it about 2 p.m. and then I thought in my innocence that we had before us merely a longish tramp across snow until we should get down to another hut on the Zermatt side and so on to Zermatt. We did set out pleasantly across a glacier and then suddenly came to the edge of one of the highest and most sheer precipices I ever saw and proceeded to go down it. I don't mind precipices in an ordinary way but such of this as was not loose shale was rotten rock, and when ever you stood on anything or held to anything it came in two in your hands or from your foot. The climax was about 2/3 of the way down, when we came to a stretch—I should think about 100 yards or more wide and still some hundreds of feet above the glacier, which was quite obviously a track for both snow and stone cavalcades. We had first to cross this track and then go down it. The guides told me to hurry, but by this time I was getting pretty tired and while I didn't say I didn't care a 2½*d.* stamp if we were all hit on the head by stones or not, it was what I felt and I replied crossly I couldn't do more than I was doing. So they waited until we had scrambled across, and down a little snow avalanche which had obviously just fallen and then they came and took me one each side and just ran me down. It was good fun as I had no bother—I slid, or walked as my legs happened to go and felt no responsibility for them. Then we had quite an easy glacier, and at last the rope off ("Gott sei Dank" said Dorsaz), then a long bit of moraine and so to the Hut which we reached about 5 p.m.—and then 4 hours walk along a very stony path down to Zermatt. It was dark before we got in and three very tired people stumbled down a half water-course, half foot-path, marvelling at the things people do for pleasure. The little Zermatt hotel received us with open arms and hot soup. Then the nice head waiter (who looked like an undergraduate) poured a cup of boiling tea over me, there were cries (not from me) of horror. I do like the Swiss. When I had had my blouse washed and told him he need no longer worry as there wasn't a mark on it, he replied briefly but fervently "Lob Gott". Fancy an English waiter saying "Praise God" when you told him he hadn't spoiled your blouse!'

Grace thoroughly enjoyed contrasted bodily sensations: and 'enjoying one's body' was part of the holiday pleasure: 'this after having walked up to an alp about 1,000 feet above a mountain inn and after scrambling in blazing sun over shale and rock to find an unexpected little lake, one end of it snow and ice, in which we bathed. It was so cold that it left one gasping, but it was lovely to come out and sun, like a sea monster, on a hot rock.'

Human interest always came by the way in Grace Hadow's enterprises and it was unending. Properly considered, the relation between guides and their clients may seem artificial enough. She would recall the remarks upon it made by her guides for their part: 'You pay a lot of money, to be made extremely uncomfortable: bitterly cold, panting with heat under the sun, tired, often hungry', in fact for expensive misery; on the other hand to the guides their charges were as nurslings for whose safety they took care in every step, whom they lighted to bed and wrapped up with blankets, whom they fed, for whose belongings they took responsibility. Themselves accustomed to the danger of mountain climbing, expert, alert, they were extremely critical of the morale of their charges and contemptuous of careless behaviour. It was worth while to stand high in one's guide's esteem, and the experiences shared in bad weather on a mountain unite men in common human feelings or separate them utterly.

'August 1928. Last Monday we set out from Lötschental to walk over three glaciers to the Concordia—just behind the Jungfrau Joch. The glaciers are very beautiful but very difficult this year as owing to the hot summer there is often no snow at all on them for some hours distance—and consequently no snow bridges —and they are tremendously crevassed. I never saw such a series of great ice cliffs and caverns as we have been walking among, or such transparent colours. As we walked over from Lötschental one of the guides suddenly dragged me to the edge of a huge and apparently bottomless crevasse and peered into it, "My brother fell into that a fortnight ago," he said, "and lost his ice axe. But" (rather irritably) "I can't see it."

'We slept at the Concordia, a much glorified Hut which calls itself an Hotel—"The highest hotel in Europe!"—since there one can get a real bed with sheets, and next morning we rose at 3 a.m. to do the Finsteraarhorn. A French Swiss doctor and his guide had left about half-an-hour before us, so we were rather surprised to come upon them on the cliff very soon after we started. "What on earth had they been doing?" I asked one of our guides afterwards. He sniffed "Throwing their lantern down the rocks and breaking it," he said. It was lucky for them we came along as without us I think they'd have been stuck till daylight. There was one place, not difficult I imagine in daylight, but not easy in the dark. The doctor—obviously very nervous—had to go first. His guide let him out on a long rope, ours perched about on bits of the cliff with lanterns giving what light they could; everybody shouting as many contradictory instructions as when a boat is coming in. Skippy and I sat waiting our turn, while from the darkness below came sounds of frantic struggles and agonies, "Sacramentos" with *rr*'s rolling. Finally he got to the bottom and from the dark shouted up encouragingly to us—in English— "Veree bad!" And with that Bumann's soothing voice said to me "Now you can go." It really was quite amusing, and the oddest way I've ever left an Hotel.'

Her guides became friends with whom she kept in touch, especially Bumann of Saas Fee, with whom the most and biggest climbs were undertaken. He introduced her to his wife and family, and they would look forward to entertaining her for a meal once each climbing season. And when she started homewards, all the little Bumanns were instructed to pray for her, commending her to the Virgin during the dangerous journey home across the Channel. Mountain risks he, like other guides, disregarded, as being only part of every day.

'Today we are going to see Bumann and his family—wife and 6 little Bumanns, the eldest 7. I think it ought to be great fun. He is a charming person. If he thinks one is at all nervous on a snow arrête he makes a point of coming to discuss the news. Yesterday when we had a quite easy, but rather a long arête he suddenly proceeded to dance on it. I wish you could have seen him— pack on back—doing a sort of bear's shuffle and shouting with laughter.

'You'd love (a picture I shall never forget) seeing Bumann in bed (we called about 9 p.m. when he had already retired, and his wife insisted on our coming in) with the dearest little 2 year old son in bed with him, and the little girls (ranging from 7 to 3) undressing preparatory to getting into a nice little padded box at the foot of the huge family bed. Everything spotlessly clean, and

such an atmosphere of happy family life. The dark haired hand-some wife, with scarlet handkerchief over her head, and the pretty, friendly children, and this great, rough, gentle man, who saves our lives at intervals daily. We had tea with him and all the family one day and it was the nicest tea-party I was ever at. . . .'
Another time she gives a character sketch of him. 'I wish you could have seen Bumann (the Saas Fee guide, on whom we called in his bed) who has a distinct gift for drama (*a*) acting to us the terror of two German men, whom he took on the glacier—he expounding on the beauties of nature and they perpetually asking in trembling tones "Aber, kommen wir wirklich (nach) dort oben?" (*b*) pretending to extreme terror himself and tottering up a tiny peak while Skippy and I offered to help him. Apparently very few of his English "Touristen" speak German (they must miss a lot) and he is so pleased that we do, that he lets himself go. When he and Dorsaz get telling stories against each other the results are sometimes grim and sometimes amusing, but always interesting. You would have enjoyed his description of how one night when he reached a Hut they told him a man and woman had gone on to the mountain and had not returned: certainly there had been an accident. He was the only guide there, but his "tourist" and three Englishmen who were there volunteered to go with him. It was a long and graphic story: in the end (at risk of his own life) he got them all right and then—delicately—he tried to convey to us that they were hardly worth it: "You see, she was not exactly his wife: an actress: Keine solide Frau." We always hope we are solid women.'

CHAPTER XI

HOLIDAYS, II

THERE were many successive holidays in the summer in the Rhône valley in Switzerland, rarely varied by a visit to French Switzerland and to the Pyrenees. To go to Brigue was like coming to a home port, and when there was no mountain climbing there were walks across passes or in some high mountain valley and there were friendships to pick up.

Dorsaz had become a staunch friend, and some of the best walking tours were across easy passes into Italy with Dorsaz in charge of the party.

'Aug. 11, 1925. We have had a second quite adorable walking tour and are very proud of having slipped into Italy and back without ever seeing a custom official or being asked for our passports. I fancy Dorsaz might have taken us an unusual way for we had a triumphal entry. At the first cottage we came to the entire family rushed out hands clasped, eyes to heaven. "We had not really walked all the way from Sempione! Impossible! Would we come in and drink coffee?" We thought not but we produced chocolate for the bambino and grandmamma ran lightly up a steep hill to get it. A little lower down we came to a tiny mountain restaurant, where the guests had to be regaled with our adventures, past, present and to come, Dorsaz showing us off in turn. I wish you had seen him guarding us. We thought of going by diligence from Domodossola to Pallanza as it was piping hot. Dorsaz decided that was too expensive and took us firmly 3rd class (I'd vowed I'd never travel 3rd in Italy again). The sight of him—mountain slouch, rope, ice-axe—leading us through the streets of a gay little lake town was something to remember. He went with us to the Islands, though he confessed it was only the 3rd time in his life he had ever been in a rowing boat and he regarded it as most dangerous. Coming back over still wilder passes his vigilance redoubled. When he heard that Lena had left her purse in her room at Veglia he just quietly locked the door and put the key in his pocket. We couldn't even get in to brush our hair. You notice one key locked us all out. It was a perfectly mad and fascinating inn 5 hours walk from the nearest road or railway. An

alp was covered with an amazing variety of extremely friendly
animals—cows, mules, donkeys, goats, dogs, cats, kittens, ducks
and hens (one hen would eat the corn in the mules' box and the
kitten sat on the edge and made nervous dabs at the hen's tail).
There was an aged goat who butted you the moment you left off
scratching his head. All round were wonderful snow peaks—a
great circle of mountains with just a cluster of huts in the middle.
. . . We had our meals in the kitchen with the guides (it was so
much nicer than the dining room which was fortunately full)—
and the cook—who had evidently been bathing for we met him
coming from the stream with dripping hair and whose age might
have been 18, came in and sat and chatted with the company after
he'd cooked a queer and most excellent dinner, and his father,
the host (who looked exactly like Mr. Pickwick) wandered in
and out and played with the babies and kittens and dogs, who
were all over the floor, and looked after us all with a grave benign
courtesy. It would be an ideal place to stay, but one would have to
speak Italian. Dorsaz and the key being found, he came upstairs
with us to look at our beds. I am quite certain he would have
changed them had he thought it necessary.

'Today we came back across a glacier, and had a fine thunderstorm on the way. It has been a wet day and I hope we may get
another fine spell when this is over.'

Festival occasions to attract a crowd of happy people giving
themselves up to the event of the hour were always of special
interest:

'Sept. 8, 1926. Saas Fee. Today has been a great Fest, one of the
prettiest sights I ever saw. Half-way down the hill lies a little
seventeenth century Chapel. It has a porch as big as itself, white-
washed with white pillars and the arches a pale yellow. Today the
pillars had garlands of green spruce and two little spruce trees
guarded the entrance. There was something Greek about it and
something very Swiss: one looked through the garlanded porch
to a hill-side of vivid green pine and above the Chapel hung the
glaciers gleaming in the sun, and the great snow fields above
again. On the little rocky platform outside were gathered
peasants from the whole valley: women in brilliant handkerchiefs
wearing elaborate gold head dresses, and aprons embroidered in
vivid greens, magentas and reds. Such of the congregation as
could not get near the Chapel were either grouped under a great

pine tree or perched on the rocks. We perched, and were interrupted by an avalanche of infant guides which descended on our
heads in the middle of service. After mass came a procession—the
priests in their vestments, acolytes in scarlet, a banner and two
girls in full peasant dress carrying a waxen image of the Virgin
and then a whole crowd of peasants—men—women and babies.'

Among the many celebrations of the national day on 1 August,
one half-way up the Furka (after a walk by the Lukmanier and St.
Gotthard Passes) is vividly recorded. A thick dry mist had fallen,
but local celebrations were not interrupted: 'Somewhere apparently in the sky—no mountain visible—a huge bonfire leaped into
flame and across it darted little black figures—obviously devils.
Rockets hissed from all sides, scattering fiery serpents, at one
moment a red Bengal light below turned the driving mist blood
red and the place looked like Hell. When the fog was at its
thickest motors appeared. Can you fancy driving up and down
the curves in a dense fog with a precipice one side of you and
often no kind of rail or fence? The whole thing was more than
weird.'

The grim valley of Andorra, with its steep mountain sides and
its strange clash between age-old customs and the modern motor-
road, stands out too as satisfying many instincts: whilst cafés and
'loud speakers (the curse of Spain)' were springing up along the
road, the side valleys remained primitive. From seeing vultures
rise suddenly above dead sheep among deserted rocks in a valley
of stone you might step out upon the road and see a smart yellow
motor filled with fashionable ladies glide by.

'Sept. 1, 1934. Lena and I had a wonderful 10½ hours walk
yesterday. We got right into the mountains where I imagine
life has been unchanged for centuries. The houses are piles of
stones: the Churches are built without mortar and the ornament
is as rough hewn as possible. We went into one tiny Church and
found a painting of the Virgin and Child in wood, which looked
as if it might have been C 13 or early C 14. Once past the village
the tracks are almost impossible to find: either they disappear
altogether or they get confused with wood cutters' paths or cow
tracks. We reached our objective all right, a pass into Spain
about 7,000 feet up, with a magnificent view, but when we tried
to follow the track which the map said led round the other side it
took us neatly through a pine wood to the edge of a cliff and then

stopped. After some discussion we decided to go back part of the way we had come and then take a track home, a short cut. We lost that first track at once and for ever. I don't know what happened to it, but we found ourselves scrambling over shale slopes and down water-courses through the pines. The worst of pines is that you can see nothing through them and you so easily lose your sense of direction. Eventually we came out not far from our short cut, but it was then 5.30 and darkness falls early and quickly here, so when we realized that it apparently led over a large mountain densely covered with forest, we decided we had had enough of pines, and we started a race back along the mule track by which we had come, hoping to reach the main road before dark. We just exactly did it, and then we had a really lovely hour's walk along the road in the starlight—the mountains which one seldom sees so late, first a wonderful series of greys, with a little white leaping torrent below, and then closing in black against the night sky. The road passes through two or three tunnels—most effective in the dark.

'The minute you are off the road you are almost in the Stone Age. The houses are just piles of stones, the hay forks are all of wood, just branches split into prongs: the hinges of the doors are of wood. No wonder the French name is Les Vallées d'Andorre.

'The population lives entirely in the narrowest valleys I ever saw. Mountains rise sheer and between them, very deep down, run brawling, foaming streams and beside each stream a primitive mule track mostly of loose stones. These wind from one valley to another. We met some young Englishmen who told us they had walked some 30 miles without finding a place where they could get any food at all. Occasionally you see one of these rough stone huts on the mountain side and can watch the peasant struggling to wrest a tiny crop from the rock. Ten houses makes a large village and I mean it when I say the Capital City is about the size of Cerney Wick: it is far smaller than Cerney.

'The people talk Catalan and are very friendly.'

However, it was in 1928, when she was expecting to hear whether or not she would be invited to become Principal of the O.H.S., that she had her most memorable holiday—an adventurous one in Albania during two months' leave. That journey also began and ended in Switzerland: a trip to show her eldest niece the Italian lakes led us on to the Engadine, and it fostered a sense of enchantment that makes itself felt every now and then in her letters and in the holiday diary which she wrote in co-operation with her companions: 'Yesterday we had a stroke of luck: we stopped to admire the flowers round a very beautiful old cottage —English flowers, sweet peas, pansies, all sorts of unexpected things crowding round it. As we talked a head appeared at the window and a voice said: "You are the first English people I have spoken to." We chatted a little and went on, but we swore to ourselves we'd see the inside of that house before we left: and we pulled it off today. It is pure fairy story. "Is it very old?" said I to the benevolent witch who lives there. "They say it is about 800 years old," she said—and it looked any age. There were old beams of that wonderful glowing brown Swiss houses turn, there were chairs of bare wood dated 1696. Little dark rooms had bowls of flowers in every corner. We went upstairs and down-stairs and into the kitchen—and we wonder if it will be there tomorrow. It is a good thing we caught it today.'

The walk on leaving the Engadine across a pass was made in an 'unbroken series of thunderstorms, rain, sleet, hail and snow; the porter fearing we should act as lightning conductors insisted on our climbing the steeper portions of the way with cold wet ice-axes clasped to our breasts under our coats. Quite beastly.' At Dissentis the party broke up, the niece and I travelled homewards while she herself and M. G. Skipworth, having got into training, had some climbs which were characterized by horrible weather 'in-congruous with human pygmies absorbed in their little concerns.' On the Petersgrat they just missed being a rescue party, when the guides of some Swiss climbers who came down from the Lauter-brunnen Breithorn behind them had to turn aside to 'fish a girl out of a crevasse': 'We wish we'd the fun of seeing how it is done'; next a Swiss Professor attached himself to their party who was of 'deadly geniality and would keep bursting into song', and when as the weather worsened 'we had to keep together to lessen the danger from falling stones, the singing Professor came too. The one consolation when it got very steep was that he couldn't sing. Everything you stepped on gave way instantly; everything you held on to at once dropped on the person below. Wet dripped over everything, oozed out of everything.' After two hours' steady climb to the top of the Schafberg the real climb up the Bietschhorn had to be abandoned. 'Here we sat on wet rock looking at a little hump of dirty snow, four guides with lanterns standing in the snow, and the Swiss singing like Christmas waits. Our two guides covered us up with knapsacks to keep out the wet and there we waited till it was obvious that it was hopeless, when we slid and bumped back to the hut for a hasty meal and then came down to the Hotel.' That 'day of rest' was followed by the climb up the Finsteraarhorn on 28 July 1928, when snow and hail blew violently and they were coated with ice from head to foot, and the wind was so strong that one could only just stand in places and waiting became 'a misery of cold'; one guide could not hear what the other said, one of them kept on making wrong shots for the way: 'He crawled a little way down the ice-slope, cut himself a big step and then lay spread eagled on his face on the ice and held his ice-axe up towards M. G. S. apparently inviting her to walk on it. Yells from an outraged Bumann. The invitation was declined.' This same guide 'got very excited' over a fragment of rope that he found near the bottom of the last slope, recognizing it as the relic of an accident when he had had a bad fall twenty years ago and saying he recognized it because it had a red thread in the middle. Bumann seemed a little sceptical, but the other remained highly pleased. So by further climbs and scrambles, across faces of sheer cliff, by huge Bergschrunds, and a premeditated fall over the edge of a cliff to the 'detestable Grimsel' where the whole valley was full of 'trains, cranes, and noise and smoke' because a huge dam was being built. 'After all the thrills it was annoying to be told that there had been only one dangerous place all day and that was a perfectly easy jump when M. G. S. followed too closely on the ponderous heels of G. E. H., neither of them realizing that they were jumping not on to solid ice but on the curve of snow over a crevasse.'

And so they were keyed up for future experiences, in strong contrast to snow and mist; by 2 September they were in Venice. 'Today we dropped in for a most amazing Regatta. The Grand Canal was gay with flags and tapestries and hangings: wonderful scarlet and green and gold gondolas manned by crews in 16th century costume processed up and down, a cheerful crowd thronged the Canal; private gondoliers resplendent in white duck with broad crimson sashes manœuvred boats of black and gold. All that was pure Gilbert and Sullivan. The actual race or races (we have still no idea if there was one race or many) was pure

Alice in the Looking Glass. Most of the crews rowed standing, but a few sitting: all—except the crews of two, who wore gondolier dress—were clad in brilliant uniform bathing dresses—crimson, blue, mauve: the members of the crews ranged from 18 to 2—and apparently all raced against all. Some of the crews really put their backs into it and seemed to think they were racing somebody (we never discovered whom), others paused to chat with the spectators as they passed. Very many of the rowing boats carried very stout passengers, presumably as ballast. The 12 to 18 oar boats—all rowed standing—were a most impressive sight. After the crews came a jostling crowd of gondoliers, shouting and pushing—family parties, each of whom had brought his or her chair; small boys by the dozen in any old tub. You couldn't see the water. One thing puzzled us at first. As we took our places beside the bank we saw what appeared to be street watering going on—a large hose playing freely on the Canal. To water the streets of Venice seemed a work of supererogation. Then we found that this was the Venetian method of keeping the course clear—the local fire-brigade plays on the general public with the fire hose. It is most effective.'

Leaving Venice they took boat at Trieste for Split and steamed 'over a blue sea past a queer rocky barren coast. The boat was so full that we slept in the linen cupboard. As its only ventilation—except for a few holes in the wall, such as you bore for caterpillars—was the door and this opened direct on to the companion way, we dressed and undressed in leaps behind a skimpy curtain which cut us off in midleg. The chief result was that we got up at 4.30 a.m. and saw the sun rise over the mountains.' They had learnt a little Serbian before starting, and though German, English, or French carried the travellers some way they were soon trying themselves in Serbian or Croatian, and found their dictionary a great resource both for entertaining inhabitants who enjoyed crowding round to read it, and for satisfying their own curiosity and making their wants understood. Split, which seemed to consist of old churches and houses grafted on to Diocletian's palace, had good bathing: 'Our language excitement was at its highest,' reports M. G. S. 'In the sea when a lady said to us in Croatian "lovely sea", when she had said it twice we grasped the situation —"Lepo more" we agreed.' 'Two things struck us specially,' adds Grace Hadow, (1) 'We came here armed with every possible device against dirt and insects and never have been so painfully and compulsorily clean. It began with our being washed down with the decks this morning, and has gone on through the washing-swilling of our bathing box with us in it, to the constant flooding of the streets. (2) There are more policemen to the square inch than one would have thought possible. Tonight we discovered why. After dinner the entire population gathered on the sea front. At intervals an excited gentleman has been shouting "Dalmatia" and at once a crowd surged round. Then the police stood in a row and leaned against them. We hoped it was a revolution, but so far we have only seen three little boys being chased by a very lovely policeman complete with sword and revolver.'

A drive by the Seven Castles to Trogir and Solan took them along roads 'bordered with hedges of pomegranate behind which lie olive yards and vineyards and on the one side a brilliant dark blue sea with the softest purple mountains beyond and on the other the queer barren rock of these parts, which goes pink and yellow and always looks unreal and almost transparent. Large spike aloes shot claws at us and the dust was feet deep, when you meet another car the only thing to do is to shut your eyes tight and not open them again until you cease to taste the dust. Trogir is an amazing little country town—barely more than a village—quite interesting and unspoiled and full of what appear to be magnificent Venetian Palaces. The winged lion is everywhere and the place resounded with a sharp crackling sound made by the women and children shelling almonds. Solan is what remains—and it is a good deal—of a large Roman city: houses, amphitheatre, burial place. There is a tiny museum, in which is preserved, among other things, the oldest book in Spalato, an English work of the 18th century written by a British architect on Spalato and the Palace of Diocletian.' For the rest Ragusa brought cheering crowds, soldiers in brown and red uniforms and, alas! a rival band dressed in red shirts, also many lovely peasant dresses, and pleasant lazy days for the travellers. A day at Mostar found them photographing the impressive single arch of its stone bridge, the clustering houses seen through it in the distance, and a group of horses in the foreground—a most successful picture.

'Mostar itself proved the most charming little town built on either side of the river—all rocks and green river and minarets. A large part of the population is Moslem, and you constantly meet

MOSTAR

ON HOLIDAY IN SWITZERLAND, 1928

terrifying veiled women: either they wear shapeless bundles of blue check and have black faces, or else—worse still—they wear long flowing black garments ending in a peak like a huge beak and under this is a straight black veil. Horrid—and must be frightfully hot. I tried to walk into one lady's private courtyard (it had a lovely covered well) and the glare I got through the veil was scorching.

'Much to our surprise we were invited into a Mosque—a very fine building (3rd century Moslem) painted in the most vivid reds and blues and with wonderful red carpets. On one side a little staircase ran up to nothing and ended in a tiny steeple. There was no furniture at all except one little modern looking bench with its face to the wall.

'A nice hotel told us proudly that it had water all day long, and the best bath outside Vienna.

'We were jolted and banged back and arrived home much shattered to be revived by a warm swim in the dark.'

A wonderful drive up a mountain side by numerous hairpin bends took them through Cattaro to Cetinje:

'We arranged to motor to Cetinje and our driver arranged that we should share the car with a Montenegrin officer and his wife. The entire quay helped and discussed and we so grossly overpaid the porter who took our luggage to the Hotel and brought it away again that he wandered round and round the motor in which we sat patiently waiting for the others, murmuring in mixed Croatian, German and Italian how much he hoped to see us again. Mixed languages are common. It was the porter at Ragusa who cried: "Ecco Schiff" as our boat appeared.

'The chauffeur, who spoke excellent French, insisted on M. G. S. sitting next to him. I was handed over to Mr. and Mrs. Officer. Mrs. Officer at first extremely cross. She thawed later and informed me that the mountains we hope to walk in are called "the damned mountains" partly on account of their natural features, partly owing to the character of their inhabitants. She also said bears and wolves were common in her part of the country. We feel very far from home and not less so when we find Cetinje full of charming people walking the streets with revolvers stuck in beautiful scarlet and orange sashes.'

Their plan was to walk across the mountains to Scutari and for this purpose to engage a local guide.

14 Sept. 1928. 'We seem to have spent most of the day with the police. The entire town is thrilled at the thought of two lunatic Englishwomen setting out to walk to Scutari. I was sitting quietly outside the Hotel this morning when a strange man leaped out of a motor car and without any preliminary rushed up to me and said: "It's 150 kilometres to Scutari—you can't possibly walk there. . . ." The Hotel keeper (who has the most villainous face we ever saw) warmly recommends a guide, one Dushan Gagović, a splendid swaggering ruffian, who assured us he had hunted brigands for years in the mountains, knew every path and could find us food for nothing everywhere. Later we met our schoolboy (a friend of the day before) who on hearing we were going with Dushan warmly advised us to motor. The chauffeur told us that Dushan was as brave as a lion. "He would think nothing of tackling four men" but "He drinks, he drinks". The police just plainly told us not to go with him; he was a marked man at the frontier and could not go into Albania. They recommended us a quiet little man, and the whole evening he and Dushan have been struggling for possession of us, Dushan coming back quite shamelessly at intervals to tell us that now it was all right, he had his papers—when we would again go round to the police and find this was a pure fairy story. The hotel sides with Dushan, having recommended him, and we feel rather in disgrace. It would certainly have been amusing to travel with him, but probably our way would have been enlivened by his readiness to tackle four at once. Vido Janović seems gentle, but also has the national passion for telling us what a fine fellow he is. The chauffeur says that any Montenegrin would die for us when once we were under his protection—but we don't want him to.'

The struggle for the possession of the travellers was continued; however, the keyword in French from an official at the passport office, 'il but, il but', settled it. The burly ruffian's dramatic gesture pointing at the rather weak-looking little man—his rival—'which will you have' was answered by the verdict of the police who would not allow them to go into Albania with so notorious a character. His last appearance was with a revolver to shake hands and say he expected picture postcards from them, to which they agreed.

They drove to Podgorica, and then started on foot with their guide, sometimes walking on a first-class motor-road, sometimes by broken paths towards the mountain pass from which there was a wonderful view of colours and lines of mountains with the lake of Scutari in the distance. Their guide regaled them with blood-curdling tales of the feuds between Serbs and Albanians, so that it seemed natural to find lying by the road a handsome revolver. As it got dark they reached Lijeva Ryeka and waited long for the preparation of their supper, which after being described as a mysterious dish needing careful preparation turned out to be tinned sardines, with hard eggs, burnt milk, sour brown bread, and cheese. The hotel was a primitive house of one story, with one room where the village met, drank, and sang, another for the family, and a third with three beds for the travellers and the guide. 'We opened the window. This so upset Vido that he went to fetch the host, who is also Burgomaster, and I shall never forget seeing this huge Montenegrin standing over M. G. S. as she lay in bed and shutting her window. We opened it again when he went, Vido groaning loudly.' The next day they met the lady of one of the previous inns, who by now felt herself to be a friend, pressing grapes on them with affectionate gestures. 'The picture of M. G. S. walking along the high road accompanied by two pack horses and two donkeys and with a dear old witch in black affectionately clasping her round the waist and murmuring "I love you. I love you" is one never to be forgotten. Nor will it be easy to forget her face when Vido, in a burst of enthusiasm today, told us he loved us like sisters. The whole journey is queerly medieval. The houses are of one storey, two rooms (one used for farm produce), no chimney, a fire in the middle of the floor; hardly any furniture. The people match. We have seen forest fire after forest fire today. "How do these fires start?" we asked. "You live next me and don't like me", returned Vido calmly, "You set fire to my wood." And a budding pope whom we picked up on the way told us that two days ago two Montenegrins had their throats cut by Albanians on the frontier. The Montenegrins have succeeded in cutting one Albanian throat in return and are looking for another. We begin to wonder if Vido regrets having left behind his real knife which weighs 2 kilo. His comment on the story is "They have no Kultur"—but he did not make clear which. What he really loves is showing us off like dancing bears at every village pub and each time the tale of M. G. S.'s appetite grows: "You walk and eat like a soldier."

'Grand Hotel, Kolasin. We got in about 5 to find the usual unspeakably dirty dining-room-bar-sitting-room, and a quite clean bedroom. The nice chambermaid is much interested in our sponges: "Do you use those to wash your faces?" Usually a request for water produces a tin basin and a kind lady with a tumbler of water which she offers to pour over our hands. We dined with the élite of Kolasin—including the Bank Manager—gathered round the bar singing patriotic songs. We thanked heaven they had not a Gurlo—they had at Lijeva Ryeka. It is the most dismal instrument on earth and you sing the same three notes to it for hours on end. Dinner presented difficulties. Our host, who speaks a little German, kept smiling and offering us "gehen"; we could not make it out. Finally, with shouts of laughter, he took us—accompanied by the entire household—into the kitchen to see what was being cooked, and none the wiser, we said "Dobro, dobro". As we were eating, he ran up to us with a cookery book and pointing to the head of a revolting-looking anatomical specimen said: "That's it! Not a man's course" and "Gehirn" flashed into our slow minds.'

Their journey back took them along 'a queerly Eastern road, dusty and sunbaked, with mountains on one side and the river below, and all the way we met trains of packhorses and mules and flocks of sheep, mountain women in blues and greens and riding astride high pack saddles, Albanians in long baggy white trousers braided with black and odd white skull caps.' Attempts to bathe could only be made in streams or rivers, and in this inhabitants took an undisguised interest, so on the occasion when a 'plump smiling person of 18 whose bare feet flashed down the river bank waved us to a wide pool in full view of several houses and a bye road and thinly sheltered trees from the main road. "Wasn't it a little public?" we asked delicately. She explained—so we gathered —that everyone was away at the market and we were quite safe. After that she sat down and watched our every movement with laughter and delight. When M. G. S. swam a few strokes, it was a climax of joy.' On another occasion a 'delightful little bare-legged chambermaid and her brother' responded to their request for hot water by voluble Croatian and dumbshow indicating did they want a bath. When she entered in triumph with a pig trough, newly scrubbed: 'a lovely bath, though a thought narrow', they had to keep on saying 'Laku Noc' before at least they could get rid of them. 'The Montenegrins are charming people but we wish they showed less fondness for collecting in our bedrooms.' Equally they peered into the windows and crowded round them: two Englishwomen, so oddly dressed, with such big boots and carrying a pack and walking so far were indeed a sensation. And the guide made the most of it. Timid by nature, he disliked exerting himself: 'Our young man begins to wilt. He is torn between intense pride in this amazing enterprise of ours—we believe the number of kilometres we have walked and the size of M. G. S.'s appetite grow at every halt—and hatred of walking. He is stiff and alternately murmurs at the pace we go and boasts of it. We wonder how long he will last out.' They hired a pony for a while and let him ride it; after about two hours' walk he'd complain: 'when soldier, must walk, but rest 10 minutes anyhow. You always quickly.' At Byelo Polye, the most Turkish-looking place they had seen as yet, matters came to a head; after he had been in search of information he declared the Albanians did not understand passports, only knives, and it was impossible to go over the frontier. It was very tiresome as their plans were altogether upset by not going into Albania that way, but it seemed equally impossible to ask him to risk his throat. To make up Vido suggested alternatives. He arranged they were to go with their host and his family to a local fair where there would be no buying and selling but only singing, dancing, drinking, and where they should take their bed.

Meanwhile, at 6 p.m. at Byelo Polye they went to hear the Call to Prayer from one of the Mosques. 'A dear old Turk came to explain it to us and then invited us in to what Vido calls "türkische Messe". It was extraordinarily simple and beautiful and dignified —a little white-washed Mosque with wonderful red carpets, dusk gathering, the only artificial light 5 big candles set on a ledge near the floor and lighting a niche in which sat a figure straight out of the Arabian Nights—turban, long beard, flowing robes; and in the dusk half a dozen worshippers listening to a monotonous chant, or squatting in silence, swaying from time to time and beating their foreheads on the floor.'

The fair turned out to be 'the most incredible day and night of our experience'. To begin with the police force visited them in a body to say that they would be under their special protection. 'The Commandant—slightly drunk at 11 a.m.—accompanied by a lady whom Vido declares to be of "die letzte Qualität" sat at our table preventing us from having lunch and assuring M. G. S. he loved her as a brother (we are collecting rather too many brothers). He then asked us to dine with him on our return. ("Say Dobro" said the lady "and never mind about it") and finally he ordered a stout and beautiful policeman with gold epaulettes and gold teeth to conduct us to the fair. Vido was furious—having arranged that we should go with the family. It is very trying to be a bone of contention but seems inevitable in Montenegro.'

They did go with the family and in the hope of not offending the police; and they found themselves joining a remarkable trek. 'A wooden car carried food, large quantities of "schnapps", a bedstead and bedding for G. E. H. and me, chairs, table and many other useful things. We joined many other similar processions along the road and after about 2½ hours' walk arrived at the fair which was held in the churchyard of an old wee ruined church (destroyed as everyone told us by the Turks). There was no village at all, only two Turkish farms stood above the church. When we started we had not been very clear what we were attending. Vido called it a market and said alternately that nothing was sold and that everything was. When we heard mass in the church the "fair" seemed to be a religious festival, when we listened to the drum and pipes and heard the shouting (I won't call it singing) it seemed to be a pagan revel, and in the distance it looked like a witches Sabbath combined with the feast of Tabernacles. The tiny church—roofless and with what looked like a pagan altar— stands on a hill-top and the open churchyard lies on the slope of the hill with the river far below. It was raining and all along one side people had built booths of green branches. Each family had its little booth, spread with red carpet, and opposite its wood fire flamed; in the hot ashes the inevitable coffee-pot heating Turkish coffee; over the fire pots hanging to cook the evening supper. Some families camped under trees swinging the baby neatly from two branches. Everywhere groups squatted round the fires; packhorses grazed; and below we saw the procession fording the river, the packhorses gay with red Serbian carpets to spread on the ground. Ours was the only bedstead (complete with embroidered sheets and a pink and blue eiderdown!) and it stood in lonely grandeur under a pear tree with branches built into a roof over us. As dusk fell there was Service in the ruin. The walls stuck with tiny votive candles and before the altar a board covered with coffee cups full of oil in which floated burning wicks. The old "pope" wore beautiful robes and the little church was packed, but outside no one paid the least attention : a drum banged (it banged from 6 p.m. till 4.30 a.m. without stopping), people uttered their piercing dismal wail which constitutes Montenegrin singing, and there was all the bustling of camping. We had the usual triumphal procession. Here we were led into one booth to sit on a red carpet (in most inappropriate mountain boots) and drink fiery liqueur and eat (in our fingers) salt dried meat : there we had cups of black coffee. Back at our own booth two forks were thrust upon us and upon the end of each a small black ball, which we swallowed grimly and found not bad. We ate mince-meat, pastry (very good), and cheese in pastry (very nasty), and drank endless coffee. We never knew when we were having a meal and when being polite to strangers. At intervals we escaped to walk round the camp and watch the fires and always we found the police keeping an anxious eye on us. My last sound as I fell asleep was M. G. S.'s voice in a tone of ecstasy "How nice to have one's bedroom full of horsey faces." Packhorses were tethered just behind us and the cheese was under our bed' (G. E. H.). 'It seemed quite natural to wake up from one of the two short sleeps possible in the din and to hear people shouting "patrol, patrol" and to see the armed police surging round our bed. There was a good deal of angry shouting and a big man was hustled out of the field by the police. We heard later that the row was the usual one of a new Montenegrin calling an "old" Montenegrin a swine or else the "old" Montenegrin was the offender' (M. G. S.). 'M. G. S. was bitterly disappointed that there was no shooting. Personally I found the sight of bayonets flashing round my bed quite sufficient. Our little watch dog gallantly rushed up to keep guard, shoved away several children and begged us not to be frightened. We weren't. He and our host slept at the foot of our bed—most mediaeval' (G. E. H.). 'We were glad after a night of drums and shouting to get up at 4.30 and to go off with the host and daughter and her friends to wash in the river, the daughter first taking her best dress from under our mattress' (M. G. S.). There was the usual intense interest in these strange Englishwomen : their clothes, which were investigated and unbuttoned by an old lady, so as to be sure what all of them were like; little boys stepped between Grace

Hadow's camera and the people whom she really meant to photograph and rushed between grown-ups' legs while everyone shoved and pushed to get a good place.

'The dancing was much more interesting in the morning than it had been the night before. A drum and two pipes made the music and at intervals led a Pied Piper procession in and out of the fires and the fruit stalls. Best of all was a wild dance of springs and leaps with arms flung over the head. One man and one woman danced at a time and as soon as a new man or woman began to dance the one already dancing dropped out. At intervals the men uttered wild yells. I thought it funny to see an umbrella clasped tightly in one hand by a leaping figure, but M. G. S. said they looked as if they ought to have a weapon of some kind—though she agreed a sword would have been better. There were lots of beautiful peasant dresses today and one beautiful group of gipsies.

'We came back on the other side of the river past the tomb of what Vido called "ein türkischer Bischof". It was in a fair-sized building with a door and on the grave lay a candle and two towels. A small peasant boy whom we met told us that every night the "Bishop" washed his hands and the towels were for him to dry them on.' The return from the fair was marked by feasting: 'we were given spoonfuls of jam, a glass of cognac, some cake, black coffee and some grapes at the house of the Director of the Gymnasium, each served us as a separate course; we had a banquet in Vido's bedroom with the Director and all the intelligentzia of the town. Vido's bedroom was filled by a trestle table groaning under dishes of fat pork, a horrible salad of raw tomato and very strong raw onion, black bread, sour cheese, and wine. Every time they felt friendly they heaped more pork on our plates. The feast at the Commandant's half an hour later at 8 p.m. was an exact repetition.' The Commandant whom they had disliked 'in his drunk and grimy condition the day before was very clean and proper in his own house. The lady of the letzte Qualität was most amusing, sang some beautiful Serbian songs and fed us with meat and much coffee. They offered us pork to take away. We stepped out of his house at 9.30 into some armed police, who evidently thought we were suspiciously late revellers. Both the lady and the President of Byelo Polye besought us to send them picture postcards from Oxford. Everybody hopes we are writing for the papers and begs us to say how well the country is getting on.'

Vido's timidity or lack of enterprise had disappointed them of
their mountain walk; however, he was given his reference un-
grudgingly: 'We wrote a testimonial for Vido, M. G. S. struggling
between exasperation with his old-maidishness and an inability to
express herself otherwise than charmingly in French. He really
did do his best for us—only he hates walking. He is now going
to fill the Cetinji paper with tales of his prowess and will be
happy.'

His fears were probably groundless, and their contention that
two women travelling as they did would be no target is likeliest
to have been correct.

'We have solved the problem of the isolated graves we so often
see on the hill side. When a man is shot he is buried where he
falls. Vido—we think to save his face—brought us in cheerful
stories of travellers recently robbed and stripped in the Accursed
Mountains. Other people tell us we should be quite safe. Anyhow it is now too late to try even if we could make Vido risk his
throat and we should have missed the fair if we had gone on.'
They returned back to a point where they could get a Montenegrin driver and a car to Scutari, through groves of wild pome-
granates and over miles of marsh where white cranes were fishing.
'At one point the military told us we must get out and walk over
the next bridge—one about 200 yards long over the marsh. It is,
said our driver, "peu solide", the wood being quite rotten and full
of large holes. We are used to leaping planks by this time, but
there were not always planks left to leap here. Later we came to
a place where we had to avoid the bridge altogether and drive
along the marsh till we could get over the river bed.' 'It has been
interesting: yesterday we saw exactly what the old passes must
have been like in Switzerland before there were roads: today we
have had the beginning of roads, hairpin bends, a wild surface,
often no room to pass anything and bridges of the sketchiest.
There are good drivers in these parts.'

In Scutari they found a fellow-countryman in charge of British
police through whom a further walk mountainwards and in
Albania itself became possible. Here they were addressed as
'sister' by an ex-patient of the Scottish Women's Hospital unit
in Serbia, and they came across traces of the Kralitze, Edith
Durham, through whom Englishwomen had won the confidence
of many Albanians, that race to whose courage and honesty

H. W. Nevinson has also testified. 'Major P.s' own house (in
Scutari) is typified in that it has a concealed spy hole from which
the owner can shoot anyone who comes to the garden gate before
he can get in. And yet, in this amazing country it is quite safe
for two women—ignorant of the language—to go alone up into
the hill tribes, and a very considerable percentage of people walk
about hung with gold and silver chains and coins.'

Their Montenegrin chauffeur and guide, however, found himself almost a prisoner in Albania where—being a Montenegrin—
he was not to be allowed to go about without the foreigners whom
he had brought. During expeditions with him there was another
interlude through which the undercurrents of frontier disputes
were seen. 'We were stopped by custom-officials outside a tiny
cluster of houses. They made endless fuss over passports and
luggage to the great interest of groups of veiled women on their
way back from market. Presently a very excited and beautiful
gentleman came up and at once held forth to Ticie while we
admired the 3 fancy handkerchiefs, pink silk and silver tied round
his waist, green and blue hanging out of one pocket and brown
silk out of the other. "What is he saying?" we asked at last.
Ticie gave one of his patient shrugs: "Ils ont manqué de nous tuer
là-bas," he said. Somewhat startled we enquired why anyone
wanted to "tuer" such harmless folk and it turned out we had
passed without seeing one of the outposts on the frontier. However everybody forgave us in the end.

'It threw a certain light on things later when we saw a shepherd
guarding his flock with his rifle slung on his back.'

The lack of language was a puzzlement to them in Albania—
for German carried no farther than just along the coastline where
Austrians visited, and French the same; they had made some
efforts to get up sufficient Serbian to get about, but Albanian—as
peculiar and isolated a language as Basque—was more than could
be managed in the time even if it had been easier to procure
Albanian grammars.

A visit to Padua and its Giottos and Mantegnas on the way
homewards led once more to Switzerland, where it proved possible
on 3 October to get a late climb up the Balmhorn (12,370 feet) and
this time to see 'the whole of Switzerland, and all white with fresh
snow standing out sharply against an intensely blue sky, everything being extraordinarily clear cut and the "Evening Glow" of

the night before deserving capitals'. It was a glorious climax to a wholly satisfying holiday.

Grace Hadow possessed great inward vivacity, and it was her way to experience her holidays as a romance that was lived indeed. European sightseeing she had undertaken in earlier years with her brother, with whom she had travelled in Italy, Greece, Austria, France, apart from the stay in Germany. In later years she rarely chose a holiday of that sort and in cities, though there was a short one at Bruges among Memlings and canals and spring-flowering trees in 1934, in which a walk to the mole recalled great things. To be with her on historic occasions was most interesting; the funeral of King Edward VII, the coronations of King George V and the present King or, earlier, the Women's Suffrage procession and the big meeting in the Queen's Hall, when 'Jerusalem', then recently composed, was sung for the first time on a public occasion after the suffrage had been gained.[1] Processions, markets, fairs, proclamations attracted Grace irresistibly; her observation and perceptions were acute, and she loved being present at the conscious making of history. To experience greatness and see by the side of it how ordinary people continue ordinary life unperturbed gave her the satisfaction of a true humorist, to whom the contrast is notable in itself. Holidays in England were necessarily tame compared to those abroad, but she missed no opportunity that she could take of experiencing remarkable events. The eclipse of the sun in June 1927 was one of those, and the account she wrote at the time conveys the scene of something marvellous flashing down upon the common-place world:

29 June 1927.

Settle by Giggleswick   (from Sheffield)

'Lena and I set out at 9 p.m. with two thermos flasks, lots of sandwiches, a tin of admirable biscuits which McVitie and Price thoughtfully sent as an advertisement just in the nick of time and all the wraps belonging to anybody we could lay hands on. At the last moment a kind Providence directed our plans, and so disregarding a nicely marked route to Richmond we took a map and a flash light and started for Settle. Lena drove during daylight through Barnsley where she put me into the driver's seat and we rushed through sleeping towns and over tram rails, by Wakefield,

---

[1] Cf. Chapter VII, p. 86.

Bradford, and Keighley where "reliable" people on bicycles (we felt them so, for who rides a mile or two in vain when tredelling) were plodding on the road and a few other cars joined us, till we grew into the Eclipse Pilgrimage: it came in motor cars, bicycles, or push bicycles and on foot along the country road, the entire male population out to explore.

'It was a very queer sight in the dark of a summer night to see this little hill-side village filling up to the brim and nice kindly burly Yorkshire police nursery-maiding us all. We found "Observation Field" about a mile away, a friendly sergeant assuring us that there "You'll be in a line with the Astronomer Royal!" but refusing to hold out any hopes that the Astronomer Royal would see anything. We got back to "Prudence"[1] about 2.45, and settled down to try sleep—but that was impossible: fresh cars arrived every minute; picnic parties were in full swing, when passenger trains were not hurling thousands more passengers at our very feet, goods trains clanked up and down. At 4 a.m. we gave it up, drank more (slightly more tepid) coffee and went back to the Observation Field. Here we climbed up a very unstable quite black wall and there we two potential grandmothers sat dangling aged legs for the next two hours or so. Eastwards lay a thick black cloud, and the whole west—from which a strong wind blew steadily—lay wrapped in thick mist and unbroken grey. It looked quite hopeless. At 4.37 a faint, watery light behind the cloud showed that the sun was there all right (and we noted and admired the tents of light shed down on the shoulder of the green hill opposite us). But more and thicker cloud kept drifting up. There followed the most exciting hour I ever spent—a race between sun and cloud. Far overhead was a big patch of blue sky: if the sun could reach it by 6.24 all would be well: if not, we should see nothing. At 6.10 it was still well hidden. (We had seen gleams of the sun, it had appeared in a crescent of gold and then mass-like in white seen through a cloud.) Suddenly at the last moment, the sun shot up, and was absolutely clear for 28 seconds of totality. There are no words to describe that. A great black ball hangs by a jewel which flashes blue and red like a diamond, a rim of light circles it, and all round burns a great flickering halo of soft brilliant fire. It is like nothing I dreamt of. (Indeed there are no words. It came as a sudden revelation quite unlike any-

[1] The car.

thing we had expected—there it flashed out in silver moonlight
sky—a jewel quivering and speaking and beautiful in its great
rim encircling blue and black.) We as mere seekers of the picturesque were specially lucky because the hour before, when the sun
played hide and seek with the clouds was wonderful. The sun
would be hidden, then all at once gigantic black rays would come
rushing across the sky: in a moment rays of light intermingled.
Then you'd get a sort of molten brass of dark and light. At
another moment some clouds would be edged with brilliant gold
and others simultaneously with the silver of full moonlight.
Once the sun shone through cloud exactly the colour and shape of
the crescent moon only about five times as large. Now and then
we saw the eclipse in process, just for a minute or two. And as the
total eclipse came, the whole sky went a sort of moon-lit white
and grey. We saw the passing of the shadow clearly all the time,
and it was full compared with the cloud effect of the coming, to say
nothing of the tension of suspense.

'(As the sun appeared clearly, the small boys in the Observation
Field clapped and cheered. But when the Corona appeared, all
was silence; the fading of the light, the uncanny grey and the
mysterious shadows were wonderful.)

'After it was all over Lena and I went back to our car and at
length succeeded in getting it out. Then we fled to the wildest
part of the nearest moor and drove 15 miles over quite impossible
roads, all boulders and huge and very sharp stones. Why we
neither broke a spring nor punctured heaven knows. It was very
lovely but as a rest-cure after a sleepless night not a complete
success (only we didn't in the least want to sleep) and then we
drove miles and miles and miles through quite hideous towns and
along tramlines—and all the time I kept seeing the sun.'[1]

[1] 'The drive back to Clithero was by Burn Moor, a lovely moorland pass. How
local the clear view of the eclipse was we realized when, before reaching the moor,
we picked up a woman for a lift. She had been on the green hillside which we saw
just opposite us, while we were on the wall, and she had seen nothing but grey
clouds.'

CHAPTER XII

WOMEN'S INSTITUTES
1916–1940

WOMEN'S Institutes claimed Grace Hadow for their own and with justice, for she identified herself with the movement till it became part of her. Was she, as has been said, 'its mainspring'? She herself would have been the first to repudiate that description as a misreading of the movement itself, as well as of her share. For her part—if she thought in such terms at all—she felt indebted to others. Breathing life into its members she found life in return. In things of the spirit there is no measure of giving and receiving, and the Institute spirit at its best was hers. In fact her relation to Women's Institutes may be described as organic, for it grew with the movement's development and with her own.

When she came to London in the spring of 1917 to work at the Ministry of Munitions she may well have found refreshment of mind in continuing to keep in touch with rural matters and with people interested in them. She had helped to start Institutes in Gloucestershire through her work for the War Agricultural Committee and was President of her own Cirencester Institute. By October 1917 she took a personal part in the historical decision by which the movement became self-governing: at the first meeting in London of representatives of the 137 Institutes then in existence she moved the resolution by which the 'Central Committee of the Women's Institutes' came into being—the forerunner of the Executive Committee of the National Federation —and shortly after, on 18 October, she attended its first meeting as one of ten representatives of Institutes and on 13 February 1918 she was made its Vice-Chairman. At her first committee meeting she had been appointed with a senior member 'to deal with all matters relating to the press and with Women's Institute literature generally'. Soon she was associated with plans for the future organization of the movement. And so she became one of those who were closely concerned with framing the constitution of Women's Institutes, a task which, in its progress, was fructified by experience in the suffrage movement both on her part and the part of others.

The higher politics of the movement in its earliest stages are not without intricacy. Institutes had been called to life by the Agricultural Organization Society in 1915 and fostered by War Agricultural Committees as part of the Board of Agriculture's plan for the management and preservation of food in war-time, this being done on the model of Canada whence Mrs. Alfred Watt had imported the idea of Institutes, so becoming foundress of the movement in England and Wales. It was necessary to adapt the idea to English rural conditions. On 3 October 1916 the Women's Institutes Sub-committee of the A.O.S.,[1] a body of nominated members, decided to invite Lady Denman to become its Chairman and further, if she consented, to ask the Board of Agriculture to appoint her governor of the A.O.S. There followed a short period of uncertainty about the position of Institutes with regard to the A.O.S. and the Board of Agriculture, during which time it became apparent to leaders and promoters that the principle of growth in the Institutes themselves gave promise of their developing into an independent movement. Under the Chairmanship of Lady Denman the Women's Institute Sub-committee of the A.O.S. decided to propose setting up in its own place the 'Central Committee of Management of Women's Institutes' consisting of a proportion of officially appointed members and a majority of representatives of the Institutes. Lady Denman was elected Chairman of this new committee which absorbed the older one, and when Grace Hadow was made its Vice-Chairman four months later there began that close association in public work between Lady Denman and her which did much to give the development of the Institute Movement its particular direction, expanding its first purpose of food production and war economies to deeper and wider aims. Henceforward Chairman and Vice-Chairman each contributed qualities that were just right for this work as well as for their specific functions. They were at one in their whole-hearted devotion to public service, in their belief in a women's movement for women and in democracy as its form of government, in their keen interest in the administration of rural affairs and their bent towards social reform. Both were ready to welcome new ideas and glad to encourage new workers and leaders; neither of them can have foreseen the great and rapid growth of Women's Institutes as an independent movement.

[1] Agricultural Organization Society.

Lady Denman's clear head for business and fine sense of fairness were great assets; her full, deep voice and commanding presence were just right for a chairman; her high sense of responsibility and force of character were reinforced by wealth and social position. Grace Hadow, for her part, bore out some of these qualities and yet stood contrasted. She had an appearance aptly described as 'often translucid', with her tall, slim frame, and voice that was high-pitched for big audiences; she contributed to the movement her intellect, her experience, her training, her gifts; and if there was little to support her that was not inherent in her personality, the use to which she was putting her powers was of high value. Her work as a Government official was equipping her with knowledge not only of departmental ways but also of the workings of social services, and it brought useful contacts. To the N.F.W.I. Chairman she gave unwavering support. That this implied no slavish agreement on particular points may be regarded as self-evident.

Lady Denman's recollections of the Vice-Chairman bring impressions of Grace Hadow vividly before the mind of memory:

'I well remember Miss Hadow when I first met her at an early meeting of the Sub-Committee of the Agricultural Organisation Society which was launching the Women's Institutes in this country. I remember how her quickness in seeing the essential point of whatever was being discussed, and her most entertaining comments made these early committee meetings stimulating and interesting. Miss Hadow's history was not known to me then and I confess I was startled when I discovered her academic record, I could not believe that anyone of Miss Hadow's knowledge could give such serious consideration to the views of anyone as ignorant as myself. I never really got used to Miss Hadow's humility of mind, and during the long years of our association I was impressed by the way in which she received suggestions from us all. She allowed committees to alter the wording of leaflets she had written and letters she had drafted, and never once implied or suggested that her command of the English language was greater than that of any of us. I do not think that she herself ever realised or appreciated that she had unique gifts both as a speaker and a writer.

'From the earliest days Miss Hadow was the leading member of the W.I. Committee. When the first meeting of the W.I. dele-

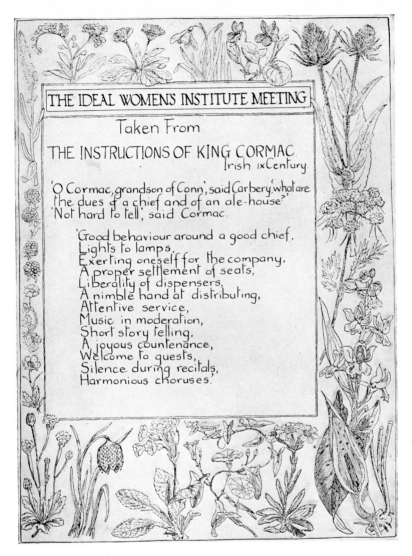

THE IDEAL WOMEN'S INSTITUTE MEETING

Taken From

THE INSTRUCTIONS OF KING CORMAC

Irish ixCentury

'O Cormac, grandson of Conn', said Carbery,'what are
the dues of a chief and of an ale-house?'
'Not hard to tell', said Cormac.

'Good behaviour around a good chief,
Lights to lamps,
Exerting oneself for the company,
A proper settlement of seats,
Liberality of dispensers,
A nimble hand at distributing,
Attentive service,
Music in moderation,
Short story telling,
A joyous countenance,
Welcome to guests,
Silence during recitals,
Harmonious choruses.'

OXFORDSHIRE'S PAGE

From the N.F.W.I. Jubilee gift-book presented to Lady Denman

The verse was chosen by GRACE HADOW

GUNFIELD, NORHAM GARDENS, OXFORD

From a drawing by HECTOR WHISTLER

gates was held it was she who had moved the resolution which formed the Institutes into a self-governing Federation; the main principles of the constitution which was adopted then have been retained ever since.

'When the W.I.s first became self-governing and elected their own Executive Committee, the Women's Branch of the Food Production Department of the Board of Agriculture was still responsible for the formation of new Institutes, and the Federation acted only for those Institutes which had been safely established and handed over by the Food Production Department. This division of responsibility was clear to me as I was working on the Government Department side and was also Chairman of the Central Committee of Management of Women's Institutes, but it had never been defined on paper, and the Executive Committee— to call it by its later name—including Miss Hadow who was Vice-Chairman, had never bothered about it.

'At an early meeting of the Executive I was absent and Miss Hadow took the chair. Unfortunately the meeting spent its time in reviewing the work done in forming the new W.I.'s and in making plans for the future. At the following meeting of the Executive I very nervously had to explain that most of the decisions arrived at at the previous meeting were out of order. I can remember now my very great relief when Miss Hadow took this to be a most comic incident. She often referred to it and years after would pretend to be relieved when she had been in the chair at a meeting that it had not been necessary to scrap everything that had been decided under her chairmanship.

'In 1936 I was unable to do W.I. work as I was ill. Miss Hadow wrote to me wishing me a speedy recovery and again referred to the joke that had become better as the years went on. After her good wishes she wrote: "Meanwhile I wonder gloomily how many things I am doing that you will reject with scorn." The letter goes on: "Mrs. Haldane, Miss Farrer and I went to interview Local Government Officials yesterday. We expected a friendly chat with three or four old gentlemen. Instead of that we were hustled into a room packed with men, shoved on to a dais and told to address them. I held forth in impassionate tones on the needs of the country women: Mrs. Haldane was her most persuasive: Miss Farrer meanly pushed across a piece of paper on which she had written, 'The Secretary will not speak.' After that it was annoying that as we left the room an exasperated little man sidled up to me and said in a hoarse whisper: 'You've come to the wrong people: these are City officials.' However it turned out that there were 17 counties represented so I hope we did some good. I went down to Blankshire the other day and was as a new born lamb among ravening wolves of dramatists raging for—and obtaining a good deal of—my blood. Mrs. Blank, the true W.I. President, told me I could use her car except in the afternoon, 'When it is wanted to take a lady-pig on her honeymoon.' I said that was putting a guest in her proper place and I hoped that pig had a white ribbon and the car a slipper." '

Undoubtedly Grace Hadow took a leading part in negotiations with various Government departments on behalf of Women's Institutes. Her work at Barnett House, after 1920, further brought her into direct touch with most of the organizations which are concerned with adult education. Often she served to represent Institutes on these bodies, and she did much to raise their status in the eyes of statutory authorities, to secure for them educational facilities, and to establish their reputation as a society which is ready to co-operate with others and which has no axe to grind. Her love for England had been stirred to its depths by the war; her affections and best associations were bound up with country things and, like many others after the war, she was ready to devote herself to building up a better England. In Institutes she saw a product of the age and a product whose roots struck far below the superficial needs of the moment: while she felt that the best guarantee of its permanency lay in its close kinship to other movements, in the fact that it moved in the great flood-tide of public opinion. And so the general line of policy for Institutes was clear in her mind. They could build on one of our best national traditions—that of voluntary public service—and could become the means of making effective the extension of social services from public funds which was to develop since the war (1914–18).

In the co-operation of voluntary societies and statutory authorities she saw the means of preserving this heritage of personal service freely given, while at the same time meeting social needs in the modern way. But the first task was to rouse the sense of responsibility towards the community in women who had been accustomed to think of themselves as bearing no share. Times were changing fast, the war produced social unrest, pointing now to infinite growth, now to chaos; the parliamentary franchise for women, however, seemed to set a seal upon the new recognition then accorded to the women's work: this last appeared as 'an island of solid achievement rising above the surge of general unsettlement', and there the stirrings of the less privileged for better education and better living could take root and flourish on the ground of home life. Over and above this there was that impulse of unity which was born of the war and was too good to lose. On the basis of all these a better England could thrive indeed: a woman's movement grounded in the country-side, based on the national traditions of home life and of voluntary public service, and furthermore welcoming opportunities for those from whom they had hitherto been withheld—such a movement necessarily commanded Grace Hadow's enthusiasm after the war and claimed her allegiance. She gave it entirely and dedicated herself to the service of what the movement stood for. Here, as elsewhere, her public service was performed the more faithfully because she interpreted it through the vision of universal truth; and her vision became clearer to herself with advancing years, as did also her power to express it in briefest and yet trenchant terms. For her and others work in Institutes brought vivid enjoyment. More than once she summed up the spirit of the movement in the words of a writer of the second century A.D.: 'Clothe thyself with cheerfulness which is acceptable with God. For everyone that is cheerful thinketh what is right and doeth what is right and despiseth pain.'

There were immediate aims which she and others have since then seen partially fulfilled. The preface to the first edition of the handbook of the N.F.W.I., published in 1921, gives these in her own words. Familiar as they must be to many Institute members, these paragraphs are sufficiently characteristic to quote as showing Grace Hadow's approach to the task of awakening the sense of citizenship within the particular setting and circumstances of country women of that day. More than twenty years have modified these last by removing the isolation of village life and familiarizing by application ideas that were then new, yet the stage of development here envisaged still fits more individual cases than is always realized at the present day when the technique of democracy is known well enough and it is easier now to turn round and question its spirit than to absorb and transmute it. By comparing this preface with the revised one of 1940 the historian of the Institute movement can register the advance in social circumstances which Institutes themselves helped to promote. A corresponding growth of awareness has developed in members, controversial questions, once firmly avoided, are no longer entirely shunned.

'Women's Institutes are gatherings of country women, who meet together once a month to discuss matters of interest to them all. Nothing could sound simpler, and yet to anyone really intimate with English rural life nothing could be more significant of the change which has permeated to remote hamlets and scattered farms, as well as to workshop and mine. As a nation we are learning to think for ourselves, not merely to accept the catch-phrases of the moment; we go about with a perpetual "Why?" in our minds if not on our lips. "Why should these things be?" And on the answer to that "Why?" depends the fate of our country, for it involves the meaning of Democracy. Democracy is not a game of grab, an attempt on the part of each individual to push to the front; its ideal is that of mutual service, of public duty as a matter of course. Pauperism is readiness to accept without giving; Patronage consists in giving without being willing to receive; but the true democrat resembles Chaucer's Clerk of Oxenford, of whom it is recorded that

"gladly wolde he lerne and gladly teche".

That exactly expresses the Institute ideal.

'All women of the village, rich and poor, gentle and simple, learned and unlearned come together with the one idea of helping each other. All pay the same subscription, have the same rights, the same privileges, the same responsibilities. Each contributes what she has to the common store. If one member has a garden she can lend it for an Institute party, another does the washing-up or brings a cherished recipe for marrow jam. There is gratitude for all, but no sense of obligation to anyone. To give and to receive are both natural and healthy when giving and receiving are not divorced, "If you know a good thing, pass it on" is one of the principles of the Institute Movement, and the result is a common bond of fellowship which unites first the women of one village and then—through the County and National Federation—the women of the County and of the Country. Nothing is more striking than that universal sense of being at home which every member has when she enters an Institute meeting no matter where it may be.

'There is, moreover, another no less far-reaching power in the movement. Country women, scattered, remote, hard-worked, up long before the dawn to get breakfast for a man who must go perhaps eight or ten miles to his work, with children to get to school, and often poultry and pigs to tend in addition to house work, have little time to read the papers and little chance of coming in contact with the world outside. City dwellers have a thousand opportunities of picking up scraps of information—however erroneous—but the country woman knows none of these; she is spared the jostling of the crowd, but she loses also the chance of hearing this and that. Institute meetings provide just the opportunity and the stimulus she requires. There is nothing terrifying about them. She comes to meet a number of her neighbours once a month or it may be oftener. They discuss the present difficulties of housekeeping; she tells them how she makes her sugar last, and someone else tells how to save fuel; there is a simple lecture on the best way to feed chickens; Miss X plays and Mrs. Y sings; the hostesses for the day provide a cup of tea and a bun all round; and the members go home feeling friendly and cheered, and that they have learned some practical method of economy, or of making something useful for the children or the husband. Bit by bit other topics are introduced. Controversial subjects, whether religious or political, are forbidden, but interest in our home leads naturally and inevitably to interest in questions of housing, sanitation, infant welfare and kindred topics. The members learn to realise their responsibilities towards the community in which they live, and from an interest in their own village and their own county, come to see the connection between their affairs and those of the nation at large. It would be difficult to plan a better training for the exercise of the vote—a training entirely free from all party or sectarian bias, based on the actual experience of home life and home needs, and working outwards through a sense of responsibility educated not to take but to give. Without the War it might have been difficult to induce women of all classes to meet together, but the War made this seem natural and simple—as indeed it is—and the spirit which it implies goes far beyond the mere details of cooking and mending : it is the basis of citizenship.'

The task of 'dealing with Women's Institute literature generally' suited Grace Hadow. Clear thinking and quick observation were natural to her, and with a marked avoidance of slogans she found the right words for the ideals of the movement, expressing them not in abstractions but in living form and as a matter of common sense. So Grace Hadow sped the development of Institute members, opening their eyes to what was taking place around them. Barriers that had been taken for granted in her own youth were being broken down by 'women who acted as hostesses to one another'. Blue and yellow, church and chapel, were no longer labels preventing personal contacts. With what pleasure she would recall a remark overheard as coming from an ardent member of the Church while washing up after a meeting: 'I always take special care of those Baptist tea-cups.' As Institutes developed, increasing attention was paid to educational facilities for members and much was done to raise the standard. In instance after instance it was found to be true that women whose natural abilities were starving began to discover their power of organization, their skill in handicrafts, their innate sense of beauty. One example was recorded by Grace, and her voice can be heard in the words: 'A few weeks ago I was chatting to a woman obviously very poor and hard worked: "Do you like poetry?" I asked, and her face lit up. "What I'd like", she said, "would be to recite, if only someone would tell me how to say words." I asked her if she had ever acted. "Only in the pageant", she answered and said softly to herself, "I'll never forget the colour of that." '

Grace Hadow believed profoundly that cultural subjects were accessible in a measure to all men, and she worked untiringly to make them available to Institute members.

Her first-hand knowledge in drama and music and her wide reading stimulated fellow members who were working to introduce these to village people and to establish a good standard in performances of pageants, plays, choral and other music as county or national events. For her own part she developed a new interest in village history and in folk-lore. In this she shared a taste that is natural to country people whose lives are lived in surroundings which contain visible and tangible links with the past. She would thoroughly enjoy sharing with Institute members her pleasure in horse-brasses and in old inscriptions or monuments, and she would stir imaginations where her own was fired. Old sayings, traditional ceremonies, and ritual dances had always appealed to her, and so had things of long ago dug up from the earth. She lectured notably on miracle plays and on roads, and these last she worked up into two series of broadcast talks given for the B.B.C. on 'Wayfaring in Olden Times' and on 'Exploration at Home'. Her interest in folk-lore led her, in another connexion, to the presidency of the Oxford University Anthropological Society where, though she always deprecated any claim to learning, she was a most successful president and one who had always something original and relevant to contribute to its discussions. 'Her special interest lay in that part of folk lore which is concerned with popular superstitions', wrote the late Dr. Marett[1] in recalling her presidency. 'Her only fault, if I may say so, was that she was apt to regard her own knowledge of the subject with an undue sense of its shortcomings; and I well remember how diffident she was when she was invited to broadcast from London, and how difficult I found it to persuade her that her matter, submitted to me beforehand, was extremely sound and valuable; while, needless to explain to her friends, her manner, with that pleasant touch of incisiveness served to emphasize the force and lucidity of her thinking.'

She put more work and thought into preparing her talks for Institutes than was realized by those who were staggered at her facility, yet it is true that she was able to get up and lecture without previous notice on almost any subject. 'One snowy night the speaker at her own Institute broke down', Miss Sidgwick writes, 'and an S.O.S. was sent to Paddington to Miss Hadow—returning as usual from a round of Committees to the meeting—to say a few words instead. She spoke magnificently, and afterwards the Secretary clearing up the table found a line or two of her notes on the back of a G.W.R. reservation ticket.' But in this faculty she would check herself severely, realizing that 'you can't give people anything that will mean something to them and they can think over afterwards without first thinking it out carefully yourself'. 'Humour', mountain climbing, and travel lectures on the many countries she had visited were among those she often gave to Institutes, and she would take great pains to procure lantern slides, though as a matter of fact her vivid and interesting talks might well have dispensed with them. But she wanted to cater also for those who never touch a book and she hated the thought of passing any one over. No doubt her talks stretched the minds of many while they roused individuals to an interest that bore further fruit.

Apart from working hard herself to bring cultural subjects to those who were starved of them, Grace drew others into this service, Oxford friends, or experts in this and that, or artists—any who shared her outlook of enthusiasm for adult education or

[1] Rector of Exeter College.

could be led to share it. Here, as in other things, 'she had', in the words of one who knew her, 'the hopefulness which her own courage in facing difficulties entitled her to hold and to impress on others who worked with her; it was impossible to suppose that any cause would fail, to which she had given her considered support.' And this spirit impressed itself also on her fellow Institute members. She trained many officers and organizers, leading larger schools and conferences for the National Federation as well as informal ones in her own county. Precise training in procedure was important in her view for effective equipment as an officer and for public work. Innumerable Institute members must have profited from her exact teaching in the conduct of public business and few, who heard them, will forget her demonstrations of how to take amendments and of the 'previous question', while many presidents will recall with laughter her impersonations of how *not* to treat the monthly letter that is sent to them by Headquarters, reading it like an incantation conscientiously observed but meaning nothing. Often officers came to conferences full of vociferous contempt for 'red tape' and returned having enjoyed themselves and having gained a new vision of procedure. Handled by Grace Hadow 'red tape' was transformed into the essential rules for an interesting game making business alive, since, in the light of those rules, it could be conducted in fairness and with common sense.

'She always "up and spoke" the right thing at the right moment whether for or against and in formal or less formal surroundings', wrote one member. 'I felt what a power of wisdom, spirit and humour she spread about.' 'What an enlarged vision of good will and impartiality and generosity one got from being with her one afternoon!' wrote another, and another delighted in 'just that combination of wisdom and fun, crispness, and understanding'.

Few could command the wit and wisdom which shone through her talks on formal business or procedure. Miss Sidgwick records: 'Her aspect was exactly the same on the platform at the Albert Hall, watching a star turn in student theatricals, or walking on competition flower-pots at a Rectory fête, intent, cheerful, knowledgeable and with a friendly eye for beginners who broke the regulations, or the flower pots. It was her love of small things and common pleasures—characteristic (whatever people say) of the scholarly mind—which is now so gratefully remembered by the humbler audiences, who had perhaps been scared by her formidable reputation. I remember sympathising with her for several weeks of strenuous night-driving to scattered districts. All she said was that she had had no idea till then how emerald green the eyes of sheep were seen in the dark by the light of motor lamps.'

Grace addressed many tiny annual meetings of Institutes in Oxfordshire, occasions when ballots are held and the formal business of the Constitution is to the fore, and she continued to do this in later years when other calls on her time were heavy. There cannot be many County Federations in England whose Annual or Half-yearly Council Meetings she did not address, and she paid visits to Wales. Her turn to take the chair at the National Annual Meeting of Institutes came round when she had to replace Lady Denman on two occasions, once in the Queen's Hall and once in the Albert Hall. In all these ways she took a lion's share in bringing home to members the importance of constitutional methods of tackling public questions. She helped them to become articulate, and relied on the ordinary countrywoman's innate sound sense to prevent her from being sidetracked by that verbosity which is a snare for the semi-educated.

Grace Hadow found tongue for what Institutes stand for by living it; and in this way the movement became bone of her bone and flesh of her flesh. She found in Institutes a means of self-expression that linked her to her fellow members, and she knew and she proclaimed that in this way Institutes give everyone her chance. In the combination of personal self-expression and social service she saw 'the keystone of the W.I. Arch'.

When she died, in 1940, Grace was entering upon the second year of her Presidency of the Oxfordshire County Federation of Women's Institutes.[1] She was by then known in pretty nearly every village in the county as 'Our Miss Hadow'. The news of her death came while her own Institute at Quarry was holding its monthly meeting, and a voice was heard to mutter, 'This is worse

---

[1] In 1939–40 the members of the Executive Committee were Miss Ashhurst, Mrs. Badger, Miss Bates, Lady Bicester, Mrs. Birch-Reynardson, Lady Brunner, the Hon. Elsie Cameron Corbett, Miss Deneke (Hon. Sec.), Miss Drummond, the Hon. Mrs. Guy Feilden, Miss Hadow (President), Miss Henman, Miss Hill, Mrs. Kreyer (Hon. Assist. Sec.), Lady Redesdale (Hon. Treas.), Miss Sandars, Miss Smith, Mrs. Stokes, Lady Wardington, Mrs. Womersley.

than the War'. Her County Federation Committee expressed a similar sense of loss in a different way:

Our President

It is difficult to believe that we shall not see Miss Hadow again. She was so full of life, so full of gaiety, and we counted on her as one counts on air, or water, or sunshine.

Whether presiding at our County meetings or taking part as one of ourselves she would be there to throw out good ideas, or flash with fun, or bring us back to the point, or direct us towards good sense. We looked to her to say the right thing when it was wanted and we were sure she would say it in the right way. And what good lectures she gave us!

One of the rarest and most brilliant women of England was ours. She gave us her fine intellect, her wit, her courage and her humour and we enjoyed them and loved them, for they were ruled by her loving kindness. She entered into the lives of many people and enriched them.

She has gone as she would wish to go, on the crest of the wave, with all her colours flying, to the next adventure. And we must be glad for her that she was spared the enfeeblement of years.

We shall see her no more. But we know that she has lighted a candle that must go on burning, and that we must tend. It will give us light for our seeing: in helpfulness, knowledge and service there is wisdom. We have seen it and we know.

CHAPTER XIII

NEW SPHERES OF ACTIVITY

1938

DURING the last years of Grace Hadow's life new spheres of activity and of interest seemed once more to be opening up. Her public speeches were attracting attention[1] and it chanced that influential people began to notice them. At a dinner given by the Oxford Society in the summer of 1938 at New College the speaker who had undertaken to propose the Vice-Chancellor's health was prevented from coming, and Grace at once consented to step into the breach. Her speech as well as its extempore character impressed Lionel Curtis, who was present, so much that she occurred to his mind when shortly after there was urgent need for a woman delegate at the second conference on British Commonwealth relations which was then being organized by the Royal Institute of International Affairs, Chatham House. He had never seen Grace Hadow before, though he had heard of her through Mrs. Curtis, and he recalls her account of his opening inquiry which she was 'mischievously fond of repeating': L.C. 'I am the husband of Mrs. Curtis and I want you to come with me to a conference in Australia on British Commonwealth relations in September next!' However this may have been, he found Grace Hadow eager to overcome any difficulties that might be in the way and to accept the invitation as long as it was understood that she went as a learner to whom the subject of the conference was new. Those responsible for selecting the delegation wanted 'some woman whose personality would impress the conference', and so it was agreed she should go. There was little time to lose. The conference was fixed for September 1938 at Lapstone, Sydney, Australia, and she got to work at once on the intricate business of removing obstacles in the shape of existing commitments. Matters were facilitated by the fact that she had anyhow applied for leave of absence in the Michaelmas Term so as to undertake her lecture tour in U.S.A. for the benefit of the Oxford Home-Student Appeal Fund and with a view to endowment of the new Library.

[1] e.g. *Sketch*, February 1938, before the Lord Mayor and H.R.H. the Duke of Gloucester in London.

Her passage to New York, which had already been booked to-gether with mine,[1] had to be cancelled, substitutes for meetings had to be found, and the tour to U.S.A. adapted where essential. The sudden invitation to undertake something new and of so interesting a kind roused all Grace Hadow's enterprise and appealed to her sense of romance, of something 'odd', as she would express it; and underlying her delight in the journey itself and its human interest there may well have been a consciousness of a special call to undertake this: 'I feel I must do this queer job' was her phrase, and this feeling would be strengthened by the fact that it chanced to be herself who was selected as the sole woman delegate for Great Britain. She put this fact before herself in the soberest terms—and with her characteristic outlook: 'I have been added at the last minute as an obvious afterthought: I deduce "A Woman" and am the only woman. Mr. Lionel Curtis, the moving spirit, broke it to me tactfully at Euston that probably I should be left out of some of the banquets as the men of Canada and New Zealand would not expect a woman. It is all very odd. I've a charming little cabin to myself, a nice smiling Irish stewardess and I hope for a good voyage' (22 July 1938).

The circumstances were nevertheless a stimulating challenge to herself. Towards fate or accident she always felt instinctive response and she delighted in the thought of the unknown. The British delegation sailed from Liverpool on 22 July for Sydney, picking up further delegates in Canada and New Zealand on the way and conferring all the while. Great Britain and Canada each provided fifteen delegates, and there were five Ireland delegates and a considerable Secretariat, so that with the addition of wives there must have been between fifty and sixty in the party by the time they crossed the Pacific. On 26 July she notes: 'We'd a meeting of the Conference this morning—interesting. The dis-cussion was on Canada—was it or was it not to her interest to remain within the British Commonwealth? How could she be free if England might involve her in War, and yet now War comes without previous declaration how could the Dominions possibly be consulted?'

Soon Canadian hospitality was experienced and much enjoyed: 4 August. 'We had a wonderful day in Montreal. We arrived about 10 a.m. and went to the Hotel Windsor where a room had

[1] I was going to Canada in September and we had agreed to travel together.

been reserved for us. The hotel promptly caught fire and 3 fire engines turned up; however it turned out to be nothing. About 12 a fleet of private cars arrived to take us out to lunch at St. Bruno Country Club, a most luxurious place in lovely surroundings, with a wide view over a fertile plain out of which shoot up sudden strange volcanic mountains. After lunch we were driven on to the country house of Mr. Birks (a wholesale jeweller and President of the local Institute of International Affairs). It was a house with every kind of comfort and beauty—a large lake beside which his children have their country houses, acres of beautiful half-wild country, exquisite flower gardens and an old mill (the actual house 200 years old) dating from the French days when one of the first obligations of a Seigneur was to build a mill.

'I came away with a sense of beauty, good taste and luxury.

'Montreal itself seemed full of flowers and with very green beautifully kept lawns everywhere.'

During the long journey across Canada she was impressed, as no one can fail to be, by the clear-cut strata of Canadian scenery, each so distinctive and so continuous while it lasts as to be unforgettable; the loneliness of the prairie farms stuck in her mind and the pleasure that books or newspapers gave when thrown from the train; also the beauty of the wide-open sky and the prairie waving in golden corn. Getting up early to go right to the back of the train so as to sit in the fresh air, she tied a handkerchief over her hair and wore a mackintosh to defy grit and smuts. And she hoped to escape reporters, who sprang up at every halt. 'Reporters at every step, but luckily chiefly interested in Mr. and Mrs. Curtis and an Irish delegate; and beyond a weary-looking lady who followed me down the platform at Winnipeg (where I was looking for the kind man who was going to take me for a drive) and asked down the back of my neck what I thought of commercial broadcasting, I've escaped, though I'm told I attract a mild amount of interest as the only woman. Everywhere people are most kind.' The Canadian delegates joined the party at Vancouver, and after boarding R.M.M.S. *Aorangi* of the Canadian Australasian line, everyone settled down to 'a routine life of deck games, conference and sleep'. 'I'm finding the Conference interesting', she wrote from the Pacific just before landing at Honolulu; 'this morning we'd a talk from one of our Labour men which led to a hot discussion. I'm beginning to see dimly where

I may some day have something to say, but so far I am just learning, learning, learning.'

Stormy petrel, dipping their wings and flying round the ship, were the prelude to Honolulu and were followed by a very interesting paper from the General, which roused explosive protests from the sister service, whose representative, the Admiral, felt the General was poaching on the Navy's preserves. When Honolulu was reached there were vivid impressions of the clash between things imported from the alien civilization of Europe and things native.

9 August. 'It is the custom in Honolulu to greet your friends with garlands of sweet-scented flowers and hardly was the ship in dock when numbers of the Pacific I.I.R. (Institute of International Relations) boarded her and hung garlands round all our necks. Professor Zimmern's bland intelligent face peering out above a wreath of pink petals was a sight to remember. One has to wear them all day and as they are common greetings among friends the streets are a most amazing sight, lined on either side by dark-skinned natives roped all over with strings of flowers in scarlet and orange and mauve and crimson and every conceivable colour and holding out armsfull for sale. People of eminence get loaded with them and I saw one elderly tubby little man who looked like a Mayor, one solid blossom from head to waist. It is not only on arrival or departure that you are decorated. You see what look like businessmen on their way to their offices hurrying along carrying gay oil silk umbrellas and hung with flowers. All the main streets are fragrant with the scent, and the colour is lovely.

'We landed about 1.30 and found the usual fleet of private cars waiting to show us the sights. I was lucky enough to fall to a man who allowed us to be unintelligent and drove us along lovely roads—mountains and below them groves of cocoa-nuts and date palms—paw paws and a riot of brilliant flowers everywhere— to a private bathing beach on the far side of the island (where it sometimes stops pouring soft warm rain on to you) and I had the most heavenly bathe of my life, on perfect sand, in deep clear water which though warm was extraordinarily buoyant and invigorating. It was like bathing in pale blue champagne.

'We drove back to a tea at the Royal Hawaiian Hotel—an appalling place, pretentious, dear, and bad, but in a lovely position opposite the surf-riding beach. There we had tea and speeches (still wearing our garlands). A kind man turned up with an offer of two tickets for a quartet after dinner and Mr. Wyndham and I accepted them. I asked if we should not go back to the ship and dress, but he said this was quite unnecessary, so I had another bathe (not very nice as the beach shelves suddenly on to sharp coral and the rollers are too big for a poor swimmer) and then Mr. Wyndham and I had dinner at a little restaurant. It poured and poured, and we came out into a street running with water. Several Honolulans told me this was so common that people frequently took off their shoes and stockings and proceeded with their shopping or whatever it might be like that. I collected my very wet bathing dress and towel and armed with an umbrella waited for our hostess to fetch us to the concert, conscious that a thin silk frock which had not only got wet several times that day but had been crushed by two hefty Irishmen in the back seat of the car, was looking as if it had been rough dried. Our hostess turned up in full evening dress—as was the rest of the audience. But it was a good concert—and at the end four charming young ladies marched in a business-like fashion on to the platform and hung garlands round the necks of the performers.'

10 August. 'Next morning Miss Harvey and I went over a Pineapple cannery. What stays in my mind is the fact that many school children work in their holidays—in all that noise and at that pace.

'We sailed at 11 surrounded by a crowd of natives (the sea, horribly oily, was suddenly full of them) who dived from the rail, and the life boats and the Bridge for dimes and caught them as they sank.'

Professor Sir Alfred Zimmern has recorded some of the happenings on the further journey to New Zealand and to Sydney:

'The next land that was sighted after Honolulu was Canton Island, where the British and United States governments had, by an agreement arrived at only a few weeks before, arranged for a joint occupation and joint flying facilities. The ship passed near enough for the passengers to be able to see the Union Jack and the Stars and Stripes flying side by side. Thence to Fiji, where the party stayed for the inside of a day and then to Auckland. Here the group separated: the secretarial staff of the conference and some of the delegates went straight on to Sydney whereas a second group whom Miss Hadow had decided to join took advantage of an invitation to spend a week in New Zealand. When the advance party arrived off Sydney the ship was boarded by reporters with instructions to seek out the Woman delegate and great was their disappointment to discover that she had been left behind *en route*. In the New Zealand party Miss Hadow was one of the most active members, undertaking long excursions regardless of fatigue. At Auckland local members of the Oxford Society organised a meeting to which several members of the party contributed impressions of present-day Oxford. Miss Hadow, felicitous and to the point as usual, carried away the palm. She was much interested in the Maoris, whom she had a chance of seeing at close quarters at Rotorua, where she was greatly interested in their dancing, and again at Wellington. Here a reception was arranged in the Parliament House at which the acting Prime Minister, Mr. Peter Fraser, the Leader of the Opposition, and the veteran Maori leader, Sir Apirana Ngata made speeches. In the evening of the same day there was a meeting of the local group of the New Zealand Institute of International Affairs, when Mr. Walter Nash spoke with great frankness about the European situation and the need of a policy of collective security, adding that, come what might, New Zealand would be by Britain's side. The discussion which followed was one of the most interesting of the whole tour and was a valuable prelude to the formal conference. The New Zealand party boarded the ship at Wellington and a most interesting group it was containing prominent leaders of both the New Zealand parties with their contrasted views on social policy.

'Honolulu, Fiji, Auckland, Rotorua and Wellington—not to speak of the constant discussions on shipboard (varied by games of darts for which Miss Hadow was found characteristically preparing herself by early morning practice) were a most stimulating experience.' Indeed friends at home hardly knew what this journey was rousing in Grace Hadow, but her mind had been engaged upon the question of rebuilding international relations even before she joined the British Commonwealth Conference, and she was moving towards seeing in some form of federal union a solution that had hitherto seemed 'too idealistic' and now seemed more workable. Her attention was drawn to the intricate considerations of specific detail that are involved in shaping the social and political world at home and overseas, and she was arrested by the impact of different civilizations in a world of nations which

were becoming more and more interdependent through the
results of mechanization. Meanwhile she had found her place in
the Conference itself.

Coming into it at the eleventh hour and without previous
preparation she had hard work to keep abreast of its subjects and
problems. Delegates were selected to represent various points of
view, and they stood for some particular group or section or service or profession. Among them, moreover, were men of high
distinction. It was interesting to be thrown together with a company of lawyers, economists, philosophers, politicians, civil
servants, business men, engineers, soldiers, and sailors, all of them
engaged upon considering a common problem and contributing
their very different experiences seen from their particular portion
of the British Commonwealth. In these deliberations Grace
Hadow held to the position of a learner and perhaps consequently
addressed the Conference more rarely than her listeners could have
wished. However, her gifts in the chair of committee and group
were invaluable. The old quickness in grasping situations and
issues inspired people of many kinds to work as a team. 'She had
the highest faculty I have ever seen in a chairman for getting
business done and perfectly done', writes Mr. Curtis; 'she had a
positive genius for keeping members to the point . . . her supreme
contribution to the conference was her personality which made the
deepest impression on the people who came from all parts of the
British Commonwealth as it was bound to do. She more than
fulfilled the main purpose that the organizers of the Conference
had in view in pressing her to come.'

This impression is confirmed by James Dillon, deputy chairman
of the United Ireland party and one of the Irish delegates:
'It is odd that perhaps the most dramatic incident of the Sydney
Conference of the Institute of International Affairs is least suscep-
tible of effective description, and the reason is I think because
that incident was the impact of a unique personality on a group of
about seventy people who had come from all over the world,
doubting the possibility of so large a group as themselves ever
being able to crystallize into a coherent committee, and suddenly
experiencing the astonishing feeling of being drawn together by
a meteoric personality concealed by the frail exterior of what must
be described as a precise-looking lady, whose name meant little
to delegates drawn from Western Australia, British Columbia,

New Zealand, but whom they quickly came to know as Miss Hadow—Great Britain.[1]

'Grace Hadow was our first chairman and that fact had an astonishing effect on the success of our subsequent deliberations. I do not think it is an exaggeration to say that it made their success possible. As we left the room for the first adjournment I remember the pessimists somewhat gloomily admitting that her success in getting the ship so triumphantly under way had dispelled all thought of failure, her work had saved a great if hazardous experiment—the overcoming of obstacles by a conference in a day when dictators were claiming that talking shops were effete and guns preferable to butter. For one who was privileged to see much of Miss Hadow during these days and in the time of returning home there remains the impression of a rare person who was given an exquisite sensitive personality by God and who had used it to acquire sublime wisdom and wonderful goodness. That these gifts were at once recognized by the young who flocked round her is evidence of their perfection; that they were hers, her friends had every reason to be thankful for, she shared them with truly regal generosity and delicacy; that they were no less unwearingly bestowed on the not so young is something for which the writer will be grateful for ever.'

Speaking further of her chairmanship James Dillon says: 'there was a general feeling amongst the fifty or sixty people present at the first meeting that putting Miss Hadow in the Chair was rather a gesture of courtesy and that we must expect a meeting which would be ill conducted and discursive for want of a strong Chairman, and I remember the growing sense of amazement and admiration around the table as Miss Hadow established herself to be a quite exceptionally competent Chairman, not only in her conduct of the meeting, but in the strange influence of sincerity and effectiveness which she diffused throughout the whole company. I remember I was sitting between the South Africans and the Canadians, some of whom, in the vernacular which used to amuse Grace Hadow were "tough guys", and it was amusing to watch them open their eyes as she proceeded to control the less relevant members of the Conference and to maintain order when our more sprightly members were inclined to stray from the fold.'

[1] The procedure of the Conference required each delegate when speaking to introduce his observations by announcing his name and the country he came from.

The Conference brought new friendships; James Dillon's for one and John McCarthey's, a young member of the Canadian Secretariat for another, whom she saw much of on the excursion to New Zealand and described as her 'adopted nephew'. On the long journey outwards Mr. and Mrs. Lionel Curtis got to know her intimately and with his godson Lionel Massey (the son of Vincent Massey) she had an affectionate friendship. There may well have been others for whom getting to know Grace Hadow had a permanent meaning, but it was never her way to speak of one friend to another unnecessarily and she has left no record. On the whole she seems to have talked most to the Irish delegates and to the Indians, to whom she listened with great interest and not out of politeness, and they responded to her sympathy. 'The conference was held at a moment when international relations were more than usually kaleidoscopic', writes Professor Zimmern, 'so that the actual discussions held at it very soon became out of date. But the contacts made were immensely valuable and certainly the good will and mutual understanding which Miss Hadow did so much to promote will bear fruit in the future. What Mr. Curtis says about her influence is perfectly true. Everyone felt it.'

It was a pity that she could not continue the journey home with the British delegation, who were travelling back across the other side of the globe, but no one could have enjoyed the beauty of the coral islands and of the Pacific more than did Grace Hadow, and there was compensation in the companionship of 'James and John'. Her friendship with James Dillon, which she valued, was formed during this passage, and the adopted nephew proved effective as a champion, rescuing her from a stifling cabin down in the boat and no doubt procuring other amenities which she would neither have sought nor found. The September crisis in Europe took place during this passage. Several letters to a friend and to her sisters give a picture and an impression of the main features of Grace in these days and an impression of the main features of this journey.

Oceanic Line, Hawaii,
South Seas, New Zealand,
Australia, America.

Sept. 17, 1938.

. . . This is one of the days when you sit—as I am doing now—with one foot pressed against the wall, and listen to the furniture fetching loose in all directions. For some odd reason they don't have fiddles on the tables and meals are a prolonged effort to keep one's food from falling into one's neighbour's lap. You can guess how thankful I am for Dr. Carling's sea-sick remedy.[1] It is simply miraculous. I was one of the very few survivors when we crossed the Tasman Sea coming, and I'm not only all right but hungry!

It has been difficult to think of anything but the news for the last week and how hateful it is to be so far away, but it is no use fussing.

I had a new experience on Thursday when a number of us were invited to lunch at a vineyard. We were given a light lunch and far more wine than was good for us. I was opposite our host and could not avoid sampling his wines, but I contrived to have only a sip or two of each; as it was I had vermouth, hock, sauterne, champagne, and burgundy (*I* who have no head). At the end he gave us what I believe is called a Rheaboam (spelling uncertain); anyhow it is a gigantic bottle which holds 10½ bottles of champagne. This was solemnly put in my custody, and I wish you'd seen the faces of the rest of the Conference when we arrived back about tea time and processed through the Lounge, I with this enormous object in my arms. We solemnly presented it to the Chairman of the Conference at dinner, and there was enough for everyone to have a glass. One of the men took a snapshot of it with me and said thoughtfully 'That would make an excellent poster': shades of Oxford forbid.

I was tiresomely seedy all the time we were at Lapstone. I think everyone has knocked up at some time with 'flu or a bad cold and mine just wouldn't go. It didn't matter, except that it took away my voice, and having to ration talking to people was difficult: also I had to refuse to take the chair once as I knew if I did I should be dumb by the end of the evening. However I did chair the conference twice so I did my duty. One of the Indians wants me to come and broadcast in India. I said, feebly, that I really had a job in Oxford. I might do it if I retired.

It has all been really interesting and I've W.I. talks for the rest of my life. I'm collecting cards to be made into lantern slides.

We have a few of the Conference on this boat, though most of them leave us at New Zealand, but Mr. Dillon (leader of the Congress party in Ireland and most entertaining) is going all the way

[1] Called Thalassan.

and so is a quite delightful Canadian boy whom I have adopted as my great nephew and who always addresses me as Great Aunt.

I'm hoping that after Auckland I may get an outside cabin. I did have one, but changed when I found I should have to share, and now I'm in one in which there is so little ventilation that even in this cold weather I'm almost suffocated. I told them they'd have a funeral at sea if I had to have that in the Tropics. However, a lot of people are getting off at Auckland and I'm not without hope. I expect I am partly jaundiced by the number of times I had to get out of bed last night to retrieve flower-vases etc. One emptied itself neatly over my clothes and I had to hang them up to dry. (Yes, I know your comment but (*a*) these are marvellous flowers I'm saving for a lady in New Zealand; (*b*) the Steward said the vase was safe.)

The Oceanic Line, Hawaii,
South Seas, New Zealand,
Sept. 22, 1938.   Australia, America.

Yesterday was Thursday Sept. 22nd and so is today. I feel like the Red Queen running 20 knots an hour to keep from slipping backwards in time.

From Sydney to Auckland we had the roughest passage this boat has had for four years. The entire contents of the shop leapt on the floor and remained there until we got to New Zealand. On the first day I watched the Shop keeper being pelted with Gramophone records and dolls and boxes of all kinds. After that he just let them lie: 'What's the use of picking them up?' he very sensibly remarked. Crockery crashed at every meal. I had some rare and very beautiful Australian flowers in my room, and the first night they emptied themselves neatly over my undies and I had to get up about 3 a.m. and hang my things up to dry. The number of times I chased vases about the floor is past counting. Meals reminded one of the Duchess in Alice, being punctuated with loud crashes, and at intervals one found oneself clinging to a pillar. Never shall I forget a long and earnest conversation with an intelligent and ardent Indian who was pressing me to come and broadcast in India and who was apparently unconscious of the fact that most of the furniture in the Lounge had come adrift and that a foam of chairs and small tables was breaking round our feet. From time to time I arose and removed one of the more excitable tables, but he did not seem to be aware of its presence. I really am an advertisement for Thalassan. I never had a qualm, and I was congratulated on being so good a sailor!

Yesterday was our last day of glory. We got a cable inviting us to lunch with Sir Harry Luke, the new Governor of Suva, and as soon as we tied up, one of the leading men in the island came aboard to ask what he could do for us. Providence had most kindly arranged that low tide should be at 11 a.m. and we arrived at 8 a.m. so with one voice we said: 'Find a boat and take us out on the reef.' The reef was amazing. From 6 a.m. we had been running beside it with huge rollers so near that it looked as if you could chuck a stone into them, and there is only one narrow entry through which a ship can pass. It passes into a world of exquisite islands covered with palm trees. Our boat—the funniest little object—arrived about 9.30 and we sat on the roof and chugged away into fairy land. Close to the reef we got into a sort of punt, and floated over coral of every shape and colour in and out of which darted myriads of brilliant emerald green and royal blue tiny fish. Now and then you saw a huge bright purple star fish, and with white sand below and clear sunshine the colour was amazing. We had to wade for the last bit and I finally sacrificed my deck shoes. Then we strolled about in blazing sun in the middle of the sea, turning over huge stones and finding more queer beasts than I knew existed, some of them like slugs about the length of a kitten, with their necks and spade-shaped heads. You can't bathe in the lovely warm sea as apart from being eaten by sharks you are stung and bitten by creatures of all sorts—but it is wonderful to look at. They give you a long tin with a glass bottom which you push into the water and which enables you to get below the surface ripple and see the bottom quite clearly.

We got back very wet and dirty, about 12.15 in time to wash and change to go to lunch in a lovely cool house all verandas (has it an h?) and big open windows looking over a beautiful garden to sea and mountain.

There our friend of the morning came to fetch us and Government House provided a second car and we were taken for a very beautiful drive, then back to our friend's house for a cool drink, and so back after a well-spent day, to sail at 5 p.m.

Tomorrow we stop at another Island, Pago-Pago, but only for two hours.

We have had such ups and downs of European news that one

doesn't know what to think. After a fortnight of living on tenter hooks I am beginning to feel a little more happy about it—but in any light it is a hateful business.

- My safest address till Nov. 10 will be Thos. Cook and Son,

587 Fifth Avenue,
New York.

Oceanic Line, Hawaii,
South Seas, New Zealand,
Australia, America.

Sept. 29, 1938.

By the time this reaches you I hope the worst may be over. It is extraordinary how even here, in mid-ocean—rumours fly about, but the wireless gives us at least the gist of the big speeches and the Ship's paper gives the Stock Market, which is some indication of how things go. Providence has been kind to me in giving me as travelling companions, John and James, John my honorary Great Nephew—James a most witty and amusing Irishman. Without them I should have gone hopping mad, as the rest of the passengers are for the most part the most appalling type of hard-faced, oozing money individuals. As it is the three of us go for excursions together when the boat stops (and this boat is always stopping) and discuss every subject in heaven and earth. James (a devout R.C.) has a lovely picture of hell as inhabited only by the devil whose punishment it is to see all souls snatched from him: 'And it's not orthodox, Miss Hadow, but I can't help thinking that at the end the Lord will say, "Lucifer, old boy, the joke is on you. Come up here." ' John had meant to go to Europe with the main party and changed his mind only the day before we sailed. It was luck both for him and for us: for us because we gained as travelling companion one of the nicest boys I've ever met, and incidentally the son of one of the biggest business potentates in Canada so that wherever we go men fall over each other to help us in every conceivable way: and for him because we saw that a number of those who meant to go by the Suez cancelled their passages at Melbourne, which means they will follow in a notoriously slow and bad boat which will probably be terribly overcrowded. I'm longing to get to the States, which by contrast will seem quite near home. I felt it would be both wrong and absurd to cancel my tour in America when by the time I got there, there might be no reason

o

for doing so—or alternatively an even better reason for carrying on, but it has all seemed queerly unreal.

Thank heaven my throat is better at last, though it is still none too safe. If I'd arrived dumb in both the English and American sense of the word, it would have been trying.

I'm getting off at Los Angeles. It saves an unnecessary journey up to San Francisco and more or less back, and the spare day should enable me to see the Grand Canyon. It is no use getting to New York a day before I'm expected, and a Sunday at that. Also my men folk are getting off over there and I should loathe a day without them. John and I think of going to the Grand Canyon together. James will—I fear—leave us.

The most marvellous adventure we've had on this trip back was at Fiji, when kind Heaven let it be low tide just at the right hour, and we hired a boat and went out on the coral reef. That in itself would be worth crossing the world to see. Yesterday in Honolulu, I met one of John's business friends whose favourite occupation is swimming out for a mile, lying face down on the water till he sees a nice fish, and then diving down some 20 feet and spearing it. A *very* odd world.

En route Pennsylvania Rail Road,
Oct. 10, 1938.

. . . It has been the queerest cinema-drama week. We ought to have got into Los Angeles about 7 a.m. on Monday morning, but we ran into a dense fog in the harbour and sat there hooting. One encouraging lady told me that she had had a similar experience off Cape Town, when the vessel sat still for 2½ days. However, we did better than that for after about 2 hours the fog began to lift and then we found we were in the midst of the American Navy—14 great battleships. You can't think how lovely it was to see one silver ship after another come out of the mist, till the whole 14 lay catching the sun—we should have been stuck in that fog anyhow, but as it transpired we should have lain to anyhow in order that a boat load of detectives and police might come and investigate a theft of £20,000 worth of jewels which took place on board on Sunday night. That made a suitable introduction to California. As usual we were met by two of John's henchmen—the poor wretches had been waiting for us since 7 o'clock and we got in about 11.30. Thanks to them we had no bother with the customs, though not unnaturally as the jewels weren't found, luggage was being gone through pretty thoroughly. The harbour is 80 miles from the town, so the henchmen's cars were useful. I wish you'd seen the queer old porter who carried our cases to the car and who addressed me as 'Girl'. We went to a very comfortable ruinous Hotel, having decided that we should never be in Los Angeles again and we would just whoop. After lunch the henchmen drove us out to Hollywood, where John (having always a friend at court) got taken to a studio, and James and I went to the Chinese Cinema where all the premières are given: outside it the impressions of the hand and feet of 'Stars' have been taken in the cement paving, with affectionate messages. You never saw anything like it. We were pretty tired that night and I firmly refused a show after dinner; we went to bed early. Next day we drove out about 12 miles to one of the country houses of a friend of John's father, and lunched there. It would take too long to describe it all to you, but picture a charming two story house on the edge of a cliff looking across 9,000 feet mountains, a garden full of roses and cactuses, orange trees, ripe figs, an elderly couple, he a cripple and she, until she married a short time ago, a Cinema director (with adventures that would make your hair curl), no children, a play room where they took us to play children's games.

We got back about 5 and the others went off to tea while I rested, partly because I wanted to rest, partly because I thought my nice men had better be free from me now and then. We'd arranged to go to a concert that night, and presently a note shot under my door conveying a formal invitation from James and John to go to a Night Club with them afterwards. Both concert (a fashionable and bad one) and Night Club were full of Hollywood stars and we saw some odd sights, including an elderly lady with a blue wig. And so home to bed about 1.45. We left on Wednesday afternoon, and since then I've had only one night not spent in the train but by this means we'd a whole day at Grand Canyon and that is an epic in itself: nothing I'd heard or read had prepared me—or could prepare anyone—for something so utterly unlike any other scenery. You can't call it lovely, or stupendous, or fantastic, other things deserve those epithets: this is as much another world as that infernal valley of Wairakei with its geysers.

Last night I spent with the dear nuns at St. Louise, and this afternoon I reach New York and begin life in earnest. . . . The trains are appalling, but I'm trying to keep from kicking against pricks. They keep the temperature at between 70 and 80 (of set choice) and *no* fresh air is ever admitted. Meals are *very* dear and rather bad: breakfast of fruit, coffee and toast costs about 3/6 and you can't get the simplest lunch or dinner under about 5/: but the conductors and porters and 'red caps' are all delightful people, so friendly and kind and helpful.

She was pledged to the American lecture tour and had booked a passage to travel home with me from Canada, at the end of November. However, when she reached the Pacific coast the September crisis of 1938 had set in, and she found herself doubtful whether to rush home at once or not. The Munich Conference cut off the immediate crisis, and as she travelled through U.S.A. she was soon besieged by questioners and it fell to her to explain England's circumstances and to defend England's outlook and action. By 15 October she writes from Baltimore:

'I've discovered at last why Providence sent me to Australia. It was to furnish me with material to answer American criticism of England now. I'm having a hot time and am enjoying it. I've just written to the Embassy at Washington to ask if they'd like to see me and give me such information as they think fit. It seems such a chance since I am in any case addressing hundreds of young Americans. I spoke to about 800 the other night, and to about 250 older people at a luncheon at New York and as a result I've been asked to go back and speak at the University in New York—and I feel I'd better be sure of my facts! However, knowing my countrymen, I think it more probable that the Embassy will say "Drat this officious woman. We will have none of her." '

The letter was followed by a visit to Washington and led to an interview followed by further engagements. Her reception was certainly not what the letter to her sisters anticipates. While staying at Government House, Ottawa, just then I sat next to one of our Embassy people at dinner who had come as a week-end guest and he spoke to me of the crisis and of having come across an Englishwoman who was doing quite excellent work in U.S.A. in these difficult days. On questioning him further I found to my amusement it was 'a Miss Hadow'. She seemed then even to me to be reaching new heights, though I had heard her times

without number and known her intimately for a lifetime. Her
speech to university women at Montreal, in its directness and
vividness, its changes from conversational simplicity to analysis
of principles was masterly—and yet it was just herself. The room
buzzed with questions and there were comments of agreement
and disagreement and the impression stayed that things were not
as simple as they seemed. The universal question was, 'What
about Czechoslovakia?' Even in the Middle West Grace Hadow
had found her life imperilled by taxi-drivers who looked away from
the wheel to ask this question; and the contrast between this state
of things and 1918 struck her forcibly, when men in the Middle
West had asked her whether there was fighting in Yorkshire.
In 1938 Americans were infinitely better informed, but naturally
they were puzzled, and Grace Hadow's days became one succession of speeches: 'I'm leading an odd life. I spend anything from
8 to 14 hours in the hottest and stuffiest of trains and arrive either
early in the morning or in the late afternoon at some unknown
place. Usually someone meets me and takes me to the Hotel or
private house where I am to stay. I am supposed to give one
lecture of about one hour, but frequently as I go round the college
I'm asked if I'd mind addressing a group of students then and
there, or saying a few words to a class. Then they mention
casually that there is a luncheon party at which it is hoped that I
will speak and after lunch a special meeting has been called of the
local branch of the Institute of International Affairs: will I talk
to it about Czechoslovakia? So I've a busy day.' Her lectures
on various subjects were offered for a fee, and with a view to
rousing interest in the appeal for O.H.S. endowment. In the
circumstances no more than the actual lecture fees came in;
though she had hopes of laying the foundation for the permanent
interchange between Oxford and U.S.A. women students, the tour
hardly proved financially worth the great effort. Speaking on
the international situation was urgent national work and attracted
everyone's immediate attention, but it was work for which no
fees could be accepted.

'I've just had a 15 minutes' wait at a junction, being heckled all
the time about Chamberlain', she writes in the train on the way to
Rock Hill, S.C. 'If I were to announce lectures on the situation in
Europe I should make a fortune.' Invitations to dine with Institutes of International Affairs met her at every turn, and she found

the information gained at the British Commonwealth Conference and its outlook had equipped her for this new role. But that tour was over-strenuous, however light she made of that aspect of it. 'I have had a specially hectic time this week, as I was in Boston on Sunday morning, left at mid-day and travelled all night, reaching Chicago Monday morning, had a luncheon party, a speech and a dinner party that day, another lunch and two speeches next day, then caught a 4 p.m. train for Albany arriving at 7.40 a.m. on Wednesday, spent the day and spoke there, caught a night train to New York where I arrived 12.30 (midnight) and another train on at 1.30 a.m. arrived at 11 and then had a luncheon party. I slept last night! and I was thankful to be in a real bed and not in one of those appalling sleepers. You have anything up to 40 and 50 people in one carriage, the windows are sealed: there is a tiny dining room for men and one for women, and the temperature is kept between 70° and 80° (often nearer 80) so that is that. Now however I have two days' holiday. I am staying in Mark Twain's native city and sat next his niece at lunch yesterday. My hostess is a Home-Student who went down early this summer and she looks after me beautifully. Tomorrow she is motoring me to my last engagement in U.S.A., Rochester, and then I go to Toronto where I hope to meet Lena. It will be quite odd to see someone I know again after the long time of incessantly meeting strangers.'

That meeting in Toronto took place in a small popular restaurant and in pouring rain, and later in the day, having been invited to address the University Women's Club, she found herself un-expectedly confronted with an audience of 2,000. She had been asked to return with me to Ottawa as the guest of Lord and Lady Tweedsmuir, who had supported the Rural Libraries scheme in Oxfordshire and had known her long. When she arrived at Government House, Ottawa, for a quiet week-end, the house-party were shocked at her looking a shadow of herself in spite of her gaiety. A glorious walk and drive in the Gatineaux district and stimulating talk on common interests were a refreshment. Lady Tweedsmuir herself, the greatest lady in Canadian Women's Institutes and also a leading and active member, had sat at Grace's feet as a learner and alternately presided over her at County meetings. Grace reports that visit as 'quite amusing', and 'I tried to remember my curtseys'. Some more last speeches, more questions on the crisis, more warm Canadian hospitality ended that journey; 'almost the nicest thing in Montreal was dining with some people who live on the hill behind the city and looking down on miles of lights! it was almost like a glow-worm upside down.'

There was a sudden fall of deep snow the night before she embarked on the *Duchess of Richmond*, the last boat to sail down the St. Lawrence that year. 'We had two days of ice- and snow-covered decks, and a temperature down to 10°, but to-day is sunny and the snow is melting. Deck hands looking like Arctic explorers in sea-boots and Sou-westers powdered with snow, go about with huge shovels scraping the deck, and I've just watched one of them thawing the steps to the boat deck with boiling water. I tried to go up there yesterday but could not stand against the wind. There was quite a tumble last night and without Thalassan I should have had a night of misery: as it is I never turned a hair and enjoyed my before-breakfast walk this morning. It is much calmer now though one still feels a gentle heave.' It was a stormy passage on a boat with a mere sprinkling of passengers; and before long she was on friendly terms with many of the crew and was making their appeal for seamen's charities in a telling speech to those who sailed.

The journey home with deck games and gymnasium revived her, and, though the boat was four days late and danced about outside Cherbourg, an even longer delay would have been welcome if it had prolonged this holiday. She never quite recovered her full physical vitality after this last American tour, though she continued her habit of paying no attention to her body in these ways. When war came in the autumn of 1939 she was already over-tired. She spent herself to the utmost on evacuation and had not had sufficient holiday to recover spring or build up reserves, and so she fell an easy prey to her last illness. In the period of reconstruction which must come after this war Grace Hadow would have had much to contribute.

CHAPTER XIV
FRIENDSHIPS AND PERSONALIA

'When a friend asks, there is no tomorrow.'
GEORGE HERBERT

IN friendship Grace was unfailing, and she meant a great deal to her friends. 'Steel-true' and warm-hearted, she always understood and that without much talk. She was ready for any enterprise, full of energy, and effervescent with fun. Caring greatly for beautiful things and exceptional people, she was very attractive herself as a companion. Hers was an effect like spring sunshine, and there was always a fund of good remarks and good stories ready to bubble up. Perhaps of all her interests the human interest was the greatest. She got at the core of people quickly, saw good points in them, appreciated gifts that were perhaps still inarticulate, and had a genius for drawing these out and strengthening them. Her belief in others would work upon them like a charm. But it was spontaneous and was based on qualities really theirs that she had appreciated. Instinctively she would set her mind on getting these recognized by others, and in this way she must have helped countless people, hardly realizing that she was doing so. With practical good sense she would set their feet in a direction where they found congenial work and would wipe cobwebs away.

There can hardly have been a time when there was not an element of detachment in her view of people, her nearest and dearest included, yet her power of belief in others expanded as years went on. When she was young there could be partisanship with its challenge and the resulting opposition. Her wit was very telling; you were aware of a high standard that was forbidding, and people could be afraid of her. In later years this anxiety subsided, and one was struck by a very wide tolerance, a growing detachment, a growing intensity of affection, and, with an undiminished sense of people's absurdities, a wonderful kindness. But the calculating or worldly minded produced a recoil which was a bar to intimacy. It is likely enough that the sufficiently subtle could take her in and abuse her, yet she could be wise as the serpent to meet their thrusts and then could be intensely entertained by topsy-turvy ideas about what was of real importance to human beings. Her sense of humour always came to the rescue. She rejoiced in people's inconsistencies and could laugh too heartily at her own to allow of malice in her laughter.

From her own life she had entirely eliminated personal ambition. As a tiny girl she had wanted to be queen; in later years she was almost morbidly averse to claiming credit for any achievement great or small, and she was an expert in attributing the credit to others. It was with incredulous surprise that she accepted proofs of affection from others. She would not, even for causes, beg a boon for personal reasons and was incapable of scheming for place or favour. She hated precautions, and 'safety first' not only met with her scorn but challenged defiance. In a little summer retreat in Catalonia after bathing, her travelling companions were amused to see her hanging out her cherished, decorous Principalian bathing-dress on a tree in the little public square to dry. Some instinct kept them from warning her; but they were sorry afterwards when they saw her surprise and heard her lament that it had been stolen in the night. No doubt her faith in the prevailing honesty of mankind was worth these risks. Yet most of us would regard it as rather silly to take them. To think highly of others was her instinctive outlook. It began perhaps as a reaching out towards qualities or graces that she felt she did not possess or had not developed. These were an attraction, an entry to friendship. In the end this power reached to pretty well everyone who had contact with her, and not least to the lame ducks. She took them on an equality and expected nothing for herself.

For the different characteristics of her many friends and for their special tastes and interests she had a rare, imaginative understanding. Her own orderliness did not, as it might have done, prejudice her against the disorderly. Something of her faculty of entering into the needs of others was seen in her flair for appropriate gifts: riding lessons for a niece or god-daughter fond of horses but with no opportunity, or objects chosen to suit the taste or way of thinking of the recipient regardless of the fact that she herself did not care for or even disliked those objects or thought them ugly. She enjoyed choosing Christmas cards for friends with an eye for what would appeal, taking trouble to get the right greeting for particular persons, often by some apposite reminder in pictures of medieval life. The greeting then came with a special appropriateness, bringing to mind her thought of a friend or a friend's thought of her.

Of her friendships with humble people of all sorts it is hard to speak: these seem to have been innumerable, and with a great many of them she kept in touch. Bumann's long winter days when snowed up at Saas Fee were eased by an interesting order to carve an oak chair to her instructions as her Christmas present to a friend in England, whose initials 'M. G. S.' and crest formed part of the design. Soldiers to whom she had written as prisoners of war and who sent her the oddest collections of post-cards; charwomen, caretakers—all these were among her personal friends. An annual motor-drive to see some beautiful garden was her way of entertaining some of the older among them. It was greatly looked forward to and long remembered.

Short motor journeys at home to explore particular places or see new ones were mostly planned to give pleasure to other people: so in later days were successive journeys in the north, to Dunstable, and to Tavistock with her brother to look up haunts of forebears, or adventurous drives in the Highlands one summer with Madge Skipworth. Left to herself she would search out rather than avoid drives under all sorts of conditions of tempest, on snow- or ice-bound roads, or through fog in Oxfordshire lanes at night, or latterly the blackout. She was a keen driver and loved trying herself in perplexing circumstances. Had finance allowed she would have been an airwoman—as it was, she seized the opportunity of a trip at the earliest moment when aeroplanes were still a recent invention and repeated the experiment occasionally, always hoping for more.

Part of every holiday was the attempt to get into personal touch with the ordinary people of the district. She loved making friends with cowherds, waiters, chambermaids, porters, village-tailors, hotel-keepers, country shopkeepers, ships' hands, and fishermen, and she enjoyed trying to talk to natives of other countries in their language. Incidental encounters with people leading to surprising talks or revelations must have been a by no means uncommon experience to her, though she rarely reported them.

An amusing example from a letter of November 1918 tells of a Canadian whom she met in the train on her way home from a lecture which she had given to munition workers: 'On the way back I met one of the humours of the war—a delicious Canadian: middle aged, taking himself very seriously, with a dash of humour every now and then: who from Ruley to Euston (thank heaven

we'd the carriage to ourselves) lectured me on Free Love (its
advantages), the "Unwritten Law" (its iniquity), the morals of
Solomon, the marriage service, and the inspiration of the Bible.
He was a complete love—and when he assured me, quite gravely,
that he liked making friends with people, "But if I go across to
speak to a lady in an Hotel I always make a point of shaking hands
with her and acting as if I know her. You see one has to consider
a lady's feelings and people might notice," I nearly disgraced myself. He found the men much stiffer than the women in England
and strongly disapproved of their attitude to their wives: "I
reckon an Englishman thinks his wife is worthy to be mother
of his children, and that's about all there is to it." At the same
time he liked the American system no better: "The girls there
expect a man to be giving them candy and flowers all the time,
and we're getting fed up with it." '

Grace could quickly establish friendly relations and had many
friends but few intimates. In ways where many others feel the
need for these she possessed an inward independence that was
unshaken by her affections, deep and constant as these were.
Friends knew they would find her steadily the same however long
they did not meet. Tenderness was not a feeling which she could
easily put into words, but it was a passion that swayed her thoughts
and actions towards others into whose lives she had entered.

Her mother apart, there are two other friendships which made
too deep a mark upon her life to be passed over in silence: the one
with her eldest brother and the other with my mother, Mrs.
Deneke.

It is hard to speak of her friendship with her brother. Undoubtedly it had much to do with her development, especially
in earlier days. Grace's weekly letters to him were destroyed,
though she faithfully continued her mother's habit of keeping his,
week by week, tied up in little bundles and dated. In course of
time she became to him something of what their mother had
been, his most intimate guide, comforter, and friend. Her brother
and she had pledged themselves not to write one another's lives,
and the outline of his is well known from the tutorship at Worcester College, Oxford, where he was also Dean, to the headship
of Armstrong College, Newcastle, and the Vice-Chancellorship
of Durham University, the war-appointment as Director of Army
Education, his knighthood and appointment as Vice-Chancellor

of Sheffield University, his work on Government Committees, and the Chairmanship of the Committee that resulted in the 'Hadow Report' on education. His later life was determined by administration, though his early love of music did not desert him, nor his interest in deepening and widening its appreciation in this country. 'A Wave of happiness' came over Grace Hadow as a wee girl in the vicarage pew when 'Harry' walked into Cerney Church. She accepted his tastes and standards without question, and this too in her earlier grown-up days, when she studied music and sang his songs to his accompaniment.

At Oxford she grew to intellectual independence and found herself still on her brother's lines but with firm roots of her own. When both of them were at college, tutors, meeting often, co-operating over a book and sharing a large part of their social life, they sparkled, exulted in good stories, and their association and companionship brought equal pleasure to them and provided a duet of flashing talk that was almost too much at times for their old friends. The years between them then ceased to have importance. They by no means took identical views of the same subject. He disagreed with her advocacy of women's suffrage, and it happened that he sat on a platform of a meeting called to oppose this measure during a time when she was advocating it elsewhere. He saw her popularity and her success with pride and came to believe more and more in her career; his weight and influence were at her service. In many ways they were greatly alike: excellent tutors and vivid lecturers with a faculty for pointed expression, delivering their college lectures extempore. Both were brilliant speakers for an occasion with much to say and a power of saying it with illustrations from their own experience and a fund of humour. Both were outstanding chairmen who could induce happy co-operation by keeping alert and interested committees which might otherwise have contained the elements of a quarrel. His amazing memory, his range, his creative vein, his command of subjects outstripped hers, yet, within her sphere, the quality of her mind matched his and perhaps hers was the even stronger character. Both broadened in their human sympathies and deepened in their conviction that all men in their measure are capable of culture and that this is the measure of a full human being. Both passed from education pure and simple to administration and there in a new way found themselves. In the

SIR HENRY HADOW AND GRACE HADOW, 1930

GRACE HADOW AND MRS. C. S. DENEKE, 1922

years when they were both engaged on the administration of adult education he used his knowledge and his influence to support her schemes, while she for her part entered into his, giving him ideas and keeping him in touch with sides of life to which he had little access. Both served on committees of the B.B.C.; his relation to the Board of Education and the Carnegie Trustees reacted favourably on hers. Both lived self-dedicated lives and strengthened one another's purposes.

For many years they shared holidays, and when these became rarer would meet in London at carefully arranged moments which they would set apart in their busy lives. Save for the brief space of time when it was possible for them to set up house together in London, while he was working on Army Education at Whitehall and she at the Ministry of Munitions, it was their lot to live full lives in close intimacy but living apart. His removal to Newcastle in 1909 and, soon after, hers to Cirencester, had meant separation, and this was confirmed when he went to Sheffield. When upon his retirement he married Edith Troutbeck in 1930, Grace entered into his new happiness. His wife predeceased him by some months, and it was Grace who was with her brother when he died in 1937. They shared friends and delightful holidays, and strange experiences which somehow sought them out, and shared thoughts which cemented them at their heart-strings. They never ceased to stimulate one another.

That Grace passed through inward conflicts no one who knew her well would doubt, nor that they proved a crucible for bringing out quality, a selflessness that nevertheless left her entirely human. 'I do believe—from my own experience—', she once wrote to her sister Margaret, 'that it is a wise Providence which helps one from depending too much on any externals—even on people: one does not love them the less—I think one loves them more truly because more holily' (1921). A casual remark from another letter gives the attitude which became characteristic with regard to her personal concerns: 'I spent an hour yesterday being towed by a load of mangold after a breakdown. We parted two ropes and a wire hawser—such are the pleasures of motoring. If you don't call in a doctor you weight the scales against the patient—I tie my camel but then commit him, without instructions, to the Lord' (1936).

When her mother died in 1917 one foundation of her life had

gone. It was with a set face and resolute decision that she then distributed or destroyed accumulated papers of one-time treasures in her study at Cirencester, determined not to prolong an existence that had lost its reality. Closely united to her family as she always remained, war work then called her and claimed a first place. Her work was compatible, however, with sharing the home of old friends, and with the short interval when she shared her brother's flat in Kensington she lived with my people as a member of the family till 1929, when her appointment as Principal demanded that she should set up a household of her own. My mother and Grace were kindred spirits and were fully aware of the pleasure they took in one another's companionship and of their profound agreement on essentials. Both were enthusiasts by temperament, and both had that integrity before which no pose can be maintained. They sized up people and situations instantly; and they had a compelling instinct for entering into and if need be shouldering the lives of other people. My mother concentrated on those at home and those who passed in and out of the home circle, and these came from a very wide acquaintance of many different kinds of people. She dealt in individual terms and retained strong likes and dislikes. Grace may have helped to open new windows for her there, yet she delighted in my mother's spontaneity which was incalculable, so that you could never tell beforehand how this or that might appeal. They both had a keen sense of humour, loved a good story and could tell it well with entirely their own ways of putting things. They took events and impressions simply and at first hand. They were great lovers, yet with a critical sense that kept them open-eyed for one another's weaknesses and made them see one another and their nearest and dearest from outside as well as in sympathy. They loved flowers and enjoyed gardening, especially rock gardening, also card-playing and foreign travel and great poetry and music, and Grace could enter into my mother's special love of this last. They counted their blessings. They respected one another's oddities. Human interest was their greatest—and so each of them had personal friendships with working-class people; they loved country people especially and the countryside. Their sense for national matters and for public questions was equally keen, though my mother had no training in dealing with these and took no active part in them. They were sportswomen; both had loved sailing—perhaps Grace's passion for mountain climbing may be set against my mother's skill as a horsewoman—but that was in the past for her. When Grace came to share our home my mother was young at seventy and Grace mature at forty-two. They had long been friends. To my mother Grace's friendship and presence meant a latter-day spring and to Grace it meant loving freely and ripening in wisdom. We fully experienced her finest qualities in times of trouble and distress and owe her thanks untold, only one got beyond thanking.

With my father Grace had an independent friendship. If she described him as the 'kindest of adopted uncles', he inscribed a gift to her 'in grateful memory of an intimate friendship'. While working at the Ministry of Munitions she occupied a flat in London at 51 Harley House which was kept for my father's convenience as a Bank Director after his retirement from Messrs. Frederick Huth & Co. He came up regularly for board meetings, and at such times they would spend evenings together. 'I wonder if you realize what it has meant to me to have so much love round me today,' she wrote from there on her birthday, 9 December 1917, to my mother in Oxford. 'It is a wonderful gift that warms my whole life. It is indeed a very great thing to know that I belong to you and that nothing—not death itself—can break the tie.' Her friendship with my mother was one of the motive powers of her life.

Acceptance of the secretaryship of Barnett House meant coming to live at Gunfield, Norham Gardens, Oxford, where my parents had moved late in life in 1916 when a tall London house had become too much for them and the old life there was broken up by the war. And so Oxford once more became her second home. Her bedroom window faced the tall elms that edge the north side of the University Parks, and from her balcony she could see the grounds of L.M.H. and beyond them open country with the ridge of Elsfield Hill. The window was always kept wide open, and just under it, in sight of the trees winter and summer alike, stood her bed. She could hear the voice of 'Tom' from Christ Church across the University Parks when the wind was right, and hard by the cawing of rooks.

Grace's plan of life was to fill every minute of the day, to accept every engagement as it came asking her to speak or do things that she could do for people or causes. She was necessarily an elusive member of a household. Her days were carefully mapped out and the times for doing things together at home were set aside and fitted in. There was always such a time, and she did much to help my parents form new attachments in Oxford, and for my mother especially she was a link to many friendships. Their Sunday drive to the country never failed, nor their regular hours for cards in which Grace was distressingly lucky; nor when she became Principal the daily morning visit to the old lady's bedroom on her way to the office. When my mother urged preventing green fly from 'leading their sinful lives' she would help her in attacks on insect pests; always they stimulated one another in good talk. In later days it was sport to go on shopping expeditions for the old lady and get her the 'exactly right thing'; or to help her discover new ways of embroidery and encourage her at eighty-four to enter a Women's Institute competition and rejoice in her gaining a first-class certificate. There were journeys to Switzerland, when part of the time was spent with her and part in climbing, short journeys in England by car, and innumerable little expeditions undertaken to provide a feeling of adventure for one in whom the zest of it had not been quenched by old age. The pleasurable excitement of taking rough tracks up a hill-side to find Llantony Abbey might serve the purpose, or drives in Oxfordshire in heavy rain to some country inn for luncheon, or going out to trace the havoc of the great storm in 1928 that snapped huge trees. Once, driving through a quiet village in Norfolk and passing a danger signal on a wall, she was delighted to hear her old lady murmur happily, 'Nice little place and danger too!' They had standing jokes together. It was a gibe of my mother's to dub Grace 'professional optimist', and Grace's easy retort on 'Deneke pessimism' would strengthen her refusal to believe in unfavourable prospects or to consider some precaution. It is true that her optimism was upheld as a matter of will, but it rested on a firm basis. She knew love without dissimulation, and believed that actions speak louder than words.

In the summer of 1939 Grace was eagerly planning the usual adventurous holiday and chose Poland. The uncertainty of the European situation checked this effectively and she decided upon Norway instead. Since the American journey in 1938 there had been no break in her activities and she was tired. However, the journey was undertaken with all the zest of reading about and seeing a new country. From the heights above Bergen we saw

a wonderful sunset in a clear sky over sea and islands; there followed a stay in Jötunheim, some bathing up there in mountain
pools, and a small climb to see what that felt like. But the air was
soft even near glaciers, and it seemed clear there would be no real
climbing that year: a walk to the foot of a great glacier stretching
surprisingly down into a green valley, a long swift ride close to
the water in the prow of a tiny motor-boat among white hills
promised further enjoyment. At Tyn we had just arranged for a
drive down dangerous looking bends of a mountain so as to
reach new parts for walking when an Englishman invited us to
listen to the wireless that he had chartered that evening. On it we
heard Lord Halifax's speech on the eve of war, and we decided
to hurry home after just about a fortnight's travel, luckily catching
the last boat before war was declared. The holiday had not been
long enough to bring the physical refreshment that Grace needed,
and a week after we reached London war came, on 3 September.
There were months of suspense between then and Christmas, with
the weary sense of besieging and being besieged. The large-scale
evacuation of London schools to Oxford and Oxfordshire involved Grace in many additional jobs (she herself housed a teacher
and two children in her house, a tax on the last remaining leisure);
planning the war activities of Institutes implied additional inter-
views and negotiations. For Christmas she travelled to Carlisle
in extreme discomfort with no seat, and from there to London to
start the new year with a week of business and some play-time for
which I was to join her. When I got there I found her very ill in
bed and speechless with the worst sore throat she had ever had.
It turned to pneumonia. The then new drug M and B produced
a check and the hope of recovery. But this hope was soon stilled.
What could be done for her was done. She was living on her
courage as Lord Dawson of Penn saw, adding sorrowfully: 'This
war will see many victims of people who have worked when over-
tired; no reserve of strength is then left when they are attacked.'
She died in London on 19 January 1940 after a fortnight's illness.
At sixty-four she was nevertheless in the prime of her maturity and
she was called away at a moment when her leadership was sorely
missed. The pattern of her life has emerged clearly in the years
that have gone by since.

After her sudden death, friends quite unknown to one another
met and recognized in her an experience which they had in com-

mon. They came from unexpected places and all ranks of society and spoke as with one voice of her kindness, of her gaiety, and of the blessing to have had her as a friend, and of her radiance: 'Her visits were like a kingfisher'; 'she was like a shaft of stimulating light which crossed the path whenever she came, and she was such fun'.

The news of her death seemed incredible, for her friends were so used to drawing freely upon her gifts that they took her for granted like the elements and it seemed as if a portion of themselves had gone. Yet the friend who described her death as 'no tragedy but a shining dawn' found the right word. She had gone on to the next great adventure, and she believed intensely that those who have really loved will meet after death.

The funeral service in the University Church of St. Mary's, Oxford, came as a fitting expression of this sense in its triumphant note: at her wish Blake's 'Jerusalem' was sung, and it was sung by many who had often sung it with her and to whom her voice was present in its words invoking 'arrows of desire' and vowing not to 'cease from mental fight' till Jerusalem had been built by the common effort of all. The church was thronged with representatives from many organizations as well as with members of the University and many friends, and though there was snow outside, it was bright with many coloured flowers. The dignity of the ceremonial upholding its agelong tradition communicated the feeling of love and peace and courage which breathed afresh in minds to whom Grace Hadow's spirit, both gallant and tranquil, seemed revealed in the love by which she lived. When she had been carried to her rest a glowing red sunset lit up the snow on her friends' homeward way.

EPILOGUE

IT had been Mrs. Hadow's constant prayer for her children that they might be spared to do useful work in the world. Grace Hadow did a great work in adult education and in the education of women. She was built to be a pioneer and at once cleared obstacles and laid foundations. She achieved much through others and much that is not necessarily associated with her name, yet in each of the main spheres of her life-work she may be described as a 'pious founder'[1] in the true sense of the word. There is little doubt that the Society of Oxford Home Students[2] would concede the claim, shocked as she herself would be to hear it made. Hers stands as a notable figure in the education of women in Oxford. And the same is true with regard to non-academic women in the country-side. The National Federation of Women's Institutes proved a sphere where she could build on a wide scale. It expanded as she herself matured, and to the last she was felt as a dynamic force in all its parts. Her personality contributed greatly to the tradition of that movement for co-operation in goodwill, and the impress of her mind is stamped upon its organization. Her work for rural community councils forms a counterpart to her work for Women's Institutes.

There was great originality in her vision of what rural life should and could be. It went hand in hand with her power to see circumstances as they are and to use them, translating them meanwhile for herself and for others in terms of her vision. She saw rural life as providing a natural basis for common interests and so as an opportunity for breaking down barriers between class and class. And this not without respect of persons, but with the respect that rests not upon class but upon intrinsic quality in men and women and upon a belief in and a love of perfect things. And it was a great part of her life-work to bring the joy of these in whatever forms to each and to all. Side by side with this there was the conscious and successful endeavour to find ways and means

[1] Cf. 'Barnett House'. Chapter VIII, p. 93.
[2] She herself wished to see the name of the Society changed and was instrumental in getting this considered, though she went no further with the idea when it was turned down through energetic opposition among a group of old members, leaving the matter 'for my successor'.

of approach and to establish an organization for the interchange of ideas and for common action. The boldness of her thought was unweakened, and the freshness of her mind remained untarnished. In the last year of her life, as her range extended by travel, she was beginning to open windows for men and women overseas as well. Her contribution to the interpretation of rural life is not at an end. It rests upon a deep faith in England and upon a broad conception of humanity.

Self-dedication was the key to her life. Heart and mind assented altogether to inward obedience and to being shown the way. The strongest influence upon her was her mother's mind and personality, which were bent upon doing God's service; and then her brother's, and these two were intertwined with home associations as well as with the actual lines on which her life was set. Close to these home affections was that which linked her to the family of her adoption whose home she shared. Her life was happy and rich in friendship, and she was creative in goodness. At first sight each move from one phase of her life to the next seems almost like starting a new career. Yet, on looking back, each appears with cumulative force as the best equipment for the next, and one experience enriched another. High hopes, often not realized, were perhaps the essential concomitant of an ardent temperament, yet they did not interfere with her shining qualities. She never ceased passionately to desire definite things, but she desired them in an impersonal way, keeping an open mind for what might come. It was not in vain that alpine climbing was a favourite holiday pursuit of hers, nor that with clear-eyed care for an exact footing she loved looking over the edge—beyond.

There was a steady coherence in her purposes, and those converged in the serenity of a reasoned faith:

> Lord temper with tranquilitie
> Our manifold activitie
> That we may do our work for thee
> With very great simplicitie.

Disinterested helpfulness was her first instinct and marked her dealings with each person: in the wider social issues for which she worked she looked to build on that same human instinct which, in her way of seeing, is the simplest and our natural outlook.

APPENDIX

SIR HENRY HADOW: SCHOLAR, MUSICIAN, AND ADMINISTRATOR

From *The Times*, Saturday, 10 April 1937.

Sir Henry Hadow died on Thursday night in his home in London, less than a month after the death of his wife, at the age of 77. His sister, Miss Grace Hadow, Principal of the Society of Oxford Home Students, was with him at the last.

Hadow was a man of extraordinarily varied abilities and interests as scholar, music critic and administrator of modern universities. To the general public he was best known as the chief author of the famous Hadow Report. The Board of Education in issuing it in December 1926 preserved a non-committal attitude, being hardly prepared for the acclamation with which it was greeted. Briefly, it paved the way for a total revolution in the education of children over 11, and when Hadow resigned the Chairmanship of the Consultative Committee in February 1934, various detailed schemes known by his name had been worked out and all that he left to his successor was the problem of the organization and interrelation of primary and secondary schools.

William Henry Hadow was the son of the Rev. W. E. Hadow and Mary Lang Cornish his wife. Born at Ebrington, Gloucestershire, on Dec. 27, 1859, he was educated at Malvern College and at Worcester College, Oxford, where he was successively exhibitioner, lecturer, tutor, Fellow and Dean; and Honorary Fellow in 1909. He was placed in the first class in both Moderations and Lit. Hum., but he did not receive his Fellowship till 1889. During the next 20 years, however, he steadily advanced in influence and authority.

A strenuous opponent of degrees for women, he served nevertheless on the Council of Somerville College, was a member of the Association for the Education of Women and to his lectures, philosophical and musical, women students came in numbers. A staunch champion of compulsory Greek and of a classical Oxford, he resisted the conversion of the University into a modern scientific school. It came therefore to many as a surprise when he left Oxford in 1909 to be the head of the institution which had been known as the Newcastle College of Science and had only just received powers to establish a literary side.

Hadow placed the finances of Armstrong College in a sound position, introduced a pension system, entered into friendly relations with capitalists and working men, established such terms with his staff and his students as had not been known for many years, if ever before, built a women's hostel, a new art school, and a school of agriculture and organized a schools council to co-operate with the University. When the War came Armstrong and Bournbrook were the only two sets of university college buildings in the Kingdom that were at once converted into military hospitals. Before the term began Hadow had housed his 16 or 18 departments in some 25 buildings throughout the city, and carried on the work with the college with the least possible interruption. Before and during the War he became known as a most effective speaker at large Sunday evening meetings in the Newcastle theatre and he was in request at church congresses. He was Vice-Chancellor of the University of Durham from 1916–1918. He served on the Advisory Council of the Board of Education, and was a member of the small subcommittee which was responsible for the interim report on scholarships for higher education in 1916. He also served on the Royal Commission on University colleges in Wales 1916–1917, under the chairmanship of Lord Haldane, and on the Committee on the Civil Service Examination for Class I, 1917. If Mr. H. A. L. Fisher had not accepted the office of President of the Board of Education in December 1916, it would have been offered next to Hadow.

On the invitation of the Young Men's Christian Association Hadow went out to France in July 1918, as their first Director of Education for the lines of Communication, and worked untiringly to bring some organization to classes for soldiers at the base camps. He realized however that he had been to some extent misinformed as to the authority and scope of the association's activities in this direction. Accordingly, when on August 22 Lord Gorell, who had meantime succeeded in getting Treasury sanction for the whole official scheme for the armies both at home and in many theatres of war, invited him to the War Office, he accepted with enthusiasm.

As Assistant Director of Staff Duties (Education) at the War Office Hadow was responsible for the initial educational framework, the early arrangements with examining bodies, and the choosing of the books to be dispatched. He remained the warmest of friends to the organization long after he had left the War Office; he was specially interested in the creation in 1920 of the Army Educational Corps and the carrying on of the work into the permanency of the Regular Army.

Hadow left the War Office in April 1919 to take up the post of Vice-Chancellor of the University of Sheffield, which he held till his retirement by reason of age in 1930. With the exception of a gymnasium and some additions in the mining departments there was no new building in his time. His regime however saw a new impetus given to the school of pharmacology on the coming of Dr. Mellanby, the creation of a Secondary Schools Council—a useful body, the full credit of which must be given to Hadow—and the foundation of a Chair of Music, which in Professor Shera's hands soon became notable.

An excellent chairman of the Senate Hadow got through business rapidly and smoothly. He was always practical, never a slave to rules, and so commended himself to the business men with whom he worked. He was for some years a valuable member of the Sheffield Education Committee and afterwards did a great work as Chairman of the Hospitals Board. His power of lecturing brilliantly on literary subjects without a note to refresh his memory was extraordinary. Of Dickens especially, whose works he had known from childhood, he had a profound knowledge and appreciation. Hadow brought distinction to the University by the position he occupied in the world of music, by his Stevenson lectures at Glasgow on 'Citizenship' (published in 1923) and by his chairmanship of important committees such as that on Chemical Studies, the Archbishop's Committee on Religious Education, the Consultative Committee of the Board of Education, which under his auspices recommended the raising of the school-leaving age to 15, the Committee on Broadcasting for Adult Education. Such duties, however, took him a good deal away from Sheffield, and so had their disadvantages. His relations with his staff were friendly if not intimate, and were chiefly confined to the walls of the University. He kept his natural impatience under control and never bore malice. The students liked him.

Hadow's position in the musical world was largely due to his denial of that world's existence. He refused to regard music as a railed-off enclosure reserved for specially qualified individuals. For him music, like literature, and cricket, was one of the absorbingly interesting factors of a full life. He was aware that it might become too absorbingly interesting to himself, so he left it rather at arm's length at first. After his schools in 1882 he spent some time in Darmstadt to enrich his experience by contact with German musical life and subsequently pursued his studies in the art with C. H. Lloyd.

'Studies in Modern Music' (1892) was Hadow's first breach in the defences of the railed-off enclosure. He never made any secret of the fact that he undertook the book for the express purpose of breaking through what he called 'the Joseph Bennett ring'. It included careful and sympathetic studies of the three artists who had suffered most from the pens of obscurantists—Berlioz, Schumann, and Wagner.

A second series, two years later, took for subjects Chopin, Dvorák and Brahms. The two last masters were then living, and Hadow went to both of them for his facts. There is in the published collection of Joachim's letters one in which he introduces this 'very charming young man' who had written about Schumann and Wagner, and who,

'I believe, has designs on you'. Joachim put Brahms into a good humour (that was necessary) and Hadow found him cordial. He saw much of him in Vienna, chiefly with Mandyczewski in the Library of the 'Gesellschaft der Musikfreunde'.

At Oxford in his year as Proctor Hadow introduced the first measure for bringing musical degrees into line with others: He lectured on music as deputy for Sir John Stainer and lent powerful support to the efforts of Stainer's successors—Parry, Paratt and Allen. He had little time for his own musical work, but the four volumes of songs which were published from Oxford disclosed a vein of genuine lyric beauty.

Two further books on music, a little one and a big one, belong to Hadow's Oxford period. 'A Croatian Composer—Joseph Haydn' shed new light for English readers on Haydn's melody by referring to its Slavonic origin. The 'Oxford History of Music' in six volumes, was the most ambitious attempt at a general history of the art made in this country since Burney. Hadow was its general editor and himself contributed the fifth volume on 'The Viennese Period' (1904). A seventh volume on the later period was published under his editorship in 1934.

After he left Oxford his advice to the Carnegie Trustees was instrumental in inducing them to undertake the publication of the great collection of 'Tudor Church Music' and also of the evergrowing body of important works by modern British composers. He was Chairman of the People's Concert Society and of the British Federation of Musical Competition Festivals, as well as a Member of the Council of the Royal College of Music. His 'Collected Essays' (1928) contain the record of his more occasional activities from the masterly lecture on Beethoven, delivered to the British Academy in 1917, to those he carried with him on his several visits to America. A comparison between Music and Poetry was the subject of his Sidgwick lecture at Cambridge in 1925 and his Romanes lecture at Oxford in 1933 was on 'The Place of Music among the arts'. To *The Times* in March 1932, he contributed an article on 'Fifty Years of Music'.

But, the end of it all with Sir Henry Hadow, as with all the best, is that the man himself was the finest element in everything he did, and also something outside and above all his doings. No one ever met him for more than a few minutes without receiving the impression of an extraordinary vitality. His brain seemed always young, alert, overflowing with energy and activity. The activity—particularly in later years—sometimes showed a tendency to degenerate a little into restlessness, the malady which so commonly besets those who love work, and too often ends their working. But ordinarily it made him the most stimulating of companions and among the most delightful.

But Hadow was by no means all brain. He had the warmest of

hearts and was one of the most loyal of friends. He was kind, too, to those who were not his friends, and was singularly free from the habit, so difficult for the clever to resist, of using his cleverness to make less clever people ridiculous. Those who knew him well noticed how seldom he mentioned other people's faults and how inclined he was to defend those who were being attacked or criticized. But he was as far as a man can be from drawing any circle of conclusion round himself. He never threw away opportunities of seeing old friends or making new ones: so that he leaves behind him many very happy memories and carries with him the affection of many men and women too.

Hadow received many honorary degrees, was knighted in 1918, and made C.B.E. in 1920. He married in 1930 Edith, daughter of the late Rev. Dr. John Troutbeck, Precentor of Westminster Abbey. She died on March 15 last.

CLARA SOPHIA DENEKE

From *The Times*, 1933.

A correspondent writes—'There died in Oxford on May 24 at the age of 86 Clara Deneke, who to generations of L.M.H. students and of others will always represent the finest fusion of all that is best in both the German and the English tradition. She cared passionately for all that is innately lovely and splendid in English literature and history; above all she cared for the English countryside, but her roots were German. She belonged to the Germany of Weimar, of Goethe, and of '48, a Germany we are apt to forget when its ideals and splendid moral qualities are temporarily overlaid with the arrogance and blatancy of Prussia. Her intense interest in the education and liberation of women (she was thrown out of a comfortable home in her twenties by a stern father for not marrying the man of his choice) has borne fruit in the lovely new buildings at Lady Margaret Hall which, called after her, are to be opened by Lord Grey this week. Her two daughters who represent so fittingly her dual personality, her fine intellect and passion for music, will have the great sympathy of many in that Mrs. Deneke was not allowed to be with us for these celebrations. Our hearts go out to these two, to whom this loss to Oxford will be hardest to bear.'

From the *Oxford Magazine*, 8 June 1933.

Last Saturday should have seen the formal opening, by the Chancellor of the University, of the Deneke Building of Lady Margaret Hall; the ceremony was naturally cancelled owing to Mrs. Deneke's sudden death. The building was called after her and for many years she had, both directly and through her two daughters, very intimate links with the college. The annual P. M. Deneke Lecture (founded in memory of her husband out of the work of her younger daughter) will, however, be given in the new hall on the evening of Tuesday next by her friend, Professor Einstein.

Born in Westphalia eighty-six years ago, Mrs. Deneke had had her home in England for nearly sixty, and in Oxford for seventeen years. In the prayer, written for the funeral service, mention was made of her as one greatly endowed 'earnestly to follow after things beautiful and true' and thanks were given 'for her life among us, her strong purpose and courage, and her gracious gift of friendship'. She was indeed a notable personality; even casual acquaintances could not but be impressed by the blend of dignity and charm, seriousness and humour, and all of them somehow quite unlike anyone else's. She held to the old things, but did not let the new pass by unheeded; an ardent lover of poetry (especially Goethe and Wordsworth), of flowers, and, perhaps most ardently of all music—with which her contacts had always been very intimate—she retained unimpaired to the end all her vivid interests and eager alertness, and also her gifts of subtly delicate manual craftsmanship. She touched life finely at many points, and those who were given the privilege of her friendship will feel that something very fragrant has become a memory.

From the *Oxford Times*, Friday, 26 May 1933.

Miss Grace Hadow, Principal of the Oxford Society of Home Students, writes: 'Clara Sophia Deneke (*née* Overweg) was born in Westphalia in 1847. She came first to England at the age of 16, and married and settled in the country in 1875. Her husband Philip Maurice Deneke (in whose memory an annual University Lecture has been founded) was for 42 years connected with the great banking firm of Messrs. Frederick Huth & Co.; in 1916 Mr. and Mrs. Deneke came to live in Oxford, next door to Lady Margaret Hall, where their elder daughter is Fellow and Garden Steward and their younger daughter Choirmaster. From the first Mrs. Deneke took the keenest interest in everything concerning the Hall and her gifts to it have been innumerable. On her husband's death in 1925 Mrs. Deneke gave Lady Margaret Hall the beautiful chased gold bowl which had been presented to her husband on his retirement from the firm, and one of her last acts was to give a beautiful picture by Lawrenson to the Senior Common Room.

Anyone who knew Mrs. Deneke must always associate her with wide interests, boundless hospitality and a gift for friendship which made those who came into contact with her even once feel the richer. Her love of music and keen critical judgment made her the friend of many artistes, and the Gunfield concerts, at which her younger daughter,

Miss Margaret Deneke, often played are known to all music lovers in Oxford. Her friendship extended to many parts of the world, and Miss Margaret Deneke's lecture tour in America brought her mother into touch with new friends on the other side of the Atlantic.

Her love of beauty was not however confined to music alone; to the very end of her life Mrs. Deneke did the most exquisite embroidery, and in 1931, when she was already 84, she won a first class prize certificate for cross stitch at the Women's Institute Handicraft Exhibition in the Town Hall.

Her love of flowers was scarcely less than her love of music and her understanding for great poetry was shown in several delicate and scholarly translations from English into German. In later years Mrs. Deneke who had earlier in life been a keen horsewoman, a walker, and a cyclist, was lamed by arthritis, but with characteristic courage and energy she used to go out alone—in an electric bath chair. No one ever more fully warmed both hands at the fire of life or shared its warmth more generously with others.'

From *Home and County Institute Roll of Honour*, 1933.

. . . How many happy and industrious conferences have met in the Gunfield music room? and blessed it in winter with its blazing fire and the row of heartening coffee cups, and in summer with its shining pianos and the green sounds and scents of Mrs. Deneke's garden. How many tired organizers have been lodged and sheltered there?

In Oxford we know that Mrs. Deneke literally rescued our music, and not a few of our musicians, in the war. But her heart was as open to the country as to the town, and to many people the best part of a Gunfield meeting was the sight of the tall, soldierly figure of our hostess coming in to shake hands at the end. No one, from the Chairman to the door-keeper, ever felt other than a guest at Gunfield. Real hospitality is like the quality of mercy, it blesses him that gives and him that takes, so said a poet well loved in England and Germany. Gunfield may live for ever—I hope—but to the Oxfordshire countrywomen the turn to the Parks will never feel quite the same again.

No one met her without feeling her remarkable quality. Apart from music she was a marvellous needlewoman (we have all seen the collars of Miss Deneke's—and also of Miss Hadow's—dresses) and when the mood and the listener were congenial she could tell inimitable tales of her fathers, the grand old gentlemen of Germany. Most characteristic was the electric bath-chair, in which she toured her garden and roamed the countryside, charging up Headington Hill with characteristic vigour. In youth Mrs. Deneke was a horsewoman. When I first knew her in Oxford she rode a tricycle (I remember the

Secretary of the Belgian Relief Fund saying 'A lady of sixty nine has offered to collect funds on her tricycle') and when she became rheumatic, at about eighty, she went out in the electric chair. A small boy, taking a dull walk in the Parks, was struck silent with admiration by the sight of Mrs. Deneke bowling magnificently out of a side walk (with a daughter artistically suppressed in the rear). He had never seen such an old lady, nor even such a bath-chair and as he went home he said 'Will she be there tomorrow?' For him and me the Parks will be less dull for that gallant memory. . . .

M. SIDGWICK

INDEX

PRINTED IN
GREAT BRITAIN
AT THE
UNIVERSITY PRESS
OXFORD
BY
JOHN JOHNSON
PRINTER
TO THE
UNIVERSITY